UNCOVERED

From the files of the British Admiralty: a report of the events of May 9, 1830, by James Stockdale, Captain of the barque *Rob Roy*

Light winds and fine clean weather. . . . Wind SSE with a light swell. Saw several large whales—some of them very light coloured. About five p.m. all at once while I was walking on the deck my attention was drawn to the water on the port bow by a scuffling noise. Judge my amazement when what should stare us all in the face as if not knowing whether to come over the deck or go around to the stern—but the great thundering big sea snake!

Now I had heard of the fellow before—and have killed snakes twenty-four feet long in the straits of Malaca, but they would go in his mouth. . . .

My ship is 171 feet long overall—and the foremast is 42 feet from the stern, which would make the monster about 129 feet long. If I had not seen it I could not have believed it but there was no mistake or doubt of its length—for the brute was so close I could smell him.

When underway he carried his head about six feet out of water— with a fin between the shoulders about two feet long. I think he was swimming about five miles an hour—for I watched him from the topsail yard till I lost sight of him in about fifty minutes. The thickened part of his body seemed to be as large round as a beef [illegible]. I hope never to see him more. It is enough to frighten the strong at heart.

STRANGE SECRETS

Real Government Files on the Unknown

NICK REDFERN
AND ANDY ROBERTS

PARAVIEW POCKET BOOKS

NEW YORK LONDON TORONTO SYDNEY SINGAPORE

An *Original* Publication of PARAVIEW POCKET BOOKS

PARAVIEW
191 Seventh Avenue, New York, NY 10011

POCKET BOOKS, a division of Simon & Schuster, Inc.
1230 Avenue of the Americas, New York, NY 10020

ISBN: 0-7434-6976-3

First Paraview Pocket Books trade paperback printing May 2003

10 9 8 7 6 5 4 3 2 1

POCKET and colophon are registered trademarks of Simon & Schuster, Inc.

For information regarding special discounts for bulk purchases,
please contact Simon & Schuster Special Sales at 1-800-456-6798
or business@simonandschuster.com

Designed by Joseph Rutt

Printed in the U.S.A.

*For Dana: my wife, soul mate and best friend.
You make every day a special one.*

ACKNOWLEDGMENTS

We would like to offer our sincere thanks to the following people for their contributions to this book: Dr. David Clarke, for generously sharing with us documentation that he uncovered at the Public Record Office; Jonathan Downes and Richard Freeman of the Center for Fortean Zoology, for a wealth of information and without whose assistance the chapter "The Monster Files" could not have been written; and everyone at Paraview and Pocket (especially our editor, Patrick Huyghe, and Louise Burke and Brigitte Smith), for their enthusiasm, support, and belief in the project.

We would also like to extend our thanks to the following agencies: the Central Intelligence Agency; the Defense Intelligence Agency; the Federal Bureau of Investigation; Her Majesty's Stationery Office; the Joint Air Reconnaissance Intelligence Center; MI5; the National Archives and Records Administration; the Provost and Security Services; the Public Record Office; the Royal Air Force; and the U.S. Army.

CONTENTS

INTRODUCTION

For almost ten years FBI special agents Fox Mulder and Dana Scully pursued UFOs, vampires, lake monsters, werewolves, ghosts, aliens, dark and sinister conspiracies, biblical mysteries, man-made flying saucers, and more. Their paranormal and paranoia-filled show, *The X-Files*, spawned the unforgettable catchphrases *The truth is out there* and *Trust no one*.

Of course, *The X-Files* was merely a work of fiction, and the idea that government, military, and intelligence agencies around the globe would take an interest in such out-of-this-world controversies is manifestly absurd. Isn't it? Perhaps not.

In the pages that follow, you will learn the remarkable facts pertaining to what could arguably be termed the real-life X-files of the American, British, and former Soviet governments. Come with us on a remarkable journey into the unknown as we reveal the FBI's records on the men who claimed face-to-face contact with alien creatures; the attempts by the U.S. Air Force to build nuclear-powered flying saucers; the true story concerning Britain's military and the Loch Ness Monster; the KGB's and the Central Intelligence Agency's plans to perfect the ultimate psychic spy; the real-life Men in Black who terrorize UFO witnesses into silence; the American military's use of vampire legends, witchcraft, sorcery, and black magic; the crop-circle secrets of the British government; FBI documents on a series of macabre and baffling cattle mutilations; official U.S. government files on spontaneous human combustion; naval reports of gargantuan sea monsters; the stranger-than-fiction world of animal espionage; telepathic experiments conducted by the CIA; unexplained phenomena reported during the Second World War; the CIA's files on Noah's Ark; and much more.

It should be noted that the nature of intelligence work requires agencies to obtain information on just about anything and everything that might conceivably have a bearing on national security. Therefore, it is really not at all surprising that documentation on "the unknown" has been created and studied at an official level.

But for years, the official files on these and other mysteries were tightly held under the strictest security. With the passing of legislation such as the U.S. government's Freedom of Information Act and the British government's Thirty Year Ruling, however, that security has, to a degree at least, begun to ease — to the extent that we can now safely say that "the truth is" indeed "out there."

And yes, you *can* trust us!

Part One

HIGH STRANGENESS

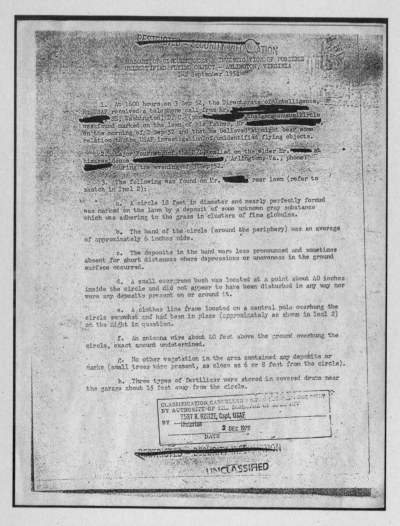

SUBJECT: SUMMARY OF CIRCUMSTANCES, INVESTIGATION OF POSSIBLE
UNIDENTIFIED FLYING OBJECT — ARLINGTON, VIRGINIA
1-2 September 1952

1. At 1600 hours on 3 Sep 52, the Directorate of Intelligence, Hq USAF received a telephone call from Mr. ███████ SS, Washington, D. C. (phone ███████ that an unusual circle was found marked on the lawn of his father, Mr. ███████ on the morning of 2 Sep 52 and that he believed it might bear some relation to the USAF investigation of unidentified flying objects.

2. Major Fournet of the D/I called on the elder Mr. ███████ at his residence ███████ Arlington, Va., phone ███████ during the evening of 3 Sep 52.

3. The following was found on Mr. ███████ rear lawn (refer to sketch in Incl 2):

   a. A circle 18 feet in diameter and nearly perfectly formed was marked on the lawn by a deposit of some unknown gray substance which was adhering to the grass in clusters of fine globules.

   b. The band of the circle (around the periphery) was an average of approximately 6 inches wide.

   c. The deposits in the band were less pronounced and sometimes absent for short distances where depressions or unevenness in the ground surface occurred.

   d. A small evergreen bush was located at a point about 40 inches inside the circle and did not appear to have been disturbed in any way nor were any deposits present on or around it.

   e. A clothes line frame located on a central pole overhung the circle somewhat and had been in place (approximately as shown in Incl 2) on the night in question.

   f. An antenna wire about 40 feet above the ground overhung the circle, exact amount undetermined.

   g. No other vegetation in the area contained any deposits or marks (small trees were present, as close as 6 or 8 feet from the circle).

   h. Three types of fertilizer were stored in covered drums near the garage about 15 feet away from the circle.

Few people will be unaware of the crop-circle mystery of the 1980s and the 1990s. U.S. government files on this subject extend back decades, however, as this Air Force Office of Special Investigations document of 1952, titled "Summary of Circumstances: Investigation of Possible Unidentified Flying Object—Arlington, Virginia," reveals.

One

AROUND IN CIRCLES

Exactly who, or what, is responsible for peppering Britain's landscape with the now familiar crop circles and the fantastically elaborate "pictogram" designs has been hotly debated for years. Indeed, worldwide interest in the subject is so intense that it even became a key aspect of the summer 2002 blockbuster movie starring Mel Gibson, *Signs*.

Official interest in these mysterious "circles" began early on. According to the *Wall Street Journal* of August 28, 1989, "British agriculture and defense officials want to know more about the mysterious crop circles which have appeared across the countryside . . . so does Queen Elizabeth, who is said to have sharply questioned Prime Minister Margaret Thatcher about the circles recently. While those talks are kept secret, a Buckingham Palace spokesman says the Queen took a hurriedly published book about the circles to her summer palace in Scotland this month."[1]

Numerous theories have been advanced to try to explain the phenomenal number of designs that have appeared throughout the country (and now, the world) since the 1980s, but opinions remain sharply divided. For the "believers," crop circles are the work of

3

UFOs, some form of vaguely defined "earth energy," or some other inexplicable phenomenon. For many, however, the human factor is overriding. Indeed, good evidence shows that many of the pictograms are the work of human beings.

In the latter part of 2000, for instance, a Welshman named Matthew Williams hit the headlines when he was arrested for causing criminal damage in a field in Wiltshire, England. Williams had created under cover of darkness a highly elaborate pictogram of the type that many crop-circle researchers believed—and continue to believe—could only be made by a currently unexplained medium. Little wonder, then, that the matter remains unresolved to everyone's satisfaction.

But what of the possibility that the circles—whatever their origin—have attracted the attention of officialdom, as the *Wall Street Journal* suggested was the case in 1989? One man who claims to have such knowledge is crop-circle researcher George Wingfield. Eton-educated and previously employed at the Royal Greenwich Observatory, Wingfield claims that in September 1990 the British government called a secret ministerial briefing to debate the circles. According to Wingfield's sources, the meeting was supposedly convened to try to determine the nature of the circles, lest the British government be placed in the potentially embarrassing position of having to admit its ignorance of the phenomenon.[2]

A similar but more personal experience comes from a Royal Air Force medic, Jonathan Turner, who was stationed at RAF Lyneham, Wiltshire, in 1991. He recalls that on July 15 of that year, a crop circle was discovered on nearby Hackpen Hill. Shortly afterward, examples of the more elaborate pictograms began appearing too. His interest piqued, Turner visited the area on an off-duty day and took some photographs of the various patterns and formations that had appeared. As he soon learned, however, Turner was not alone.

Parked near a run-down farm building was a car: a Royal Air Force Police car. Turner subsequently had a brief conversation with

the police officer and questioned him about his presence. This provoked a cryptic response from the RAF policeman, who admitted
that he was "monitoring the activity on the downs regarding the
crop circles."[3]

And the stories continue of official interest, in one form or another. The film director John McNeish claims that he received an
order from Buckingham Palace for a copy of his book *Crop Circle
Apocalypse*.[4]

But to what extent can such tales of official interest in crop circles
be validated? Do governmental, military, and intelligence files exist
on this topic? The answer is yes—at least, to an extent.

The earliest documented example of official interest in unusual
crop formations dates not, as might be expected, from the 1980s or
1990s, but from the 1940s and the battle-scarred landscape of
wartime Britain. This example implicates one of Britain's most secretive intelligence agencies, MI5, in the mystery.

In March 1909, the British government instructed its Committee of Imperial Defense to consider the dangers posed to British
naval ports by German espionage agents. On October 1 of that year,
Captain Vernon Kell of the South Staffordshire Regiment and Captain Mansfield Cumming of the Royal Navy jointly established the
Secret Service Bureau. To fulfill the Admiralty's requirement for information about Germany's new navy, Kell and Cumming divided
their work; Kell became responsible for counterespionage within
the British Isles, while Cumming coordinated the collection and
analysis of overseas intelligence data.

Between March 1909 and the outbreak of the First World War,
more than thirty spies were identified and arrested by the Secret
Service Bureau. At the time the bureau had a staff of only ten, but it
was rapidly mobilized as a branch of the War Office and in January
1916 became part of the new Directorate of Military Intelligence
and was known thereafter as MI5.

In early 1941, Sir David Petrie was appointed the first director
general of the Security Service and was given substantial resources

to rebuild the organization. As a result MI5 became one of the most efficient agencies of the war. After the defeat of the Nazis in 1945, it was learned that *all* of the Nazi agents targeted against Britain had been identified, and in some cases recruited as double agents, by MI5—something that contributed to the success of the Allied landing in Normandy on D day on June 6, 1944. But what, you may ask, does this have to do with the crop-circle mystery?

In 2001 a number of files pertaining to the wartime activities of MI5 were declassified and made available for inspection at the Public Record Office, Kew. One dealt with MI5 investigations of "markings on the ground," "suspicious pieces of paper and messages," "marked maps," and "markings on telegraph poles." According to the report:

The early days of 1940 and 1941 produced an avalanche of reports about the spys [sic] and fifth columnists who many people thought were roaming the land unhindered. Each village boasted of "enemy agents" in their midst, and it is only by recapturing the atmosphere of those days that one can see the matter in its proper perspective. Everyone had heard of the activities of fifth columnists on the continent and of the alarmingly successful part they had played in the overthrow of France and Belgium. It was therefore natural with everyone tense for the threatened invasion that so many reports came in. Each had to be investigated, even if only to put the minds of the public and the services at rest.

The report outlines the nature of its content:

This account is not concerned with the activities of fifth columnists such as sabotage, capturing airfields and key points, and harassing the defending army, but in the methods used in communicating to each other and to the enemy. Reports from Poland, Holland, France and Belgium showed that they used ground markings for the guidance of bombers and paratroops (and of lights by night). Such ground markings might be the cutting of cornfields into guiding marks for aircraft, painting of roofs and the inside of chimneys white, setting haystacks on fire, and laying out strips of white linen in pre-arranged patterns. For guiding and giving information to advancing troops they would conceal messages behind advertisement hoardings and leave markings on walls and telegraph poles.

For the most part, the unusual markings on telegraph poles, roofs, and chimneys were dismissed as having perfectly innocent explanations and indicates how rumor and misperception can run wildly out of control at times of hostility and high stress. But what of the "ground markings" in cornfields?

From interviews conducted with personnel who had taken part in the hostilities in Poland, MI5 had determined that one of the ways that Nazi spies were communicating with German Luftwaffe pilots was by "beating out signs," twenty meters in diameter, "on harrowed fields or mowing such signs on meadows or cornfields." Crop circles, in other words!

In a section of the report titled "Examples of Ground Markings Investigated," a still-anonymous MI5 employee wrote:

1. Field at Little Mill, Monmouthshire.
In May 1941 a report was made that an unusual mark was visible amongst the growing corn. Near one of the gates was a mark in the form of the letter "G," some 33 yards long. This mark had been made by sowing barley transversely through the grain. Air photographs were taken and it was seen that the tail of the marking pointed towards the Ordnance factory at Glascoed. The farmer, a man of good character, was interviewed, and admitted that he had sown the field himself. He explained that he had sold the field in April. Shortly after, having a drilling machine nearby which had a small quantity of barley

seed in it, and wishing to empty it as he had to return it to the
farmer from whom he had borrowed it that night, he turned
his team of horses into the grain field and drilled it into the
ground thickly to get rid of it. He did this because it is extremely difficult to remove the grain in the machine by hand,
and to sow it was the quickest way of getting rid of it. He
agreed to plough up this part of the field. As a satisfactory explanation had been reached, the case was carried no further.

2. Field, north of Newquay, Cornwall.
Aircraft noticed, in May 1940, strange marking in this field
and it was photographed. Enquiries were made and it was
found that the lines were formed by heaps of lime used for agri-
cultural purposes. The farmer concerned was above reproach
and removed the lime heaps.

3. Field, near Staplehurst, Kent.
In October 1943, aircraft saw a faint white circle on the ground
with the word MARDEN inscribed in it. Enquiries were made,
and it was discovered that before the war the field was used as
an emergency landing ground by Imperial Airways; the mark
was made by them, and they paid a small yearly rent to the
farmer. At the beginning of the war the mark was obliterated
in some way, but this had worn thin. Steps were taken to oblit-
erate it again.[5]

So these examples of unusual wartime formations found in cornfields were determined not be related to the activities of the Nazis
and instead had wholly down-to-earth explanations. But this intriguing aspect of MI5's wartime activities is notable for one key
reason: it demonstrates that official bodies within Britain *have* investigated unusual crop formations to determine if they are in any
way representative of a threat to the British Isles.
   In the postwar period, the next example we have of official in-

volvement in crop-circle-like phenomena dates from early 1964.
On March 23 of that year, the Reverend T. E. T. Burbury of Clifton
Rectory, Penrith, England, wrote to the National Physical Labora-
tory at Teddington, which in turn forwarded his letter to the British
Air Ministry via the Meteorological Office at Bracknell, about a
crop-circle-forming blue light he had seen.

Does an apparent column of blue light about eight feet in diameter and about fifteen feet high which disperses and leaves a
mark of very slightly disturbed earth, the same diameter,
mean anything to you?

I examined the ground which is about one hundred yards
from the nearest building and there are no pylons near. There
was no sign of burning, either by sight or smell; the grass
growing between the exposed ground appeared quite normal.
There were no signs of bird tracks or droppings; the ground
simply appeared to have been lightly raked over in almost perfect circle.

In this case, the Air Ministry seemed less than impressed with the
report and suggested in an internal memorandum that the encounter probably had more to do with the condition of the liver of
the witness than it did with anything else.[6]

The key witness in this 1964 encounter was eventually tracked
down by the crop-circle investigator Paul Fuller. Robert Ellis informed Fuller that at approximately 9:30 P.M. on the night in question the family's dog began to howl in the vicinity of an outbuilding
where it slept at night. Thinking that some stock might have broken
loose, Ellis went to check and noticed that the tops of two nearby
apple trees were lit up by a blue light. He told Fuller:

"Approximately one hundred yards from where I stood was a
vivid 'electric blue' light. Its shape was elliptical. It stayed in a horizontal position, remaining motionless and making no audible
sound. I could see no detail within the light; in fact I had to shade

my eyes with my hand, the light was so intense. I was quite frightened—being alone—and quickly went indoors. By that time I had calmed down and opened the curtains and shutters of the front window to look out again in that direction, all was in darkness."

According to Ellis, an inspection of the area the following morning revealed a circular depression as described by Burbury. "In some places the disturbance was two inches deep as if the area had been vigorously raked. The roots of the grass were damaged and the circle remained visible well into May of that year."[7]

The lack of official interest in this 1964 case is in direct contrast to the concern shown over the wartime 1940s cases. Would MI5 be interested in the crop-circle phenomenon since the 1980s? We don't know. But we have found one aspect of the current phenomenon very interesting.

Most of the crop circles in the British Isles have been found in the county of Wiltshire, which is also home to Porton Down, the British government's Chemical and Biological Defense Establishment; Salisbury Plain, an area used for military training purposes; Boscombe Down, from where new and experimental aircraft are flown; and RAF Rudloe Manor, a secretive military establishment that until 1998 was home to an elite body of the Royal Air Force known as the Provost and Security Services.

Could the crop circles be coded messages left for terrorist or subversive groups intent on disrupting activities at Porton Down, Boscombe Down, Rudloe Manor, and Salisbury Plain? Or could the phenomenon be produced by the British military itself?

Let us now turn our attention to the United States. A report titled "Summary of Circumstances: Investigation of Possible Unidentified Flying Object—Arlington, Virginia, 1–2 September 1952" was found at the National Archives, Maryland, in the now declassified UFO-related investigative files of the U.S. Air Force's Office of Special Investigations. It is of interest and relevance because it deals with the discovery and investigation of an "an unusual circle."

1. At 1600 hours on 3 Sep 52, the Directorate of Intelligence, HQ USAF received a telephone call from Mr. Storm, SE, Washington, that an unusual circle was found marked on the lawn of his father, Mr. Storm, on the morning of 2 Sep 52 and that he believed it might bear some relation to the USAF investigation of unidentified flying objects.

2. Major Fournet, of the D/I, called on the elder Mr. Storm at his residence, Arlington, Va., during the evening of 3 Sep 52.

3. The following was found on Mr. Storm's rear lawn:

a. A circle 18 feet in diameter and nearly perfectly formed was marked on the lawn by a deposit of some unknown gray substance which was adhering to the grass in clusters of fine globules.

b. The band of the circle (around the periphery) was an average of approximately 6 inches wide.

c. The deposits in the band were less pronounced and sometimes absent for short distances where depressions or unevenness in the ground surface occurred.

d. A small evergreen bush was located at a point about 40 inches inside the circle and did not appear to have been disturbed in any way nor were any deposits present on or around it.

e. A clothes line frame located on a central pole overhung the circle somewhat and had been in place on the night in question.

f. An antenna wire about 40 feet above the ground overhung the circle, exact amount undetermined.

g. No other vegetation in the area contained any deposits or marks (small trees were present, as close as 6 or 8 feet from the circle).

h. Three types of fertilizer were stored in covered drums near the garage about 15 feet away from the circle.

4. Mr. and Mrs. Storm were interviewed and offered the following information:

a. Mr. Storm cut the grass in the area in question around 1800–1900 hours on 1 Sep 52. The clippings were left where they fell.

b. At 2300 hours on 1 Sep 52, Mr. Storm put his dog in the basement for the night. (Note: the dog barks at anyone who comes into the yard, and, until that time, had not sounded off.)

c. (As related to Mr. Storm later by Mrs. [deleted] a neighbor immediately in the rear of the Storm residence and adjacent to the lawn in question.) Mrs. [deleted] was awakened at about 0400 hours on 2 Sep 52 by barking of dog "which seemed to be in distress." She looked out of a window in the rear of her house but failed to see anything (it was a rather dark night).

d. Upon going out to his car at 0730 hours 2 Sep 52, Mr. Storm noticed the circle and walked over to examine it. He describes it as having at that time a brown, oily-sandy appearance with what seemed to be a very fine granular structure (as though a fine sand mixed with light oil had been spread to form the ring). He rubbed some of the substance between his fingers and found it faintly gritty and definitely oily. Mrs. Storm corroborates this description.

e. During mid-afternoon of 2 Sep 52 Mrs. Storm reexamined the ring and found that the color had changed to grayish blue, and it no longer appeared to be oily. However it still felt oily but no longer felt gritty. She detected no odor upon smelling it.

f. Upon returning from work at 1700 hours 2 Sep 52, Mr. Storm again examined it with his wife. He describes the color as purplish-gray; Mrs. Storm describes the color as bluish gray. Both agree that the substance had begun to form small, closely-packed globules on the blades of grass and that it had begun to "crystallize." Mr. Storm states that it then felt slick (like graphite) when rubbed between the fingers; Mrs. Storm describes it as a powdery feel. (NOTE: There has been no rain since before the evening of 1 Sep 52, and there was a hot sun all day on 2 Sep 52. However, there was a heavy rainfall during the night of 2/3 Sep 52.)

g. During the morning of 3 Sep 52, Mr. Storm reexamined it and "was surprised to find it there after so much rain." He describes its appearance as darker (a slate gray) and still formed in globules on the grass blades. It still felt about like graphite. Perhaps a bit "thinner" than the preceding evening.

5. Mr. and Mrs. [deleted] were not at home and, therefore, were not interviewed.

6. Samples of grass, leaves and soil, and of three types of fertilizer stored nearby were removed for analysis.

7. Mr. and Mrs. Storm were very cooperative and appeared to be completely sincere. They stated that they have not recently evinced much interest in the subject of unidentified flying objects nor had they discussed the subject with anyone, thereby eliminating any obvious motive for a practical joke.

The Air Force recommended that the relevant samples be forwarded to the FBI laboratory for analysis. While this was done, followed by some discussion of the possibility of contamination from fertilizers, the case was left frustratingly unresolved.

Forty years later, official interest in such phenomena continues on the part of U.S. intelligence. Files released by the ultrasecret National Security Agency, for example, detail accounts of crop circles appearing in fields in northern Germany in the 1990s and claims that they were made by human beings. Additional papers from the same time frame declassified by the NSA refer to "mysterious, small circles" that had appeared on the walls of tunnels in Japan's underground railway system that were believed to be caused by a plasma emanating from high-voltage railway power lines.

These records clearly demonstrate that crop circles and crop-circle-like phenomena *have* been investigated at an official level on both sides of the Atlantic from the early 1940s to the mid-1990s. To what extent similar investigations may have continued since then, however, still has many researchers of the puzzle going, quite literally, around in circles.

Two

THE ARARAT ANOMALY

History was made on June 17, 1949. That's when a U.S. Air Force Europe (USAFE) plane taking part in a classified mission that included aerial imaging of the 16,945-foot-high Mt. Ararat, Turkey, inadvertently stumbled across what may have been the remains of the mighty Ark of Noah described in the Bible. As the aircraft reached a height of around fifteen thousand feet and a distance of approximately one mile from the frozen mountain, its cameras captured two extraordinary images of a large structure—perhaps five hundred feet in length—that protruded from an ice cap located at the southwest edge of Ararat's west-facing plateau.

The crew quickly swung the aircraft around and headed to the north of the mountain and continued to take photographs. Astonishingly, these revealed (from a distance of two miles) the existence of yet another large, unidentified structure on the western plateau and three symmetrical, but badly damaged, protrusions that pointed skyward out of what looked like a wing-style section of the structure. Needless to say the photographs were carefully and quietly processed and duly classified. And thus was born the legend of the Ararat Anomaly—as it is unofficially known throughout

``We have looked into this matter in some detail and we regret that we are unable to provide any information''.

In September/October 1974, Admiral Showers of the Intelligence Community Staff, in re sponse to a query from Lieutenant Commander Lonnie McClung, asked about the availability of intelligence information concerning the location of Noah's Ark. He was told that a search had been made of aerial photography with negative results.

On 30 January 1975, Dr. John Morris again wrote Congressman Bob Wilson noting that aerial photos ``were taken in August 1974, as a result of my request. They were not to be classified, but have been classified since and are not available.'' Congressman Wilson again contacted solicited the Agency with the request. On 27 February 1975, Mr. Hicks again denied the request. On 11 March 1975, Dr. Morris was notified that the photography of Mt. Ararat was classified and, therefore, could not be provided. On 5 March 1975, an additional request made through Dr. on 5 March 1975 Charles Willis of Fresno, California to Mr. Arthur C. Lundahl, retired Director NPIC was also denied on 31 March 1975.

On 3 April 1975, NPIC Section Chief ████████████ sent a memo to the Chief, IEG, detailing the efforts of Messrs. ████████████ and ████████ who had searched unsuccessfully all available U-2 and satellite imagery for possible evidence of Noah's Ark. This search had been prompted by the visit to the Center, on 14 March 1975, of Captain Howard Schue of the IC Staff with a ground photo ``showing a long range view of the purported Ark.'' The ████████████ Division of NPIC was tasked to determine if the Ark's features in the photo had been altered; tests failed to identify any manipulation. Attempts to compare the ground photo with satellite imagery for identification and location purposes also proved negative.

From 27 March to 5 April 1975, a French archeological explorer, Fernand Navarra was at Iverson Mall in Washington, D.C. publicizing his book Noah's Ark I Touched It. As part of the sales pitch for the book, there was a display which included a supposed wood fragment of the Ark.

The CIA has declassified a number of files relating to the so-called Ararat Anomaly—an unusual feature on Mt. Ararat, Turkey, that some believe may be the remains of Noah's Ark. This CIA document dates from 1982 and reveals some of the CIA's findings on the Anomaly.

the U.S. intelligence community in general and the CIA in particular.

Any mention of the Central Intelligence Agency inevitably conjures up images of sinister-looking characters conducting covert espionage operations, political assassinations, and James Bond–like escapades. The truth is often different. Granted, the CIA's history has at times been both dark and controversial. But for the most part, CIA employees do not run around the world with gorgeous girls on their arms while ordering their drinks "shaken and not stirred" and simultaneously saving the planet from some deranged madman in 007-style. In reality, the CIA makes use of numerous personnel in a wide and varied body of disciplines. Scientists, engineers, economists, linguists, mathematicians, secretaries, accountants, and computer specialists are but a few of the professionals that the CIA employs.

The CIA was established on July 26, 1947, by President Harry Truman as a result of the passing of the U.S. government's National Security Act. It had its origins in the wartime Office of Strategic Services and the Central Intelligence Group (which had been created in January 1946 under the directorship of Admiral Sidney Souers). With its primary mission to collect, evaluate, and disseminate foreign intelligence data, the CIA assists the president and senior U.S. government policymakers in making decisions relating to national security. The CIA does not make policy, however. It is an independent source of foreign intelligence for those who do.

A common misconception is that the CIA's budget is unlimited. While exempt from disclosure to the public and the media alike, the specific budget and the size of the CIA are known in detail and scrutinized by the Office of Management and Budget and by the Senate Select Committee on Intelligence, the House Permanent Select Committee on Intelligence, and the Defense Subcommittees of the Appropriations Committees in both houses of Congress. In 1997, for example, the aggregate figure for *all* U.S. government intelligence and intelligence-related activities—of which the CIA is

only one part—was made public for the first time and amounted to
$26.6 billion. And as the CIA's remarkable history shows, at times
that budget has been applied to some distinctly unusual topics—as
we shall now see.[1]

In a situation that mirrors the allegations of conspiracy and
cover-up regarding the assassination of President John F. Kennedy
on November 22, 1963, a whole host of claims, counterclaims, and
assertions regarding the Ararat Anomaly have surfaced both privately and publicly. Many of these maintain that the CIA and a
number of other official bodies have collated a wealth of data and
imagery on the Anomaly that are exempt from public disclosure.

Sources tell of Indiana Jones–style, U.S. government–funded ex-
peditions to Turkey to try to locate the Ark's remains. Others maintain that remnants of the Anomaly *have* been found and spirited
away to classified military and governmental installations and institutions in the USA. And there is talk of intimidation by Men-in-
Black-type characters warning those with knowledge of the
Anomaly to remain silent. But can such claims be validated? Is the
Anomaly really the Ark of Noah? Or is it simply a natural structure?
And if so, should we relegate the entire story to the worlds of fiction,
rumor, and misperception?

The best place to begin our investigation is, obviously, the Bible.
"God said unto Noah . . . Make thee an ark of gopher wood . . . And
this is the fashion which thou shalt make it of: The length of the ark
shall be three hundred cubits, the breadth of it fifty cubits, and the
height of it thirty cubits." A cubit is approximately twenty inches in
length—which would make the Ark five hundred feet long, eighty-
three feet wide, and fifty feet high.

Moreover, it is alleged that the Ark was strong enough to with-
stand the catastrophic worldwide flood that supposedly encompassed the globe and lasted for forty turbulent days. So the story
goes, when the flood waters began to recede, the Ark settled on its
final resting place: the permanently snowcapped Mt. Ararat.

Needless to say, if the U.S. intelligence community *has* located the remains (or the suspected remains) of such an impressive vessel, it would undoubtedly be the archaeological find of the century. But would such a discovery be made public? Certainly there is no shortage of accounts positing a link between the Ararat Anomaly, Noah's Ark, and the secret world of officialdom.

In 1952, William Todd, a photographer's mate chief with the U.S. Navy, viewed an object "of huge size" that appeared to be a "rectangular, slate-colored boat," while flying near the summit of Mt. Ararat.[2] And in 1955, a French explorer, Fernand Navarra, located a five-foot-long piece of ancient, carved wood high on Mt. Ararat, just several hundred meters from the site shown in the historic photographs taken in 1949.[3]

According to Gregor Schwinghammer, formerly of the U.S. Air Force's 428th Tactical Flight Squadron based in Adana, Turkey, he saw the Anomaly as he was flying near the mountain in an F-100 aircraft in the late 1950s. Moreover, he said that it looked like "an enormous boxcar" lying in a gully high up on Mount Ararat and added that photographs had been taken of the structure by U-2 spyplane pilots. He further revealed that the object seemed to be banked—something that indicated it had become caught there as it slid down the mountainside. "I think most of the time it is covered with ice and snow and that we just saw it at a time when part of it was protruding from the snow," Schwinghammer told author Charles Berlitz. "I know that I saw a rectangular structure that looked like a ship. It was at a period in time or history and we were there at that time. Other pilots in the squadron remember having taken part in flights over Ararat or having heard that other pilots had seen a shiplike object on the mountain."[4]

Similarly, the noted authority on the Ark, Robin Simmons, has secured the testimony of a man who worked at the Smithsonian in the fall of 1968. After being there for approximately a month, the man said that "several crates were delivered to our section which seemed to cause quite a bit of interest among the directors."

The crates were duly opened, and contained within them were

"several artifacts like old wood and some old-style tools." There were photographs too, reportedly taken from a balloon, that showed "a shiplike object down in some ice. So I took a look at them and talked some, and I was told it was Noah's Ark."

The man said this caused a lot of excitement among the staff, but after about five days, things began to change. "They didn't talk anymore," he said. "They started taking the stuff out. The questions we'd ask, they just kind of ignore us, and finally they pretty well came out and told everybody to just keep their mouth shut."

After portions of his story were published in the book *Has Anyone Really Seen Noah's Ark?* (written by the author Violet Cummings), the man said he was visited at work by two men who identified themselves as FBI agents. "They told me my statements were making waves at the Smithsonian. And that I had been somewhere where I shouldn't have and seen something that didn't concern me. They didn't threaten me, exactly."

This prompted the man to phone his boss at the Smithsonian. "I asked him some questions about all that stuff from Ararat and the Ark. He said, 'You know, I really can't talk about it,' and kind of laughed."[5] And the accounts do not end there.

In September 1973 on the eve of the Yom Kippur War, a CIA reconnaissance satellite allegedly obtained imagery of a "boatlike" object on Mt. Ararat. "The pictures are real clear," according to Dino Brugioni, a retired CIA photographic specialist directed to study the high-resolution imagery, and quoted in the *Washington Times*. "You see the whole summit and lots of rock formations. We measured things, but none of them fell within the dimensions given in the Bible. If you didn't have the biblical dimensions in cubits, you could pick up those pictures and say they look like a ship. But when you measure it, it doesn't come out right. At no time did we say we saw an ark."[6]

Echoing these words, an anonymous, former high-ranking intelligence official who had seen the 1973 satellite images informed the *Washington Times* that one photograph showed close-ups of what seemed to be three large, curved wooden beams. While there was disagreement on the part of CIA analysts over what the photograph showed exactly, he was careful to state, "I have felt from the beginning the thing ought to be looked at more carefully. It's worth looking into."[7]

The late George A. Carver Jr., the former deputy for national intelligence in the CIA during the 1970s, made a similar statement in 1993: "Well, I don't recall the CIA working on Noah's Ark, but I do remember that at the time there were some pictures taken, and there were clear indications that there was something up on Mt. Ararat, which was rather strange."[8]

Having reviewed a wealth of testimony both on and off the record, let us now turn our attention to what can be determined officially about the Ararat Anomaly and its potential relationship to the Ark of Noah.

In the story of the Ark, the Anomaly, the CIA, and the U.S. intelligence community, one name stands out more than any other: that of Professor Porcher Taylor III, of the University of Richmond. He has diligently pursued this story for a decade and originally heard rumors pertaining to the Anomaly while a junior cadet at the U.S. Military Academy at West Point in 1973.

Having begun to seriously research the Ararat Anomaly in 1993, Taylor cultivated good contacts and links within U.S. intelligence. He struck gold on March 14, 1995, when the Defense Intelligence Agency made available to him a single sixteen-by-nine-inch copy of one of the black-and-white photographs taken of the Ararat Anomaly by the U.S. Air Force forty-six years previously. By October 1995, further images were released to Taylor by the DIA. But what, exactly, do they show?

According to Peter Hsu, a principal naval engineer, the "dense linear-shaped object" might be "man-made." Similarly a former colleague of Carver's informed Taylor in 1995 that he had both seen and evaluated photographs taken of the Ararat Anomaly for the CIA in 1959–60 and thought that in the photographic evidence secured by Taylor from the DIA the object was "too linear to be natural and that most of the structure appeared to be under ice."[9]

Not everyone is in agreement, however, in particular the Defense Intelligence Agency:

The anomaly identified by Mr. Taylor on photographic enlargements . . . is located at approximately 39 42' 10"N 044 16' 30" at an elevation of approximately 14–15000' and approximately 2.2 KM horizontal distance West of the summit. This position is map derived and should not be considered geodetically precise.

The "anomaly" is located along an unstable precipice near the edge of the permanent glacial ice cap atop Mt. Ararat. The instability of this feature is evidenced by the observation of an avalanche in progress just to the east of the "anomaly" on frame 2. The accumulated ice and snow along this precipice obviously fall down the side of the mountain at frequent intervals, often leaving long linear facades. It appears that the "anomaly" is one of these linear facades in the glacial ice underlying more recent accumulated ice and snow. Further, the tone and texture of the "anomaly" and avalanche debris immediately below are consistent with the shadowed snow, ice, and debris prevalent along the face of the precipice.

And the controversy continues. On several occasions in late 1999 and mid-2000, photographs of the Anomaly were taken by the private satellite of a Colorado-based company: Space Imaging. A seven-person team examined the images and again there was a divergence of opinion. Some favored the theory that the Anomaly was artificial and others leaned toward accepting that it was a natural rock formation. Intriguingly, however, one of the team members concluded that the Anomaly had "shifted" slightly and was "broken" in several places—something that suggests it is not simply a formation of rock.[10]

But let us now turn our attention to the crux of the matter: the CIA's knowledge of the Ararat Anomaly. In February 2002, the CIA released to us via the terms of the Freedom of Information Act a package of material concerning the Anomaly, Mt. Ararat, and Noah's Ark. The file is illuminating in what it tells us, what it doesn't tell us, and what it implies.

Certainly one of the most intriguing entries in the file is a four-page document titled "Noah's Ark, 1974–1982," which provides a time-line for significant events in the Agency's involvement in the controversy.

According to the records, on May 13, 1974, the then director of central intelligence, William Colby, wrote a letter to Sayre Stevens, of the Agency's Directorate of Science and Technology, asking if the CIA had any evidence in its possession of the existence of Noah's Ark on Mt. Ararat.

Mr. Colby said that Lieutenant Colonel Walter Brown of the US Air Force Academy had asked "whether it would be appropriate or possible to exploit satellite photography to examine the glacier systems there to see whether any evidence of the Ark could be found." On 21 May, the Center responded that no evidence of the Ark could be discerned on U-2 photography acquired on 10 September 1957 or on any satellite imagery available at the Center.

While the response to the inquiry from Lieutenant Colonel Walter Brown provided nothing of substance, it is perhaps of significance, however, that the reference to U-2 photography of the region taken in 1957 does correlate somewhat with the account of Gregor Schwinghammer, who asserted, long before this CIA document surfaced, that the U-2 spy plane had been utilized to photograph both Mt. Ararat and the Anomaly.

On 6 August 1974, Congressman Bob Wilson asked the Agency whether any aerial photos of Mt. Ararat could be released to a friend of his, Dr. John Morris, son of Dr. Henry Morris, the head of the Institution of Creation Research of San Diego, California. Mr. Hicks stated in a letter to the Agency legislative liaison staff that several U-2 photos dated 1957 were available but were still classified "Confidential." The younger Dr. Morris wrote to the Agency later requesting the photos. His request was denied by Angus Theurmer, the Agency's press spokesman, who stated, "We have looked into this matter in some detail and we regret that we are unable to provide any information."

Further rumors were apparently leaking outside the corridors of power to the effect that photographs of the Ark had been obtained for the CIA on U-2 spying missions. And still the requests for the declassification of evidence that many believed the CIA to be in possession of continued.

In September/October 1974, Admiral Showers of the Intelligence Community Staff, in response to a query from Lieutenant Commander Lonnie McClung, asked about the availability of intelligence information concerning the location of Noah's Ark. He was told that a search had been made of aerial photography with negative results.

On 30 January 1975, Dr. John Morris again wrote Congressman Bob Wilson noting that aerial photos "were taken in August 1974, as a result of my request. They were not to be classified, but have been classified since and are not available." Congressman Wilson again contacted the Agency with the request. On 27 February 1975, Mr. Hicks again denied the request. On 11 March 1975, Dr. Morris was notified that the photography of Mt. Ararat was classified and, therefore, could not be provided. An additional request made through Dr.

Charles Willis of Fresno, California, to Mr. Arthur C. Lundahl, retired Director NPIC [Note from the authors: National Photographic Interpretation Center] on 5 March 1975 was also denied on 31 March 1975.

This particular reference to classified aerial photographs taken of Mt. Ararat in 1974 indicates that some officials were working hard to resolve the controversy. And that controversy continued unabated.

On 3 April 1975, NPIC Section Chief [deleted] sent a memo to the Chief, IEG, detailing the efforts of Messrs. [deleted] and [deleted] who had searched unsuccessfully all available U-2 and satellite imagery for possible evidence of Noah's Ark. This search had been prompted by the visit to the Center, on 14 March 1975, of Captain Howard Schue of the IC Staff with a ground photo "showing a long range view of the purported Ark." The [deleted] Division of NPIC was tasked to determine if the Ark's features in the photo had been altered; tests failed to identify any manipulation. Attempts to compare the ground photo with satellite imagery for identification and location purposes also proved negative.

Obviously the CIA was as much in the dark as everyone else about the nature of what was, or was not, situated on Mt. Ararat, but the reference to the NPIC being "tasked" to determine the nature of the Schue photograph, however, demonstrates that additional files or memoranda on this matter have been generated. To date, they have failed to surface into the public domain.

We return to the CIA document.

From 27 March to 5 April 1975, a French archeological explorer, Fernand Navarra, was at Iverson Mall in Washington, D.C. publicizing his book *Noah's Ark: I Touched It*. As part of the sales pitch for the book, there was a display which included a supposed wood fragment of the Ark. Several NPIC analysts concerned with the Ark problem visited the display but found nothing that would help their search effort.

That the CIA's NPIC would be sufficiently involved in analyzing Ark-related data to stealthily check out a public display promoting a book on the subject suggests strongly that the possible existence of something truly extraordinary on Mt. Ararat was being seriously addressed. It may also be notable that, as we revealed earlier, the location where Navarra found his potentially historic piece of wood was only meters from where then still classified Air Force imagery of the Anomaly was taken in 1949.

Then on 10 April 1975 another development in the affair surfaced.

Colonel Paul Tanota and Captain Howard Schue, of the IC Staff visited NPIC to discuss Mt. Ararat and to see the August 1974 aerial photography of the mountain. At the request of Captain Schue, a print of Mt. Ararat showing the 13,000 and 14,000 foot elevations was provided.

On 5 July 1975 a book entitled *The Ark of Ararat* by Thomas Nelson was released. Mr. Nelson maintained that the CIA had photos of Mt. Ararat and that they had been analyzed in the search for the Ark.

On 12 October 1975, Tom Croster from a group known as The Holy Ground Mission of Frankston, Texas showed a ground photo supposedly of the Ark taken during their 1974 expedition to Mt. Ararat. Sometime in 1977, Bill Chaney Speed of Search Foundation, Inc. requested the aerial photos of Mt. Ararat. His request was also denied.

The references to the Holy Ground Mission and to the Nelson book again demonstrate that the CIA was keeping a watchful eye on

any and all developments. And the CIA continued to be dogged by
the specter of the Ark.

Senator Barry Goldwater wrote DCI Turner on 1 September
1978, "You may think this is a screwball request and it may
be, but I would like to know if you can do anything about it."
The letter went on to ask if satellite photography could be
searched "to determine whether or not something in the way of
an archeological find might be located near or on top of the
Mount." Goldwater explained that a letter he had received had
come "from a man in whom I have great confidence, who certainly is no nut, who knows Turkey rather well but who feels
that there is reason to believe the Ark may be resting at or
near the top of the mount. I assure that I will keep this at any
classification you want it kept and if you desire me to go to the
devil, I know the way." DCI Turner replied, "We have been requested on several occasions if we could determine whether
there was remains of the Ark on Mt. Ararat. We have, as a result, carefully reviewed the photography of the area but have
not found any evidence of the Ark."

At the turn of the 1980s the controversy surrounding the CIA and
the Ark of Noah continued.

On 27 May 1981, [deleted] of the Center received a telephone
call from Air Force Tallent Control Officer, Major Ray Abel, requesting information on Noah's Ark. Major Abel said he had
received a request from General Lew Allen, Air Force Chief of
Staff, who, in turn, was answering a requirement from Congressman Bill Archer of Texas.

Congressman Archer had indicated that some of his con-
stituents from Houston, Texas were going on an expedition
to Mt. Ararat and would like to have as much information as

possible. [Deleted] told Major Abel that NPIC had conducted a
study of Mt. Ararat in the 1970s and had found no evidence of
the Ark.

In February 1982, former Astronaut James B. Irwin of the
High Flight Foundation, a Christian group in Colorado Springs,
Colorado, called former NPIC official Dino A. Brugioni, at his
home and asked about the aerial photos of Mount Ararat. Irwin
was informed that no evidence of the Ark had ever been seen
on aerial photography.

Since 1982 the amount of documentation on the Ararat Anomaly that the CIA has declassified into the public domain is limited.
Indeed, the next entry we see in the file dates from 1992 and is a letter from one Charles P. Aaron, described as chief pilot and director
of operations for the Tsirah Corporation. He wrote to the CIA requesting Agency assistance in the corporation's search for Noah's
vessel, a search that had been in progress for a number of years
and that had the support of astronaut Jim Irwin and several U.S.
senators.

It is noteworthy that Aaron informed the Agency that a number
of qualified officials had informed him that the U.S. government
possessed a restricted-access satellite surveillance system that was
capable of looking through ice.

Aaron sensibly advised the CIA further that he was not interested
in obtaining first-hand knowledge of what might very well have
been classified surveillance technology, but simply wanted to know
if the CIA could lend help to Tsirah's quest. A June 2, 1992, memorandum titled "Noah's Ark" and designated for the Agency's Office
of Imagery Analysis (OIA) reveals the response to the Tsirah
request.

We reviewed a video—for assistance in locating Noah's Ark on
Mt. Ararat in northeastern Turkey. The request made by
Charles Aaron of the Tsirah Corporation, was sent to the Di-

rector of Central Intelligence. . . . Mr. Aaron's letter stated a belief that the Agency had the technical capability to look
through hundreds of feet of ice and asked that we use this
technology to aid his search for the Ark. To the best of OIA's
knowledge, there is no such existing technology.

The OIA added that, having looked at existing imagery of Mt.
Ararat, they were unable to confirm the existence of the Ark or its
proposed location and suggested that the Tsirah Corporation
should be informed likewise. Again, we have a firm denial of anything positive having been determined from an analysis of imagery
of the alleged final resting place of the Ark of Noah.

On January 21, 1993, however, a formerly secret CIA memorandum contained within the file makes a curious reference to
"a request to declassify imagery of Noah's Ark for a TV production" that was, to quote further, "turned down" by the CIA. It
may be nothing more than a slip of the keyboard, but the specific
reference to imagery of Noah's Ark (rather than, for example, imagery of the Anomaly or imagery of an unidentified formation on
Mt. Ararat) is something that we should bear in mind as potentially
telling.

Of equal interest is a February 7, 1994, document from the CIA's
Office of the Deputy Director for Science and Technology to the director of central intelligence stating in part that they had "no efforts
currently underway to conduct additional searches for Noah's Ark
in the Mt. Ararat region." Of course, the reference to "additional
searches" can only mean that at some point in its past, at least, the
CIA *had* undertaken a quest to try to locate the Ark.

The final document of any significance contained within the declassified material is a February 1, 1994, memorandum from an unknown source within the office of the Director of the CIA to the
Science and Technology office. The purpose was to obtain a status
report to determine what the CIA had on file in the form of imagery
on both Mt. Ararat and Noah's Ark.

OIA and NPIC has no active project searching imagery of Mt. Ararat, Turkey, for evidence of Noah's Ark. . . . At the direction of DCI [Robert] Gates, OIA in 1992 searched for the Ark on imagery routinely collected of the Mt. Ararat area between November 1990 and January 1992. That search revealed nothing conclusive; only two areas of apparent rock formations protruding through existing snow and ice.

We doubt that a thorough search of imagery of Mt. Ararat for evidence of the Ark would be conclusive. With its summit over 15,000 feet of elevation, Mt. Ararat is snow and ice covered virtually year round.

A few scant documents aside, there ends the CIA's file. But are we any closer to understanding the nature and origin of the curious anomaly of Mt. Ararat? The answer has to be no. However, a curious trend runs throughout this entire story. On the one hand, the officially released files for the most part fail to indicate the presence of anything truly unusual on the mountain, while retired CIA and military personnel for the most part suggest otherwise. Is this simply coincidence or is there a missing piece to the Ararat Anomaly puzzle that has led to this curious situation? Is it possible that the Ark *was* located after the Anomaly was first photographed by the U.S. Air Force in the summer of 1949? And if so, is it feasible that remnants of the Ark have been retrieved—as Robin Simmons's source suggests?

Perhaps the answers to those questions can be found buried deep within some impenetrable vault of U.S. intelligence. Equally, the harsh, snowcapped peaks of Mt. Ararat may continue to hide their secrets from one and all. For now, at least (and until such time as the Turkish government allows it to be examined in detail and at close quarters), the Ararat Anomaly will continue to remain precisely that: an anomaly.

Three

ASHES TO ASHES

Of the many and varied ways to meet that grimmest of reapers, few can be more horrific than being burned to death. To do so in a house fire or a car wreck would be bad enough, but to simply burst into flames for no apparent reason and at any given moment is positively horrifying. But such is the nature of spontaneous human combustion (SHC).

For centuries people have pondered this worrisome phenomenon and have advanced numerous theories to explain precisely why someone might, literally, go up in smoke, for no apparent cause. Possible explanations include having excessive amounts of body fat, being alcoholic, built-up static electricity, a lethal combination of chemicals in the stomach generated by a poor diet, even divine intervention.

One of the earliest references to spontaneous human combustion dates back to 1673, when Jonas Dupont of France published a collection of SHC reports and investigations in his book, *De Incendiis Corporis Humani Spontaneis*. He had been inspired by a Parisian case that almost led to a murder conviction for the unfortunate victim's spouse. Similarly, on April 9, 1744, Grace Pett of Ip-

REPORT
of the
FBI LABORATORY

FEDERAL BUREAU OF INVESTIGATION
WASHINGTON D. C.

To:

Mr. J. R. Reichert
Chief of Police
St. Petersburg, Florida

July 11, 1951

There follows the report of the FBI Laboratory on the examination of evidence received from your department.

This examination has been made with the understanding that the evidence is connected with an official investigation of a criminal matter and that the Laboratory report will be used for official purposes only, related to the investigation or a subsequent criminal prosecution. Authorization cannot be granted for the use of the Laboratory report in connection with a civil proceeding.

John Edgar Hoover, Director

Re:

Mrs. ~~~~~~~~~~, Deceased
Burned to Death in Apartment
1200 Cherry Street

YOUR FILE NO.
FBI FILE NO.
RECORDED #96   95-1112 - 1
~-3053 cc

Examination requested by: Addressee

Reference: Letter dated July 7, 1951

Examination requested: Chemical Analyses - Miscellaneous - Microscopic Analyses

Specimens:

- Q1   Glass fragments found in ashes
- Q2   Six small objects believed to be teeth
- Q3   Metal from near body
- Q4   Fibers believed to be part of nightgown
- Q5   Particles of bones found in ashes
- Q6   Charred fabric believed to be from chair
- Q7   Cotton material from chair
- Q8   Charred wood
- Q9   Charred legs from end table
- Q10 Charred fabric from rug
- Q11 Unburned section of rug heavily soaked with grease substance
- Q12 Remainder of ashes
- Q13 Shoe from foot not consumed by fire
- Q14 Chair springs

Enclosure

1-Miami

78 AUG 6 1951

(continued next page)

An extract from an untitled, official FBI file of 1951 on one of the
strangest of all mysteries: spontaneous human combustion.

swich, England, was found on the floor of her home burned like "a log of wood consumed by a fire, without apparent flame."

More than two hundred years later, on May 18, 1957, Anna Martin of West Philadelphia, Pennsylvania, died after being incinerated in temperatures that reached almost two thousand degrees. All that remained of Anna Martin were her shoes and a small part of her torso. And almost a decade later, the remains of Dr. J. Irving Bentley were discovered at his home in Coudersport, Pennsylvania. Another victim of SHC, he had apparently burned with such intensity as to create a three-foot-wide hole in the floor of his bathroom where he had fallen.

The most famous fictional account of death by SHC is surely that of the character Krook, in Charles Dickens's celebrated novel of 1852, *Bleak House*. Dickens expanded on the theory postulated at the time that SHC was linked to alcoholism and based his character's death on that of alleged real-life SHC victim Countess Cornelia de Bandi Cesenate. Interestingly, in the second edition of his book published in the following year, Dickens asserted that he had researched the subject of SHC thoroughly and had uncovered more than thirty such cases.

The real-life details of the countess's death are not pretty. According to the August 1832 edition of *The Saturday Magazine*, "This lady, who was in the sixty-second year of her age, retired to bed in her usual health. Here she spent above three hours in conversation with her maid, and in saying her prayers; and having at last fallen asleep, the door of her chamber was shut. As her maid was not summoned at the usual hour, she went into the bedroom to wake her mistress; but receiving no answer, she opened the window, and saw her corpse on the floor, in the most dreadful condition. At the distance of four feet from the bed there was a heap of ashes. Her legs, with stockings on, remained untouched, and the head, half-burned, lay between them. Nearly all the rest of the body was reduced to ashes. The air in the room was charged with floating soot. A small oil lamp on the floor was covered with ashes, but had no oil in it; and in two candlesticks, which stood upright upon a table, the cotton wick of both the candles was left, and the tallow of both had disappeared. It has been generally supposed that an internal combustion had taken place; that the lady had risen from her bed to cool herself, and that, in her way to open the window, the combustion had overpowered her, and consumed her by a process in which no flame was produced." .

The most intriguing case of all, however, and one that provides the official answer to the mystery of SHC, occurred in St. Petersburg, Florida. At 9 P.M. on the evening of July 1, 1951, sixty-seven-year-old Mary Hardy Reeser was alone in her apartment. Indeed, the only people in the building that night were Reeser and her landlady. She took a sleeping pill, lay back in "an overstuffed chair," and lit a cigarette. What happened next has been the subject of heated debate for years.

All that can be said for certain, however, is that at 8 A.M. the following day, her landlady, Patsy Carpenter, took a telegram to Reeser's room but found the doorknob too hot to turn. She quickly shouted to two painters working nearby to lend assistance, which they duly did, and the door was forced open. A blast of hot air filled the building and the three were confronted with a shocking scene. Where Reeser had been sitting and relaxing the previous evening was a fire-destroyed chair, a pile of ashes, and a few remnants of teeth and bone. These looked suspiciously like the shrunken remains of a human skull. There was also an undamaged left ankle and foot—complete with shoe, no less, in pristine condition. Not only that, but the wall nearest the victim and the floor in the immediate vicinity were only slightly scorched, and newspapers on a nearby table had failed to ignite. There was no evidence in the room of any flammable material, and despite the intense temperatures, the room itself was unscathed.

Dr. Wilton Marion Krogman of the University of Pennsylvania was fascinated by the case and addressed a whole variety of theories and explanations in a published article titled "The Strange Case of the Cinder Lady." "The local police," wrote Krogman, "kept referring to it as 'weird,' 'fantastic,' 'unbelievable,' and even the conservative FBI ventured 'unusual,' 'improbable.' As for me, were I living in the Middle Ages I'd mutter something about 'black magic' . . ."

Krogman did not come outright and support the SHC theory but admitted that "the case still haunts me." He concluded with the words of the local chief of police, J. R. Reichert, who said, "The case is not closed and may never be to the satisfaction of all concerned."

But were some people satisfied the case could be explained in rational terms without the need to invoke SHC? Indeed some were, at the FBI.

The roots of the Bureau can be traced back to July 1908 when Charles J. Bonaparte, attorney general under U.S. president Theodore Roosevelt, created a force of special agents within the Department of Justice (DOJ) that ultimately evolved into the FBI. With its headquarters in Washington, D.C., the FBI has offices in every U.S. state and employs thousands of people.

The primary function of the FBI is law enforcement, something that encompasses organized crime, civil rights violations, kidnapping, bank robbery, foreign counterintelligence, white-collar crime, and drug trafficking. On various occasions, however, the FBI has found itself immersed in the murky and controversial world of the unexplained.

On July 7, 1951, Chief Reichert forwarded to J. Edgar Hoover, the director of the Federal Bureau of Investigation, a package of material related to the Reeser death that included glass fragments found in the ashes, six small objects that were believed to be teeth, pieces of metal discovered near the body, fibers from part of her nightgown, Reeser's shoe (which had been retrieved from her one remaining foot), and charred fabric believed to be from the chair.

Reichert provided all the details of the remarkable burn scene for J. Edgar Hoover.

The body of MRS. REESER was partially cremated with the exception of the left foot which was burned completely in two, about 4" above the ankle. The chair in which she had been sitting was completely burned away, leaving just the springs. A small end table was completely burned away, with the exception of 2 legs. The carpet was burned in an area of approximately 3 ft. We also request any information or theories that could explain how a human body could be so destroyed and the fire confined to such a small area and so little damage done to the structure of the building and the furniture in the room not even scorched or damaged by smoke.

Reichert's request was handled by the FBI Laboratory, which produced a report on the death of Mary Hardy Reeser.

As regards the destruction of the deceased's body which occurred in this case it is entirely possible that the body was consumed to the extent shown in the photographs and as indicated by the bone fragments and other debris without the aid of any such material as gasoline.

It is not generally realized the extent to which the human body can burn once it becomes ignited. While such cases are not common, there are on record numerous instances of bodies burning with almost complete destruction. It was formerly believed that such cases arose from spontaneous combustion or the burning was sometimes attributed to preternatural causes. There is, however, absolutely no evidence from any of the cases on record to show that burning of this nature occurs other than when the body is ignited by some external means. The unusual aspects of such cases of burning have been heightened by the fact that in many instances little damage from burning occurred in the room or area directly surrounding the victim. As in this case, the remains of the victim were found reclining in the wreckage of a chair, sofa, bed or in one instance sitting on a stairway. In the last-named case the victim was a woman who had been clad in rather voluminous garments. Not a vestige of clothing was found remaining in that case although no extensive damage was done to the stairs.

The FBI Laboratory elaborated on the death of Reeser and offered a scientific explanation for alleged cases of SHC.

These cases are explained by the fact that the body becomes ignited from some outside cause such as burning clothing, a burning mattress, chair or other means. Once the body starts to burn there is enough fat and other inflammable substances to permit varying amounts of destruction to take place. Sometimes this destruction by burning will proceed to a degree which results in almost complete combustion of the body.

In this case, the absence of any scorching or damage to furniture in the room can only be explained by the fact that heat liberated by the burning body had a tendency to rise and formed a layer of hot air which never came in contact with the furnishings on a lower level. This situation would have occurred particularly if the fire had smoldered rather than burned freely.

The FBI's evaluation seemed to be perfectly sound, and more than half a century on, it still offers a logical explanation for a phenomenon that many continue to believe belongs in the realm of the unexplained. Indeed, perhaps some cases of SHC *cannot* be explained via the circumstances posited by the FBI, and, if so, those incidents should continue to be examined in their own right. For the death of Mary Hardy Reeser and the half a century of persistent rumors that she too was a victim of SHC, this, at least, is one file that should firmly and conclusively be stamped: *Case Closed.*[1]

Part Two

SAUCER SECRETS

C
O
P
Y
- - - - - -

UNITED STATES DEPARTMENT OF COMMERCE
WEATHER BUREAU

Report

Information on "Ball Lightning"

I. Origin

Various theories and suggestions have been proposed to explain ball
lightning, most of them being without well-established physical foundation. There is still doubt in scientific circles regarding the
origin of a number of reported cases of ball lightning.

Briefly, the explanations of the origin of ball lightning may be
broken down as follows:

(1) Brush discharge (St. Elmo's fire).

(May be stationary over sharp-pointed objects, or
moving along or near the surface of wires, roofs,
rocks, etc., especially on mountains. Conditions
most favorable for brush discharge occur during
thunderstorms, but the phenomenon may occur even
during clear, dry, dusty weather. When a lightning
stroke is approaching an object, the brush discharge
becomes especially intense.)

(2) Intensely ionized, incandescent volume of air forming end of lightning stroke and lasting for short
interval of time.
(This would occur mainly during thunderstorms following the passage of a lightning stroke. At the
ground end, the terminal flash is intense, and vapors,
smoke or molten material from objects fused at points
struck may enhance and extend the duration of incan-
descence. After-image formed on the retinas of the
eyes of a person looking at the brilliant flash at
the point of discharge may give spurious effects.)

(3) Brush discharge in air containing high concentration
of dust or other aerosols, during thunderstorms.
(If this occurs, it probably is associated with the
path taken by a real lightning stroke, and presumably
involves corona discharges from suspended particles
and possibly combustion in some cases.)

*For almost a century there has been official interest in unexplained
weather phenomena and unknown aerial objects, as this document,
"Information on 'Ball Lightning,' " written in 1948 by the U.S.
Department of Commerce, Weather Bureau, makes abundantly clear.*

Four

GREAT BALLS OF FIRE!

It is well-known that the so-called modern era of UFO sightings began on June 24, 1947. But years, and in some cases decades, before, encounters with unknown aerial objects occupied the minds of the British military and government.

One of the most notable pre-1947 reports lies in the files of the old British Admiralty and dates from, incredibly, 1915. Prepared by Lieutenant Colonel W. P. Drury, Garrison Intelligence Officer at Plymouth Garrison, Devonport, England, the four-page paper is titled "Report on the Dartmoor Floating (or Balloon) Light" and details a series of curious events that occurred on the wilds of Dartmoor. Lieutenant Colonel Drury informed his superiors at the Admiralty that on June 28, 1915, he and a colleague, Lieutenant C. Brownlow of Naval Intelligence, had interviewed a Miss Cecilia Peel Yates at Dolbeare Cottage, Ashburton, about an unusual experience.

She informed us that a few mornings previously, just before dawn, having been awakened by the barking of dogs, she saw from her bedroom window a bright light in the sky, bearing N., and apparently suspended a short distance above the earth. It was too large and bright for a planet, and, as she watched, it swung to the N.E., and disappeared. Haytor is due North of Ashburton and 4 miles distant as the crow files.

Initially, the report reveals, Lieutenant Colonel Drury and Lieutenant Brownlow were decidedly skeptical of Miss Peel Yates's experience.

Although we had entirely failed to shake the lady's evidence by cross-examination, we deemed her story so wildly improbable that we excluded it from our official report. But shortly afterwards reports of a similar phenomenon were received from the neighbourhood of Hexworthy Mine, which is 5 miles to the N.W., across Dartmoor.

On July 12th, Lieutenant Brownlow and I proceeded to Sherril, near Hexworthy, and interviewed Mrs. Cave-Penny and her daughter, from whom the report emanated. Their house, an isolated form on the moor, commands a clear view of the mine, which is two-and-a-half miles distant. They stated that on several occasions they had watched a bright white light rise from a point a few hundred yards to the Eastward of the mine, swing across the valley to about the same from Totnes, and a paddock some distance West of it, and disappear. The light sometimes rose above the skyline, at others it showed against the moon of Down Ridge, on which the mine is situated. On each occasion it rose from the same spot and followed the same course. Mrs. Cave-Penny is a rather excitable, irresponsible Irish lady, but we had no reason to doubt her evidence in the main, and her daughter's testimony (which fully corroborated that of her mother) was most clear and definite. This floating light against Down Ridge has been reported from the Hexworthy district on several occasions since, the last being a few nights ago.

One month later, Lieutenant Colonel Drury advised the Admiralty that sightings of the unidentified light were being reported from other locations on the moors.

About the middle of August this peculiar light was reported from two other points, viz., a meadow at Dartington Manor, about two miles belonging to Barton Pines, a large country house on high land overlooking Paignton. Dartington Manor is the home of the Champernownes: Barton Pines is owned by a Mr. William Whitley, formerly of the Life Guards. On more than one occasion Mrs. Whitley had reported that she and other witnesses had seen the floating light immediately above the belt of fir trees which screen the paddock from the garden and house. Brownlow, the Detective Police and I have separately interviewed Mrs. Whitley on various occasions, and we have all found her perfectly consistent in her story. For some time Mr. Whitley was sceptical, but, having seen it himself, he is now as convinced of its existence as his wife. The paddock commands an extensive view of Tor Bay in one direction and a long chain of the Dartmoor Tors in the other. The Dartington "floating light" was reported by Mr. Falkland Ricketts of Gatcombe Manor, who had also seen the Barton Pines occurrence. After several further reports from this witness, I obtained the sanction of the G.O.C., to watch one of the three points enumerated until I saw the light myself. I selected the Dartington Point, and, accompanied by Mr. Brownlow, began to watch from a position immediately opposite near the main Totnes-Newton Abbot road. On the third night we both saw the phenomenon precisely as it had been described at Hexworthy and Barton Pines.

And what, exactly, was it that the intelligence officer of Plymouth Garrison saw on the wilds of Dartmoor on the fateful evening in question?

About 9:30 that night (September 4th) we observed a bright white light, considerably larger in appearance than a planet, steadily ascend from the meadow to an approximate height of 50 or 60 feet. It then swung for a hundred yards or so to the left, and suddenly vanished. Its course was clearly visible against the dark background of wood and hill, though, the night being dark, it was not easy to determine whether it was a little above or beneath the skyline. We were within a mile of the light and both saw its ascension and transit distinctly. The Dart flows between Dartington and our post of observation, and, unfordable, it was impossible to reach the meadow from which the light arose.

Demonstrating that he had carried out a number of stakeouts of the area in the hope of seeing the unidentified intruder, Lieutenant Colonel Drury provided yet more pertinent data.

I have watched Down Ridge, Dartington Manor, and Barton Pines by night on several occasions before and since September 4th, but that date is the only time I personally have seen this "floating light" which has so often been reported by other and reliable witnesses.

It is to be observed that a ruler-edge laid upon the map will pass through the three indicated points, and that the suspect Buckfast Abbey (which harbours some 40 un-naturalized Germans of Military age) lies on the centre of the line. The line runs from the direction of Princetown to the Coast of Paignton. These lights, which are presumably lifted by captive balloons, are of an entirely different character from that of the stray fire balloon reported over Ashburton.

Lieutenant Colonel Drury then concluded his report on the curious encounters for the Admiralty.

It is suggested that the former may be employed to lift an aerial for wireless purposes. In any case it is difficult to find a normal cause for the credibility attested and oft recurring phenomenon, unless it be some form of illicit signalling. The proposed methods of detecting it I have dealt with in my former report "Suspects and alleged Illicit Signalling on N.E. Dartmoor."

W. P. Drury.

Lieut. Colonel, R.M.L.I.

Intelligence Officer.

For a full three months after the events chronicled in this report, sightings of the unknown light continued regularly and prompted Lieutenant Colonel Drury to submit a confidential message to his superiors at the Admiralty. Titled "Abnormal Lights on Dartmoor," it states:

With a view to detecting the origin of the above (and especially of the "floating light") I have recently submitted a scheme, which has been approved by the C.O.C., for rounding up one of the most active areas of the Moor at night. This scheme can only be carried into effect under certain conditions, for which I am writing. Meanwhile, and as an essential preliminary measure, I am awaiting the sanction of the War Office to my application to have certain correspondence in that area secretly examined. The application which was made a month ago, has been recently renewed, but no reply has so far been received.[1]

Available documentation pertaining to these incidents and events shows that whatever the true nature of the strange aerial lights of Dartmoor, the matter was never fully resolved. Were the curious lights the result of the actions of the "40 un-naturalized Germans of Military age" at Buckfast Abbey or was something far stranger occurring?

No evidence has surfaced in the Public Record Office's archives to suggest that this was the work of the Germans. Investigators David Clarke and Granville Oldroyd, however, have suggested that the curious Dartmoor light phenomena may have been some form of "earthlight" or "spooklight." As they have noted, at least *some* of these objects "are plasmalike blobs of energy created by frictional discharges from rocks in zones of geological faulting. In this way spooklights are 'created' by electromagnetic leakage from the strain generated in faultlines during the period leading up to an earth tremor."[2]

This theory has its merits. Unidentified luminous objects have been witnessed time and again in areas with a reputation for being geologically unstable. A number of minor earth tremors have occurred in the West Country over the last one hundred years—as have other sightings of unknown aerial lights. In 1932, for example, an incident similar to those of 1915 occurred near the River Torridge, North Devon. From the archives of the *Western Morning News* comes the following account titled "Will o' the Wisp?"

Sir. A few nights ago, another man and I were, one dark November night, at about eleven o'clock, on a hillside near the River Torridge far from any road, footpath or house. We were long-netting rabbits. Between us and the river lay a stretch of marshy ground, perhaps one hundred yards wide. On the other side of the river the ground rose abruptly covered in timber. Suddenly, we saw quite near us apparently about fifty feet above the marsh, an oblong object floating in the air. I cannot describe it better than saying that it looked like a conglomeration of very dim stars. It appeared to be about three feet by two feet in size and was clearly outlined against the dark background of the opposite hillside. It sailed about with a sort of circular motion, something like a swallow hawking over a pond. For five minutes or so, we watched it as it swept around in ever-widening circles; finally, it sailed off up the river and we saw it no more. I have sent this letter, before forwarding it to you, to the man who was with me at the time, and he corroborates all that I have said.[3]

As the author Jonathan Downes notes, will-o'-the-wisp (or jack-o'-lantern, as it is also referred to) is "an incandescent form of methane that rises above rotting vegetation"—marsh gas, in other words. However, in response to the account that appeared in the *Western Morning News*, one E. E. Rudd of Torrington asserted, " 'Jack' does not dance fifty feet above the ground. You will not see him on a dark November night, neither does he move with a circular motion. As a youth, I was lucky to see a superb display over some bogland on our common. This land has since been reclaimed and cultivated. What [the writer] and his companion saw was a white owl."[4]

The notion that this witness had been fooled by something so ordinary as an owl is manifestly absurd. But, it is important to note that a local man who had lived in the area for his entire life was also dismissing the marsh gas explanation.

Although "earthlights" and "spooklights" seem to be an entirely real phenomenon, one major problem surfaces time and again when trying to apply this explanation to the events of 1915. Quite simply, in the Admiralty's reports, there is little doubt that the lights were under some form of intelligent control.

For example, according to the official documents at our disposal, Mrs. Cave-Penny and her daughter had seen, on what was described as "several occasions," a bright white light "rise from a point a few hundred yards to the Eastward of the mine, swing across the valley to about the same . . . distance West of it, and disappear." Whatever the nature of this phenomenon, the description conjures up images of something undertaking deliberate—as opposed to entirely random—movements time and again and from the exact same location.

Likewise, the testimony of Mrs. Whitley of Barton Pines referred to repeated sightings of the curious light "immediately above" a belt of fir trees on her property. Again, this suggests the presence of some form of aerial phenomenon undertaking a planned reconnoiter of the area by way of an established route. In other words, there was demonstrable evidence of an intelligence behind the mystery light.

Nearly ninety years later, it seems extremely unlikely that this intriguing affair will ever be truly resolved. We can be certain, however, that unusual aerial phenomena were highly active throughout Dartmoor in 1915, and Britain's military was keeping a careful and concerned watch on the situation.

On numerous occasions throughout the latter stages of the Second World War, military pilots from the United States, Britain, Germany, Japan, and Poland reported seeing strange, seemingly intelligently controlled aerial globes of light that would pursue their aircraft and even at times engage in "dogfights" with the mystified—and at times terrified—pilots and aircrews.

The pilots of the Second World War had their own nickname for this mysterious precursor to the flying saucer. They called them Foo Fighters. And they were a mystery that attracted considerable interest on the part of the British Royal Air Force, which collected a number of notable and intriguing reports and files on encounters with these elusive objects. But first some necessary background.

According to UFO investigator Harold T. Wilkins, a pilot, chatting in a mess hall of the 415th U.S. Night Fighter squadron, stationed at Dijon, France, spoke to other pilots who had encountered weird balls of light in the skies over Europe and who had been derided by intelligence officers after filing their reports.

"This pilot had a brain wave," said Wilkins. " 'Let's call the so-and-sos Foo Fighters!' he said. This nickname was taken up and stuck. It appears that it was suggested by a comic strip in a New York newspaper, at the time. One Smokey Stover said, 'Yeah, if there's foo there's fire!' Probably the word *foo* is a corruption of the French *feu*, or 'fire' "[5]

Several remarkable Foo Fighter reports surfaced during the latter part of the Second World War. One case is reported by the researcher Timothy Good. "In late 1943," Good writes, "Staff Sergeant Louis Kiss was a tail gunner on the *Phyllis Marie*, a B-17 Flying Fortress bomber of the 390th Bombardment Group, Third Division, Eighth Air Force, when a Foo Fighter was encountered over central Germany."

Kiss observed an "odd-looking" sphere that closed in on the aircraft from the rear. Basketball-sized and gold in color, it approached the aircraft slowly and hovered above one wing, passed over the top of the aircraft, and hovered over the other wing. Kiss was tempted to fire at the device, but decided against the idea. The sphere then moved to the rear again and disappeared rapidly into the remainder of the B-17 formation.[6]

Some might argue that Staff Sergeant Kiss had merely viewed some rare form of natural phenomenon. But this possibility can be dismissed simply because dozens of such reports surfaced around the world in what was a brief and clearly delineated period.

To illustrate this, consider the following eye-opening revelation from British UFO investigator Jenny Randles: "UK comedian Michael Bentine, then an intelligence officer supervising the free Polish forces, told me of the debriefing he carried out in late 1944 on an aircrew who had seen the lights during raids on the secret V-rocket base at Peenemunde and the intense interest in them shown by U.S. intelligence staff. Despite feeling they were dangerous, no crewman ever described a single harmful effect caused by them."[7]

On December 13, 1944, the *South Wales Argus* newspaper reported that a new player was making itself known in the skies over Europe and elsewhere: "The Germans have produced a 'secret' weapon in keeping with the Christmas season. The new device, which is apparently an air defense weapon, resembles the glass balls which adorn Christmas trees. They have been seen hanging in the air and are apparently transparent."

The *South Wales Argus*, however, was not the only newspaper to report on Foo Fighter activity. The *New York Herald Tribune*, on January 2, 1945, asserted, "On Dec. 13, 1944, newspaper men were told that the Germans had thrown silvery balls into the air against day raiders. Pilots then reported that they had seen these balls, both individually and in clusters during forays over the Rhine. Now, it seems, the Nazis have thrown something new into the night skies over Germany. It is the weird, mysterious 'Foo Fighter' balls which race alongside the wings of Beaufighters flying intruder missions over Germany. Pilots have been encountering this eerie weapon for more than a month in their night flights. No one apparently knows what this sky weapon is. The 'balls of fire' appear suddenly and accompany the planes for miles. They seem to be radio-controlled from the ground, so official reports reveal."

With so many highly qualified military pilots of both Allied and Axis nations having viewed the activities of the mysterious Foo Fighters, one would assume that some form of official project—or projects—would have been launched to ascertain the truth behind the phenomenon. Indeed, evidence suggests such studies were conducted.

According to the journalist Warren Smith, the Office of Strategic Services (the forerunner of the CIA) started investigating Foo Fighter sightings. Agents in France, Germany, and Italy were asked to report on any secret weapon the Germans or Italians might be using, but they drew a blank. As a result the OSS decided that Foo Fighters were unusual, but harmless, phenomena and took no further action to try to resolve the mystery.[8]

Half a century later we would learn the official conclusion of the Office of Strategic Services' investigation of Foo Fighter reports. It appeared in the CIA's declassified paper "CIA's Role in the Study of UFOs, 1947–90," written by Gerald Haines, who has been historian for both the CIA and the National Reconnaissance Office (NRO), one of America's most secretive bodies. Haines wrote, "Fearing they might be Japanese or German secret weapons, OSS investigated but could find no concrete evidence of enemy weapons and often filed such reports in the 'crackpot' category."[9]

It has to be said that Haines's "crackpot" comment is a gross disservice to those highly qualified Allied pilots who simply reported in good faith the curious objects they had seen while trying to eradicate the Nazi threat. Consider, for example, the following reports from the official files of the U.S. Army Air Force during the latter stages of the war, from aircrews, none of whom, we are sure, would have taken kindly to Gerald Haines's "crackpot" comment.

November 27, 1944—The following weird excerpt comes from Lt. Schluter's report of an intruder mission: "Upon returning to base saw a red light flying through area about 35 miles ENE of Pt. A. Came in to about 2000 feet off Starboard and then it disappeared in a long red streak."

December 15, 1944—The following is an excerpt from the operations report: "Saw a brilliant red light at 2000 feet going E at 200 MPH in the vicinity of Ernstein. Due to AI (Air Interceptor Radar) failure could not pick up contact but followed it by sight until it went out."

December 18, 1944—I quote from the operations report: "In Rastatt area Sighted five or six red and green lights in a 'T' shape which followed A/C thru turns and closed to 1000 feet. Lights followed for several miles and then went out. Our pilots have named these mysterious phenomena which they encounter over Germany at night Foo Fighters."

December 23, 1944—More Foo Fighters were in the air last night. The Ops' report says: "In vicinity of Hagenau saw 2 lights coming toward A/C from ground. After reaching the altitude of the A/C they leveled off and flew on tail of Beau for 2 minutes and then peeled up and turned away. 8th mission sighted 2 orange lights. One light sighted at 10,000 feet, the other climbed until it disappeared."

December 24, 1944—The Foo Fighters were active again according to the pilot's report: "Observed a glowing, red object shooting straight up. It changed suddenly to a plan view of an A/C doing a wing-over and going into a dive and disappearing."

December 28, 1944—The Ops' report says: "1st patrol saw 2 sets of 3 red and white lights. One appeared on port side, the other on starboard at 1000 to 2000 feet to rear and closing in. Beau peeled off and lights went out. Nothing on GCI scope at the time." And then again: "Observed lights suspended in air, moving slowly in no general direction and then disappeared. Lights were orange, and appeared singly and in pairs. These lights were observed 4 or 5 times throughout the period."

January 30, 1945—Foo Fighters were at it again last night. This is operations' report: "Halfway between Wissenburg and Langau sighted amber lights at 2000 ft. One light was 20 to 50 feet above the other and of about 30 seconds duration. Lights were about a foot in diameter, 1000 feet away and following Beaus'. Lights disappeared when Beaus' turned into them."

Let us now turn to the crux of the matter, Foo Fighters and the British government. An account of one daytime encounter comes from Gordon W. Cammell, who served as a bomber captain with the British Royal Air Force during the war. In May 1943, Cammell was the captain of a Lancaster bomber aircraft and recalled that while crossing the English Channel after a bombing mission over Germany, all of the crew viewed what appeared to be a "huge, orange ball" on or near the sea at a height of around seven or eight thousand feet below that of the Lancaster.

The object appeared stationary and was seen by those on board for about ten minutes, during which time it didn't change in its brightness or intensity. Discussions among the crew determined that the light was not from an aircraft nor a ship in distress.

After landing back at their base at RAF East Wrentham, Suffolk, the crew reported their sighting to the debriefing officer, who also had no idea of what it was that the crew had seen. The incident remained unresolved.[10]

Cammell is not the only Royal Air Force source to speak out publicly about his knowledge of Foo Fighter activity in the European theater. Another such account comes from former Lancaster pilot George Barton, who had a memorable encounter with one of the mystery objects in June 1944.

"I was flying from Elsham Wolds, in Lincolnshire, with 576 Squadron, 1 Group Bomber Command," writes Barton. "I remember the incident very well; the raid was just after 'D-Day,' June 1944 and was the second of three raids we made on Stuttgart. Bomber Command never flew direct to the target but flew a series of 'doglegs'; the idea being not to let the Germans known where we were heading for, until the last possible moment. Anyway, on this particular night, it seemed that 'Jerry' knew every move we made, as he had dropped fighter flares at regular intervals along each of our 'dog legs' and our losses were quite heavy.

"When we eventually got back to base and into debriefing, I was pretty tired and not really paying much attention to the chap who was debriefing us and in fact my mind was wandering. It was for this reason that I became aware of what the guys at the next table were saying. One particular chap was rather excited and was therefore talking in a loud voice [and] I took him to be the rear gunner.

"Apparently as they were approaching the Target Area, he became aware of spheres following behind them; it was as though they were caught in the aircraft's slipstream. He thought it was a new German secret weapon so he asked his skipper to take violent evasive action, while at the same time, he tried to shoot them down. Neither action did any good, as the spheres easily kept their position behind the aircraft. I got the impression that the spheres were the size of a large football. I had no idea of what he was talking about at the time and it was not until after the War that I heard about Foo Fighters and put two and two together!" [11]

But to what extent were such accounts taken seriously and acted upon by British authorities at the height of the Second World War? For decades rumors have circulated that extremely rigorous investigations were made into the Foo Fighter phenomenon by an elite team of Air Ministry and Royal Air Force operatives.

But Air Marshal Sir Victor Goddard, the first deputy director of air intelligence to the Air Ministry in 1935, raised an excellent point. "To the best of my knowledge," he stated in 1988, "there has never been any official study made [of the Foo Fighters]. This implies Treasury sanction; it suggests that in the middle of the war against Germany when we had our hands full and it was far from certain that we could survive, the Air Ministry was concerned that a UFO menace existed; it most certainly was not." [12]

Nonetheless previously classified files *do* now reveal that British officialdom at least had a deep awareness of the Foo Fighter mystery and sometimes acted on those reports.

The earliest documented indication of what might conceivably have been Foo Fighter phenomena is noted in a formerly secret Bomber Command document of August 11, 1940, titled "Phenomena Connected With Enemy Night Tactics." While the document focuses much of its attention on encounters with what could only have been German aircraft, it also refers briefly to other "unexplained phenomena" reported by Royal Air Force crews from May to June 1940, largely in the vicinity of the Ruhr and near the coast of Holland.

It is difficult to assess the degree of accuracy of some of the reports, where enemy aircraft have not attacked, or have not approached close enough to be identified with certainty, and where the reports have not been substantiated by more than one member of the crew.

The strain upon a member of the crew maintaining a vigilant lookout for long periods of time is intense, and, under such conditions, the stories of "shadowing" are apt to stimulate the very natural tendency to think that any unidentified shape seen, or imagined in the sky, is an enemy aircraft.

In this connection it is interesting to note that, except on occasions when fire ensued, only one report of the 92 considered can be definitely confirmed by more than one member of the crew. It is appreciated that the reason for this is probably the limited view from crew positions, but it is, nevertheless, not without interest.

. . . It is quite a well known practice for the Germans to test experimental apparatus under active service conditions and it appears highly probable that some of the peculiar incidents reported by pilots have been due to some new detection device or searchlight installed for experimental purposes.[13]

The foremost thought on the minds of Bomber Command personnel was that the more "peculiar incidents reported by pilots," the things of an "unidentified shape," and the "unexplained phenomena" *were* connected to the activities of the Nazis. However, this document does serve as an indicator of what was to come.

On September 25, 1942, a document titled "A Note on Recent Enemy Pyrotechnic Activity Over Germany," was prepared by the British Air Ministry's Operational Research Section.

Crews have reported encountering various strange pyrotechnic devices recently over Germany. An investigation covering No. 3 and 5 Groups was undertaken in collaboration with the Flak Liaison Officer of No. 5 Group, in an endeavor to determine the probable purpose of these devices. M.I.14(e) is also looking into the matter in other Groups and a further report will be issued later.

There appeared to be at least two different phenomena, said the Air Ministry, which had collectively become known as Chandelier Flares. Here is how the Air Ministry described "Phenomenon 1."

These objects are undoubtedly shot up from the ground, either by a rocket with damping to render its trail invisible or by some form of mortar. It is possible that they are projected by heavy flak guns but unlikely owing to the size of the resulting object.

The object first makes its appearance in the sky as an orange red ball of fire and its arrival is definitely not accompanied by any blast in its vicinity. It persists as a "ball of fire" about 50 to 60 feet in diameter for a period of about 5–10 seconds after which period it begins to "drip" multicoloured fragments which fall for about 150 feet before burning out. This cascade continues for about half a minute or a little longer, after which the whole thing appears to burn out.

These flares emit very little light and it is very unlikely that they are intended to illuminate our aircraft. The enemy seems to make no attempt to aim them at our bombers, in fact the reverse seems to be the case. They are only found over gun defended areas, principally over such targets as the Ruhr and Bremen and are invariably accompanied by heavy flak.

Most aircraft report that they are shot up to the height at which they are flying although some crews have seen them both below and above them, up to 19000 feet.

The enemy does not seem to use them in the very early stages of an attack but waits until it is well developed and then shoots them up to the height at which the majority of aircraft are flying, and it is unusual to see more than one in the sky at once. No cases are known in which an aircraft has been attacked by or has seen an enemy fighter either immediately before or after seeing one of these firework displays.

Aircraft have been very close to them (150–200 yards)

when they have appeared and no ill effects at all were noticed. At a distance they are reported to look very similar to aircraft falling in flames and it is thought that they are intended to give crews the impression that a large number of aircraft are being shot down in flames and that the defences are stronger than they really are.

It is almost certain that these devices are used purely as a deterrent and not intended to be lethal although, of course, if an aircraft happened to collide with one it might be lethal. This view is supported by the fact that the Germans have always placed great value on horrific devices. However, the deterrent value of such devices is much reduced and even destroyed once it is realized that they are practically harmless.

These objects have been described by some stations as "aerial minefields," but it is very misleading as it appears that they are certainly not mines, since (a) no aircraft is known to have sustained damage from them and (b) it is thought that the whole object of an aerial mine would be defeated if its position were indicated by such a luminous object.[14]

As with many of the Foo Fighter–style reports, "Phenomenon 1" did not apparently exhibit any outward form of hostility. The displays were not precursors to enemy attacks and were, in the words of the Air Ministry, "practically harmless," which leaves numerous questions unanswered about their nature and origin. The British Air Ministry's Operational Research Section then described "Phenomenon 2," the second form of unidentified aerial activity that was being reported.

These flares have been seen both over this country and over enemy territory and it therefore seems probable that they are always dropped from aircraft. They are a form of multiple flare, usually a minimum of 3 or 4 in number which give out a large amount of light and are probably designed to assist fighter attack. It is not known whether they are all fixed together on a cable support by a parachute or whether each flare drifts down independently after being ejected from some form of container.

Besides Phenomenon 1 and 2, one other aspect of the mystery puzzled the Air Ministry.

There appear to be track indicating flares which may either be on the ground or be projected up to moderate heights and also small coloured balls which are reported to come up slowly to heights of 6 or 7 thousand feet. The latter are in all probability light flak tracers. Several references have recently been made to "Flashless Flak" and this subject was also investigated.

But the Air Ministry seemed rather uncertain about their conclusions.

Phenomenon 1 is probably purely a "scarecrow" and is not lethal.

Phenomenon 2 is probably a flare to assist enemy fighters.

"Flashless flak" if it exists exhibits all the normal characteristics of flak except the brilliance of the flash.

None of the above mentioned phenomena are considered to be in any way connected with aerial mines.

It is suggested that suitable names should be bestowed on "Phenomena 1 and 2" to facilitate reporting and an attempt to do so will be made in a [deleted] report shortly to be published jointly by M.I.14(e) and this section.[15]

While the Air Ministry report concluded that any and all unusual aerial phenomena observed were strictly the work of the Nazis, in some cases that possibility (however logical) seemed distinctly doubtful, as the following document of December 2, 1942, makes strikingly apparent. The report, titled "Report by the Crew of 61 Sqdn. A/c 'J,' Captain W/O Lever, of object seen during raid on TURIN, night of November 28/29th, 1942," was classified secret.

The object . . . was seen by the entire crew of the above aircraft. They believe it to have been 200–300 feet in length and its width is estimated at 1/5th or 1/6th of its length. The speed was estimated at 500 m.p.h., and it had four pairs of red lights spaced at equal distances along its body. These lights did not appear in any way like exhaust flames; no trace was seen. The object kept a level course. The crew saw the object twice during the raid, and brief details are given below:

    (i) After bombing, time 2240 hours, a/c height 11,000 feet. The aircraft at this time was some 10/15 miles South-West of Turin traveling in a northwesterly direction. The object was traveling South-East at the same height or slightly below the aircraft.

    (ii) After bombing, time 2245 hours, a/c height 14,000 feet. The aircraft was approaching the Alps when the object was seen again traveling West-South-West up a valley in the Alps below the level of the peaks. The lights appeared to go out and the object disappeared from view.

The Captain of the aircraft also reports that he has seen a similar object about three months ago North of Amsterdam. In this instance it appeared to be on the ground and later traveling at high speed at a lower level than the heights given above along the coast for about two seconds; the lights then went out for the same period of time and came on again, and the object was still seen to be traveling in the same direction.

Precisely what this object was remains unknown, and declassified documents do not support the notion that the mystery was ever satisfactorily resolved. It's worth noting that a covering letter signed by the air vice marshal, commanding, No. 5 Group of the Royal Air

Force, states, "The crew refuses to be shaken in their story in the face of the usual banter and ridicule." It must also be stressed that at no time during the Second World War were either the Allied or Axis forces flying aerial vehicles two to three hundred feet in length that were capable of speeds of five hundred miles per hour. Like so many UFO reports filed through official channels in the last sixty years, this one remains unexplained. And unidentified aerial activity continued unabated throughout the war.[16]

Formerly classified at secret level, the following document, titled "Bang On," acted as a newsletter for one particular outfit of the British Royal Air Force, 115 Squadron, and told a remarkable story.

Under this heading there occur from time to time reports of weird and wonderful apparitions seen during our (and the American) attacks on Germany. We have asked our local Inner Circle bloke to comment on the latest species of wizardry. Here is his story . . . believe it or not.

On the 11th December the Yanks paid one of their daylight visits to Emden. Visibility was good and the weather clear. "An unidentified object was seen in the target area. It was about the size of a Thunderbolt and passed 50–75 yards beneath the formation. It flew straight and level (No chaps it was not a Lanc. gone mad . . .) at a terrific speed, leaving a streak like a vapour trail which remained visible for a long time. The object passed so quickly that the observer could not determine it more accurately.

Suggestions will be welcome . . . serious ones . . . as to what this Loch Ness Monster of Emden might have been. (Prize . . . one year's free issue of this News Sheet . . . if the publication survives as long.)

Another of the attacking aircraft was hit by a length of wire which bit deeply into the nose. Twenty feet were coiled around the nose and something caused the bomb door to open. The wire may have been towed behind a fighter which had just made an attack upon the bomber; some form of explosive charge or weight may have been attached to a parachute fired from a rocket projectile, though no parachute was seen. An examination of the wire is taking place and it is hoped that this will shed some light on the occurrence.

In another attack, this time on Bremen, there were many reports of "silver and red discs above the formations." These have been seen before but up to now no one has been able to decide their purpose. Suggestions please.[17]

Although this report was written in a somewhat lighthearted vein, two points are worthy of comment. The entire report was classified secret. It is revealed that "these have been seen before," meaning that such reports were on file with the British Air Ministry by 1943. The statement that "up to now no one has been able to decide their purpose" suggests that attempts had, indeed, been made by officials to determine the origin and intent of the Foo Fighters.

For years, rumors and stories have circulated in books and magazines on UFOs about an alleged sighting of "scores" of Foo Fighters during a raid on Schweinfurt, Germany, on October 14, 1943. The first person to have postulated a link between the Schweinfurt raid and unidentified aerial phenomena was the late writer Martin Caidin.

According to Caidin, as the bombers of 384th Group swung into the final bomb run, pilots and top-turret gunners, as well as several crewmen in the Plexiglas noses of the aircraft, reported seeing a cluster of disks in the path of the 384th's formation that appeared to be closing in on them.

The disks were silver in color, approximately one inch thick and three inches in diameter, and appeared above the bombers, gliding down in uniform clusters. Suddenly, Boeing B-17 Number 026 closed rapidly with a cluster of the disks. The pilot maneuvered the aircraft violently to evade an imminent collision. At an intelligence briefing, the pilot stated that "my right wing went directly through a cluster with absolutely no effect on engines or plane surface," and added that at about twenty feet from the disks, the crew watched an unusual mass of black debris of varying sizes, and in clusters of three by four feet, floating past their aircraft.[18]

Despite the intriguing nature of this encounter, no confirmation for its reality was ever forthcoming—until the summer of 2000 when an official report pertaining to the Schweinfurt raid was discovered at the Public Record Office. The document was circulated to Colonel Kingman Douglas, Wing Commander Smith of AI (Air Intelligence) 3, and Wing Commander Heath of AI 2 at the Air Ministry.

Annexe to intelligence report mission Schweinfurt 16 October 1943. 306 Group report a partially unexploded 20mm shell imbedded above the panel in the cockpit of A/C number 412 bearing the following figures, 19K43. The Group Ordnance Officer believes the steel composing the shell is of inferior grade. 348th Group reports a cluster of discs observed in the path of the formation near Schweinfurt, at the time there are no E/A [Authors note: "enemy aircraft"] above. Discs were described as silver coloured—one inch thick and three inches in diameter. They were gliding slowly down in very uniform cluster. A/C 026 was unable to avoid them and his right wing went directly through the cluster with absolutely no effect on engines or plane's surface. One of the discs was heard striking tail assembly but no explosion was heard. About twenty feet from these discs a mass of black debris of varying sizes in clusters of 3 by 4 feet. Also observed 2 other A/C flying through silver discs with no apparent damage. Observed discs and debris 2 other times but could not determine where it came from.[19]

Interestingly, references to the Foo Fighter incident reported by Martin Caidin and cited in the official report reproduced above also appear in an allegedly official document dealing with UFO encounters and supposed UFO crashes in the 1940s. While the document was supposedly leaked by "insider sources," it has been widely denounced as a hoax by many UFO researchers, along with a whole variety of similar papers that, collectively, have become known as the Majestic 12 documents, so named after the purported secret U.S. government group established in the wake of the notorious incident at Roswell, New Mexico, in 1947. Nevertheless, as this is directly relevant to the issue at hand, we present the material for consideration. Extracted from a lengthy document titled "The 1st Annual Report" and—purportedly—prepared by the supersecret Majestic 12 group, it asserts:

Aerial interference with military aircraft has demonstrated the ability to observe our air operations in war and peacetime conditions. During the war over 900 near-miss incidents were reported by allied pilots and crews in all theaters of operations. One of the most dramatic near-miss encounters occurred on 14 October 1943, 8th AF Mission 115 over Schwienfurt [sic], Germany. B-17 crews reported many formations of silvery discs flying down into the B-17 formations. Several times during the bombing mission, large objects were seen following the discs descent into the formations. Unlike previous reports, no engine failures or airframe damage was reported. After the surrender of Nazi Germany, GAF fighter pilots were interviewed by AF intelligence concerning Mission 115. GAF did not have any aircraft above our bombers at that time.

While this document may indeed be the hoax that some believe it to be (and the misspelling of *Schweinfurt* is perhaps notable), it is intriguing that the author chose to cite the Caidin-Schweinfurt encounter. At the time that the "1st Annual Report" surfaced, the official records on the case at the Public Record Office had not been located. Therefore, the author of the "1st Annual Report" was taking a considerable risk by citing an encounter that was unverifiable at the time and that might have been uncovered as a hoax. And, of course, had the case been proved bogus, then so would the "1st Annual Report." That the author of the "Report" chose to cite a case that was ultimately vindicated is an indication that the Majestic 12 controversy might not be as insignificant as many believe.

A secret document of January 29, 1944, titled "Rocket Phenomena" shows that reports of encounters with unknown aerial objects continued to be filed by Royal Air Force crews.

At 52 32N 13 03E, 2037 hours, 20,500 ft., heading 082 degrees True. A red ball leaving trail of yellow/red flames and black smoke at about 1,000 yards and at the same height dead astern. It was seen closing in. I dived to starboard and the object followed, appearing to fizzle out and then immediately to reappear. I turned hard to port and it followed us round in a tighter turn than we were in. When within 100 yards or less of the aircraft, it finally fizzled out.[20]

In this case, as in so many others, the object closed in on the aircraft yet curiously and carefully avoided any hostile action. Another report surfaced on February 3, 1944.

It was a ball of red fire on port side 2 miles away at same height with yellowish red flame coming out behind and black smoke. It was 30/40 m.p.h. faster than the Lancaster. It went like this for a period of ¾ to 1 minute. It did not explode at any time. Fizzled out and not seen again. The smoke was very black and showed up well against grayish night background. It followed when Lancaster went into a dive and again on corkscrewing. It seemed to go out once but sprang into life again when Lancaster changed from dive to starboard into a corkscrew.[21]

Since these reports remained buried among the myriad documents at the Public Record Office for nearly half a century, it is entirely possible that other, similar reports remain untouched and await discovery by researchers and archivists alike. The reports currently in hand, however, demonstrate amply that not only were unusual and unexplained objects flying around the war-torn skies of Europe during the Second World War, they also baffled and concerned the finest minds of the British Royal Air Force.

Having analyzed a variety of witness accounts and official Royal Air Force documentation relating to one of the most confounding mysteries of the Second World War, are we any nearer to understanding the nature, origin, and intent of the phenomena? Since the majority of encounters were reported in the European theater and most of the activity as reported in official Royal Air Force files seemed to be directed at Allied pilots, it can be argued with some degree of rationale that the Foo Fighters were a form of highly advanced weapon developed and deployed by the Nazis.

But if the Foo Fighters were German, why then, asked the renowned investigator of UFOs Aime Michel, "did they never display the slightest disposition to attack? Although the accounts given by the airmen differed in detail, the investigators did not discover a single case of the mysterious machines showing fight. Surely Hitler would not have used such a weapon so kindly at the very time when the V.1's were pounding London." [22]

Author Harold T. Wilkins expresses a similar opinion. "Any facile theory that these Foo Fighters were secret experimental devices emanating from Nazi Peenemünde was dispelled by the fact that Russia, who in 1945 seized the station and laboratories of Peenemünde, in 1950, set up a secret commission to inquire into the mystery of the flying saucers and Foo Fighters." [23] In other words, if the Russians had succeeded in uncovering data from the ransacking of the German factories and airbases to show that the Foo Fighters were indeed Nazi in origin, an inquiry would hardly have been needed to try to determine their point of origin.

Further doubts about the Nazi origins of Foo Fighters come from the recollections of the late Michael Bentine. Bentine had spoken with a number of Allied pilots who had had close encounters with the Foo Fighters and was keen to secure their opinions. When they suggested to Bentine that the Foo Fighters were possibly Nazi weapons, Bentine, quite reasonably, asked, "Okay, what did the weapon do to you?" When the reply "Nothing" was offered, Bentine perceptively noted, "Well, they're not very effective weapons, are they?" [24]

And this is the problem: it seems patently illogical for the Nazis to have expended so much money and effort on developing a truly fantastic technology that they failed to put to practical and offensive use.

More than half a century later, the Foo Fighter mystery remains unresolved. Were they indeed some form of tactical device employed by Hitler's minions? Were they the product of an incredibly well-hidden agency of the United States or the United Kingdom? Or were they possibly the first wave of visitors from a distant world— curious and concerned at the carnage that was taking place below them as they soared around the globe? Whether hidden, lost, or never fully determined, the answer to that question remains—publicly, at least—unknown.

Only three years after the close of hostilities, however, elements of the U.S. government were implicated in the investigation of a phenomenon that was, in many ways, similar to that of the Foo Fighters. It was the summer of 1948, and while the U.S. Air Force was busying itself trying to determine if UFOs were alien spacecraft, Soviet inventions, or even the work of an ultrasecret department buried within the bowels of the American military and intelligence community, the Weather Bureau of the Department of Commerce (DoC) was taking a distinctly different approach in a search for the answers and was digging deep into that most mysterious and rarely observed natural phenomena known as ball lightning.

In a technical report published in August 1948 by the U.S. Air

Force's UFO investigative unit, Project Grudge, the Department of Commerce revealed its findings on ball lightning.

Various theories and suggestions have been proposed to explain ball lightning, most of them being without well-established physical foundation. There is still doubt in scientific circles regarding the origin of a number of reported cases of ball lightning.

Having discussed eight theories centering on the phenomenon's likely connection to standard lightning and electrical discharge, the DoC, under the heading "Forms," described the appearance of ball lightning. Numerous students of the UFO mystery suspect that it may be the cause of many perceived UFO encounters. According to the DoC, ball lightning is

spherical, roughly globular, egg-shaped, or pear-shaped; many times with projecting streamers; or flame-like irregular 'masses of light.' Luminous in appearance, described in individual cases by different colors but mostly reported as deep red and often as glaring white.

And the phenomenon was capable of manifesting itself in other ways as well.

Some of the cases of "ball lightning" observed have displayed excrescences of the appearance of little flames emanating from the main body of the luminous mass, or luminous streamers have developed from it and propagated slant-wise toward the ground. In rare instances, it has been reported that the luminous body may break up into a number of smaller balls which may appear to fall towards the earth like a rain of sparks. It has even been reported that the ball has suddenly ejected a whole bundle of many luminous, radiating streamers toward the earth, and then disappeared. There have been reports by observers of "ball lightning" to the effect that the phenomenon appeared to float through a room or other space for a brief interval of time without making contact with or being attracted by objects.[25]

While this document suggests that *some* UFO sightings *have* been due to the still-mystifying phenomenon known as ball lightning, its contents demonstrate that an agency even as relatively innocuous as the Department of Commerce's Weather Bureau can find itself immersed in the world of the unexplained.

Five

WHO FLIES THE SAUCERS?

Of the many rumors that surround the UFO puzzle, one has long persisted. According to some, UFO encounters and reports are not due to the activities of extraterrestrial creatures operating on our planet, nor are UFOs the work of hoaxers and fantasists. Rather, they are the result of sightings of highly advanced, and highly classified, earth-based aircraft modeled on radical and groundbreaking technology captured from the Germans by American and Soviet forces in the closing stages of the Second World War.

The sheer number and diversity of UFO reports filed throughout the world since 1947, the year in which the term *flying saucer* was coined, tends to rule out this theory as adequately and definitively explaining the intricacies of the *entire* UFO subject. However, enough credible reports and official files exist to demonstrate that at least *some* UFOs originate far closer to home than many devotees of the unidentified flying object mystery might initially suspect.

Our story begins with the pilot Kenneth Arnold, whose June 24, 1947, encounter over the Cascade Mountains, Washington State, kicked off the modern era of UFO sightings. At approximately 3 P.M. that day, Arnold was searching for an aircraft that had report-

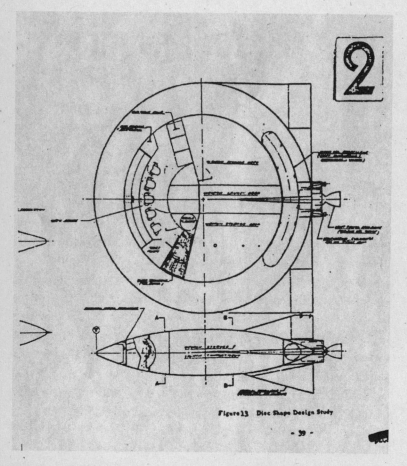

Figure 13 Disc Shape Design Study

- 39 -

A diagram taken from an official U.S. Air Force file of 1962 titled
"Environment Control Systems for Manned Space Vehicles."
The document concerns a USAF plan to build a flying-saucer-style
spacecraft for use in warfare.

edly crashed on the southwest side of Mt. Rainier. Arnold's encounter attracted the keen interest at the time of not just the public
and the media but also of the all-powerful Federal Bureau of Investigation. The following account by Arnold comes from previously
secret FBI records of 1947 that confirm the Bureau's deep interest
in the Arnold affair.

I hadn't flown more than two or three minutes on my course
when a bright flash reflected on my airplane. It startled me as
I thought I was too close to some other aircraft. I looked every
place in the sky and couldn't find where the reflection had
come from until I looked to the left and the north of Mt. Rainier
where I observed a chain of nine peculiar looking aircraft flying from north to south at approximately 9,500 feet elevation
and going, seemingly, in a definite direction of about 170 degrees.

Arnold stressed that the objects were approaching Mt. Rainier
rapidly and was puzzled by their physical appearance.

I thought it was very peculiar that I couldn't find their tails but
assumed they were some type of jet plane. . . . The more I observed these objects, the more upset I became, as I am accus-
tomed and familiar with most all objects flying whether I am
close to the ground or at higher altitudes. . . . The chain of
these saucer-like objects [was] at least five miles long. I felt
confident after I would land there would be some explanation
of what I saw.

No explanation for Arnold's sighting has ever surfaced, and the
mystery regarding what he did, or did not, see has raged for more
than half a century. Even the FBI, which was monitoring UFO activity somewhat ad hoc in the summer of 1947, came away impressed by the report.

It is difficult to believe that a man of [Arnold's] character and apparent integrity would state that he saw objects and write up a report to the extent that he did if he did not see them.

So what, precisely, *did* Kenneth Arnold see on that fateful day in June 1947? Were the objects really alien spacecraft undertaking a covert study of the earth? Or were they—as even Kenneth Arnold himself suspected initially—a newly designed and revolutionary aircraft of the Army Air Force?

As UFO sightings reached epidemic proportions across the United States in the summer of 1947, the military swung into action and various initial studies and operations were formulated that ulti- mately unified into an official UFO investigation known as Project Sign. That project would, in 1948, make way for Project Grudge, and finally, Project Blue Book, which continued until 1969. To- gether the three projects concluded that no UFO sighting investi- gated had ever had a bearing on national security, and no evidence indicated that any UFO sightings represented alien visitations.

Of course, numerous claims, counterclaims, arguments, and counterarguments have been put forth by a variety of authors and commentators on whether some UFOs are indeed alien spacecraft and whether elements of the U.S. government, military, and intelli- gence community have systematically hidden evidence in support of that theory from the public and the media alike.

We will concentrate our study on determining if at least *a part* of the UFO controversy can be explained via a series of ultrasecret American and Russian military projects that had their beginnings in the closing stages of the Second World War and that, in some fash- ion, continue to this day. To do so, we need to first turn our attention to the official UFO files of the Federal Bureau of Investigation.

Two weeks after the encounter of Kenneth Arnold, Brigadier General George F. Schulgen, Chief of the Requirements Intelli- gence Branch of Army Air Corps Intelligence, met with Special Agent S. W. Reynolds of the FBI to determine if the Army Air Force could regularly solicit the assistance of the Bureau in investigating the UFO mystery.

General Schulgen advised SA Reynolds that "every effort must be undertaken in order to run down and ascertain whether or not the flying discs are a fact and, if so, to learn all about them."

It becomes clear from accessing the relevant files of the FBI that, in the weeks following Arnold's encounter of June 24, 1947, the foremost thought on General Schulgen's mind was that the saucers were Russian. He confided in SA Reynolds that "the first reported sightings might have been by individuals of Communist sympathies with the view to causing hysteria and fear of a secret weapon." For this reason, the Army Air Force had sought the FBI's assistance.

General Schulgen guaranteed the FBI "all the facilities of [my] office as to results obtained" and outlined a plan for the FBI to locate and question witnesses of UFOs to ascertain whether they were sincere in their sightings or if their statements were prompted by a desire for publicity or political reasons.

Schulgen was careful to advise Reynolds, "It has been established that the flying discs are not the result of any Army or Navy experiment." There is evidence, however, that his statement may not have been entirely correct.

Following the meeting between Schulgen and Reynolds, FBI director J. Edgar Hoover instructed his agents to begin investigations into UFO sightings in the manner suggested by General Schulgen. As a result of these investigations, the FBI learned, on August 15, 1947, that the U.S. military's involvement with UFOs possibly extended beyond mere observation.

In a memorandum to Edward A. Tamm, the FBI assistant director, D. M. Ladd of the Domestic Intelligence Division wrote:

The Director advised on August 14, 1947, that the Los Angeles papers were carrying headlines indicating that Soviet espionage agents had been instructed to determine the facts relative to the flying discs. The article carried a Washington date line and indicated that Red espionage agents had been ordered to solve the question of the flying discs, the Russians being of the opinion that this might be some new form of defense perfected by the American military. The article further recalled that during the recent war pieces of tin foil had been dropped in the air for the purpose of off-setting the value of radar being used by the enemy forces and that these aluminum discs might be a new development along this line. The Director inquired as to whether the Bureau had any such information.

Suspecting that, if the Russians were snooping around, the saucers had to be of U.S. origin, SA Reynolds of the FBI's Liaison Section was directed by J. Edgar Hoover to make further inquiries with the Air Force. On August 19, 1947, Reynolds met with a colonel (whom we will call X, since all references to his identity are still classified by the FBI) from Air Force Intelligence and the entire secret-weapon issue was frankly discussed, as were the possible consequences should the Bureau uncover details of a top-secret research-and-development program that, presumably, had implications for the national security of the Western world. Following their candid discussion, a remarkable memorandum captioned "Flying Discs" was prepared by Reynolds for the attention of Hoover. This document, perhaps more than any other, indicates that the U.S. military *was* test-flying UFO-type aircraft in the summer of 1947.

Special Agent S. W. Reynolds of the Liaison Section, while discussing the above captioned phenomena with Lieutenant Colonel [X] of the Air Forces Intelligence, expressed the possibility that flying discs were, in fact, a very highly classified experiment of the Army or Navy. Mr. Reynolds was very much surprised when Colonel [X] not only agreed that this was a possibility, but confidentially stated it was his personal opinion that such was a probability. Colonel [X] indicated that a Mr. [Deleted], who is a scientist attached to the Air Forces Intelligence, was of the same opinion.

Colonel [X] stated that he based his assumption on the following: He pointed out that when flying objects were reported seen over Sweden, the "high brass" of the War Department extended tremendous pressure on the Air Forces Intelligence to conduct research and collect information in an effort to identify these sightings. Colonel [X] stated that, in contrast to this, we have reported sightings of unknown objects over the United States, and the "high brass" appeared to be totally unconcerned. He indicated this led him to believe that they knew enough about these objects to express no concern. Colonel [X] pointed out further that the objects in question have been seen by many individuals who are what he terms "trained observers" such as airline pilots. He indicated also that several of the individuals are reliable members of the community. He stated that these individuals saw something. He stated the above has led him to the conclusion that there were objects seen which somebody in the Government knows all about.

SA Reynolds then pointed out to the colonel that if UFOs were indeed a highly classified domestic project of the military, it was wholly unreasonable for the FBI to be expected to "spend money and precious time conducting inquiries with respect to this matter."

The colonel duly concurred with Reynolds and indicated that it would have been extremely embarrassing to Air Force Intelligence if the saucers proved to be American in origin.

Perhaps sensing that he was getting close to uncovering the truth behind the UFO puzzle, Reynolds then made inquiries with the Intelligence Division of the War Department for an opinion on the theory that some shadow government operation was responsible for the many flying-saucer-type objects seen over North America.

The War Department, however, issued a flat denial that it was in any way implicated in the UFO issue. In a report written up later, Reynolds noted that he was given "the assurance of General Chamberlain and General Todd that the Army is conducting no experiments with anything which could possibly be mistaken for a flying disc."

Nevertheless the rumors persisted, and throughout its liaison with the Air Force, the FBI continued to express concern and unease about the nature and origin of the UFO mystery. But if some UFOs were indeed man-made, *who*, precisely, was flying them and from *where* were they flying them?

Several years before the outbreak of UFO sightings in the United States in 1947, the Nazis had been working to perfect a circular-shaped, offensive aircraft that would broadly fit the classic flying-saucer description. This can be demonstrated easily by examining a series of papers released officially under the terms of the U.S. Freedom of Information Act by a variety of agencies. The following U.S. Air Force report of January 3, 1952, from Brigadier General W. M. Garland to General Samford, Air Force director of intelligence, makes the Nazi connection amply clear.

The continued reports of unusual flying objects requires positive action to determine the nature and origin of this phenomena. It is logical to relate the reported sightings to the known development of aircraft, jet propulsion, rockets and range extension capabilities in Germany and the USSR. In this connection, it is to be noted that certain developments by the Germans, particularly the Horton wing, jet propulsion, and refueling, combined with their extensive employment of V-1 and V-2 weapons during World War II, lend credence to the possibility that the flying objects may be of German and Russian origin. The developments mentioned above were completed and operational between 1941 and 1944 and subsequently fell into the hands of the Soviets at the end of the war. There is evidence that the Germans were working on these projects as far back as 1931 to 1938. Therefore it may be assumed that the Germans had at least a 7 to 10 year lead over the United States.

The CIA showed similar concerns in its report of May 27, 1954:

A German newspaper (not further identified) recently published an interview with George Klein, famous German engineer and aircraft expert, describing the experimental construction of "flying saucers" carried out by him from 1941 to 1945. Klein stated that he was present when, in 1945, the first piloted "flying saucer" took off and reached a speed of 1,300 miles per hour within 3 minutes. The experiments resulted in three designs: one designed by Miethe, was a disk-shaped aircraft, 135 feet in diameter, which did not rotate; another designed by Habermohl and Schriever, consisted of a large rotating ring, in the center of which was a round, stationary cabin for the crew. When the Soviets occupied Prague, the Germans destroyed every trace of the "flying saucer" project and nothing more was heard of Habermohl and his assistants. Schriever recently died in Bremen, where he had been living. In Breslau, the Soviets managed to capture one of the saucers built by Miethe, who escaped to France. He is reportedly in the U.S. at present.

More information continued to fall into the hands of the FBI to the effect that the saucers were man-made and linked in part to the work of the Nazis. For instance, an American wrote the following letter to the FBI in 1947; it was kept on file in the FBI's archives for decades before declassification.

Recently I have heard and read about reports of disc-shaped aircraft, or whatever they are, in our Western regions. They reminded me of a nearly forgotten incident in Germany, after the war. I report this to you because I feel this may be of international scope.

My buddy and I went on pass to see a friend of his. One evening the three of us were driving along some back roads when I sighted a strange-looking object in the sky from eight to ten miles to our front and approximately 5,000 feet high. I immediately stopped the jeep for a better look. The object rapidly came toward us, descending slowly. About a mile away it stopped its horizontal motion but continued a slow-oscillating descent similar to a descending parachute. Then it stopped in a spiral motion.

Immediately I drove to where it had dropped. It took almost five minutes to reach the place but we saw nothing. After ten minutes of cruising around the area it became too dark to see so we went back to town.

I am not sure my companions saw this because it happened so quickly it could easily have been missed, but I described what I had seen so vividly that they were as excited as I was. My first impression was that it was a cloud, but it was traveling at right angles to the wind.

The locale of this incident was approximately 120 miles north west of Habberbishophiem. If necessary, I will swear to the authenticity of this and to the shape of the object.

During the summer of 1947, the FBI also interviewed one Edwin M. Bailey of Stamford, Connecticut, who had concerns about man-made saucers and their use against the United States by an offensive nation. Bailey's comments were the subject of a memorandum to FBI director Hoover.

Bailey prefaced his remarks by stating that he is a scientist by occupation and is currently employed at the American Cyanamid Research Laboratories on West Main Street in Stamford, Connecticut, in the Physics Division. Bailey further indicated that during the war he was employed at MIT, Cambridge, Massachusetts, in the Radiation Laboratory which Laboratory is connected with the Manhattan Project. Bailey advised that he is thirty years of age and is a graduate of the University of Arizona.

Bailey stated that the topic of flying saucers had caused considerable comment and concern to the present day scientists and indicated that he himself had a personal theory concerning the flying saucers. Prior to advancing his own theory, Bailey remarked that immediately after the conclusion of World War II, a friend of his [censored], allegedly observed the flying saucers from an observatory in Milan and Bologna, Italy. He stated that apparently at that time the flying saucers had caused a little comment in Italy but that after some little publicity they immediately died out as public interest. Bailey stated that it is quite possible that actually the flying saucers could be radio controlled germ bombs or atom bombs which are circling the orbit of the earth and which could be controlled by radio and directed to land on any designated target at the specific desire of the agency or country operating the bombs.

Five years later, in July 1952, the FBI uncovered information, from a source whose credentials remain hidden to this day, about the CIA's knowledge of potential Soviet involvement in the UFO phenomenon.

[Source] said that more recent reports have been received from representatives of the Central Intelligence Agency in Southern Europe and Southern Asia to the effect that the Russians were experimenting with some type of radical aircraft or guided missile which could be dispatched for great distances out over the sea, made to turn in flight and return to the base from which it was launched. He related that this information was extremely worthy of notice as experiments in this country have so far only developed to the point where we are concerned with delivering a missile to the required point of impact and no consideration has been given to imparting to that missile the ability to return. [Source] also advised that it is a known fact that the Russians are attempting to develop some type of nuclear energy, that they received a wealth of information concerning nuclear energy at the time of their occupation in Germany, and that they have at their disposal a limited supply of fissionable materials. [Source] pointed out that the Russians have some very capable scientists in the field of atomic energy and that, in addition thereto, they took into their custody some of the most-advanced and capable scientists of the German nation.

Two of the most persuasive accounts that reached the FBI that posited a direct link between the Nazi war machine and unidentified flying objects came via two individuals interviewed by Bureau agents in 1957 and 1967 respectively. In the 1957 case, agents at Detroit recorded that they had spoken with a man who was

born February 19, 1926, in the State of Warsaw, Poland, and was brought from Poland as a Prisoner of War to Gut Alt Golssen approximately 30 miles east of Berlin, Germany, in May, 1942, where he remained until a few weeks after the end of World War II. He spent the following years at Displaced Persons Camps at Kork, Strasburg [sic], Offenburg, Milheim and Freiburg, Germany. He attended a radio technician school at Freiburg and for about a year was employed in a textile mill at Laurachbaden, Germany. He arrived in the United States at New York, May 2, 1951, via the "SS General Stewart" as a Displaced Person. According to the man, during 1944, month not recalled, while enroute [sic] to work in a field a short distance north of Gut Alt Golssen, their tractor engine stalled on a road through a swamp area. No machinery or other vehicle was then visible although a noise was heard described as a high-pitched whine similar to that produced by a large electric generator.

An "SS" guard appeared and talked briefly with the German driver of the tractor, who waited five to ten minutes, after which the noise stopped and the tractor engine was started normally. Approximately 3 hours later in the same swamp area, but away from the road where the work crew was cutting "hay," he surreptitiously, because of the German in charge of the crew and "SS" guards in the otherwise deserted area, observed a circular enclosure approximately 100 to 150 yards in diameter protected from viewers by a tarpaulin-type wall approximately 50 feet high, from which a vehicle was observed to slowly rise vertically to a height sufficient to clear the wall and then to move slowly horizontally a short distance out of his view, which was obstructed by trees.

This vehicle, observed from approximately 500 feet, was described as circular in shape, 75 to 100 yards in diameter, and about 14 feet high, consisting of dark gray stationary top and bottom sections, five to six feet high. The approximate three foot middle section appeared to be a rapidly moving component producing a continuous blur similar to an aeroplane propeller, but extending the circumference of the vehicle so far as could be observed. The noise emanating from the vehicle was similar but of somewhat lower pitch than the noise previously heard. The engine of the tractor again stalled on this occasion and no effort was made by the German driver to start the engine until the noise stopped, after which the engine started normally.

This account is particularly notable because numerous witnesses have reported that their car engine has been adversely affected when in close proximity to a UFO. For many UFO investigators this is prime evidence in support of the notion that UFOs represent a technology far in advance of our own and must, therefore, be from some distant world. But the reality, as this document firmly demonstrates, is that there is an equally strong argument in support of the notion that vehicle interference cases, as they are commonly known, are the result of encounters with distinctly terrestrial craft.

The report continues:

Uninsulated metal, possibly copper, cables one and one-half inch to two inches in diameter, on and under the surface of the ground, in some places covered by water, were observed on this and previous occasions, apparently running between the enclosure and a small concrete column-like structure between the road and enclosure. This area was not visited by the man again until shortly after the end of World War II, when it was observed the cables had been removed and the previous locations of the concrete structure and the enclosure were covered by water. The man stated he has not been in communication since 1945 with any of the work crew of 16 or 18 men, consisting of Russian, French and Polish POWs, who had discussed this incident among themselves many times. However, of these, he was able to recall by name only one, no address known, described as then about 50 years of age and presumed to have returned to Poland after 1945.

The second document concerns a man who appeared at the Miami Office of the FBI on April 26, 1967, and furnished information relating to a flying-saucer-like object that he allegedly photographed during November 1944.

Sometime during 1943, he graduated from the German Air Academy and was assigned as a member of the *Luftwaffe* on the Russian Front. Near the end of 1944, he was released from this duty and was assigned as a test pilot to a top secret project in the Black Forest of Austria. [Authors' note: This data is particularly important since it identifies this source as an expert and highly trained witness.] During this period he observed the aircraft described above. It was saucer-shaped, about twenty-one feet in diameter, radio-controlled, and mounted several jet engines around the exterior portion of the craft. He further described the exterior portion as revolving around the dome in the center which remained stationary. It was his responsibility to photograph the object while in flight. He asserted he was able to retain a negative of a photograph he made at 7,000 meters (20,000 feet).

According to him, the above aircraft was designed and engineered by a German engineer whose present whereabouts is unknown to him. He also assumed the secrets pertaining to this aircraft were captured by Allied Forces. He said this type of aircraft was responsible for the downing of at least one American B-26 airplane.

Again, we see the forever-circling rumor that UFO-style technology was captured from the Nazis by Allied personnel at the close of hostilities. The report concludes:

He has become increasingly concerned because of the unconfirmed reports concerning a similar object and denials the United States has such an aircraft. He feels such a weapon would be beneficial in Vietnam and would prevent the further loss of American lives which was his paramount purpose in contacting the Federal Bureau of Investigation.

Meanwhile, British authorities had uncovered a similar body of data. A 1957 secret Air Ministry report, for example, states, "A review by the *Daily Worker* newspaper of a book recently published on German wartime weapons contained references to a German flying saucer which was flown at a speed of 1,250 mph to a height of 40,000 feet."[1]

But that is not all. In 1998, the British government declassified a

two-volume document—titled *Unorthodox Aircraft*, previously
withheld at top-secret level and dating from 1948 to 1951—that
dealt with British intelligence interviews with former prisoners of
war who had seen unusual and radical aircraft in the vicinity of German and Russian airfields and military installations.

Interestingly enough, interspersed throughout the reports are a
variety of foreign newspaper clippings on both UFOs and the attempts of the Nazis to build and utilize such craft. Moreover, copies
of the file were distributed to a whole host of British agencies and
departments, including the Joint Intelligence Bureau, the Air Ministry's Scientific and Technical Intelligence office, MI10 at the War
Office, Air Intelligence, and an elite Air Ministry division known
as A13.[2]

In other words, several key departments in the British government during the late 1940s were extremely interested in knowing
the extent to which the Nazis had made advances with respect to
flying-saucer-type aircraft designs.

If, as the available documented evidence strongly suggests,
Hitler's hordes *were* working to construct flying-saucer-like craft
in the early 1940s and that at the close of World War II some of
that technology fell into the hands of the Soviets, then to what
extent did the U.S. military also acquire similar technology from
the Nazis?

Without a doubt the most famous—or rather infamous—man-
made flying saucer was the Avrocar. In 1953, the *Toronto Star* newspaper revealed that the aerospace company Avro Canada was
working to perfect a flying saucer. The Avrocar made its first unteth-
ered and largely unsuccessful "flight" in December 1959. Two years
later it had still barely gotten off the ground, and the U.S. Department of Defense—which had expressed considerable interest in the
project and had been working closely with Avro—severed its ties
with the project. An official U.S. Air Force document on the Avrocar, dated from 1961, amply sums up the situation:

From 1958 on, Aircraft Lab had many doubts about feasibility as expressed in correspondence and project reviews. On basis of various tests, the Aircraft Lab noted in Feb 1958 that the Avrocar probably would not be capable of supersonic flight. A few months later, Aircraft Lab statements [said] that the concept was feasible, but that much work had to be done before it would ever be operational—serious mechanical problems, engine problems, aerodynamic problems, and flight factors unknown.

Later evaluation of wind tunnel tests were unsatisfactory and the project was finally disbanded. Of course, this situation creates a major problem. If both the Nazis and the Soviets *had* succeeded in creating seemingly near-flawless UFO-like aircraft, what prevented the Americans from doing likewise? The answer, quite simply, is nothing at all. At the close of the Second World War, the U.S. government's Operation Paperclip ensured that a wealth of German scientists were brought to the United States to continue the research that they had been conducting on a variety of aircraft and rocket technologies during the war. In other words, the United States had the expertise to continue the UFO work that the Nazis had begun several years previously. Perhaps there really was a secret postwar UFO project by the U.S. military, and perhaps it was almost compromised by the FBI's Special Agent S. W. Reynolds in the summer of 1947.

Moreover, persuasive evidence in the form of official files shows that the Avrocar—which largely became little more than a joke in the worlds of both aviation and the media—was in reality a carefully executed cover for far more in-depth and secretive U.S. programs designed to build and—in theory—fly UFO-style aircraft. In other words, the Avrocar project was a planned failure to create the impression with the Soviets that the U.S. military had failed to successfully develop and put into service the ultimate flying war machine.

Evidence exists to support such a scenario. Documentation de-classified in 1995 shows that from 1952 to 1961, a Special Projects Group from Avro worked on a series of sensitive flying saucer programs that were far in advance of the Avrocar. One such project, known as Y2, was purchased by the U.S. Air Force and renamed Project Silver Bug.

A technical report (Report TR-AC-47) on Silverbug prepared on February 15, 1955, by the Air Technical Intelligence Center at Wright-Patterson Air Force Base, Dayton, Ohio, reveals the extent to which truly radical research was being undertaken. Stressing that the document contained information that affected the national defense of the United States "within the meaning of the Espionage Law," the report clearly spelled out its purpose.

This report presents factual technical data on A. V. Roe, Canada, Limited, proposed development, Project Y2 (Secret). This proposal is the second of two designs which can be classified as radical aircraft designs. The ultimate purpose of presenting this is two-fold; to correct the distorted picture presented in previous releases, both classified and unclassified, and to acquaint the intelligence community with the current state-of-the-art facts thereby alerting them to any air intelligence information which may become available indicating Soviet interest in this specialized field.

Obviously the Air Force was concerned about Soviet advances in this area and the classified information on the matter. This amply reinforces the sensitivity from an official perspective of man-made saucers in the United States.

The author of this proposal, by one of Canada's most progressive members of the aircraft industry, AVRO Aircraft Limited, a member of the Hawker-Siddley group, wished to disassociate it from connotations related to the object's shape.

[The design] should in no way be associated with any science fiction or "Flying Saucer" stories because of its external appearance. The configuration was a result of an engineering investigation into the solution of a particular problem. An examination of the AVRO proposal shows that the potential for a very high performance weapon system exists in the not-too-distant future. Although this proposal offers the USAF a potentially advanced weapon system having both vertical take-off and military performance capabilities, there are numerous technical problems which must be solved before a successful development can be realized. The proposal is for the design of a supersonic research aircraft having a circular planform and VTO characteristics. One version provides for the use of several conventional radial-flow type engines. Another unusual feature of this proposal is that the control of the aircraft is accomplished by selective direction of the exhaust gases which eliminates the necessity of conventional aerodynamic control surfaces.

Although the author of the report was careful to distance himself, and by definition, the entire project, from flying saucer stories, the proposed vehicle did display many of the characteristics of UFOs — the circular shape, the ability to travel at supersonic speeds, and the capability of taking off vertically. Not only that, control of the aircraft was accomplished by selectively directing the exhaust gases, which would have given the vehicle maneuvering capabilities far in advance of standard aircraft technology. Needless to say, accounts of UFOs carrying out incredible midair, ninety-degree turns abound in the annals of ufology. Perhaps we now know why.

The following section of the document reveals why, from a strategic perspective, the Air Force had such a pressing need to construct and utilize a flying-saucer-style device.

This proposal offers a possible solution to the USAF requirement for achieving dispersed base operations. There appears to be no fundamental reason why this proposal should not ultimately result in a weapon system; however there are several technical areas which must be investigated before a full-scale development program is initiated. The simplicity of airframe construction should alleviate many of the manufacturing and logistic problems normally associated with new aircraft developments. Based on the above conclusions, a two-fold intelligence program is justifiable.

a. The technical information on this project should be followed by direct liaison between WADC and ATIC personnel.

b. A collection effort should be initiated to determine whether the Soviet Bloc is or has been conducting research efforts on a similar project, when this work began, and the present state of the Soviet development.

A. Background

There is a USAF requirement to develop a means of operation from dispersed bases. This requirement stems from the growing and possibly catastrophic vulnerability of conventional air bases. The major feature of conventional air bases is the runway, which has grown wider, thicker, and longer as aircraft have become heavier and faster. The operational necessity of runways leads to concentrations of aircraft which have become critical targets. The logical approach to dispersed base operation would appear to be toward reducing the length of runways or to their total elimination. Numerous schemes have been proposed, investigated, and some developed to reduce the take-off distance of aircraft. Among them are water ejection, afterburning, and RATO. Drag chutes and methods of thrust reversal have been developed for reducing landing requirements. Attempts to eliminate runways completely have resulted in helicopters, convertiplanes and what is known as VTO aircraft. There are two general types of VTO aircraft—"tail sitters" and "flat risers." A flat-riser takes off in the vertical direction in a normal horizontal flight attitude, while the tail-sitter takes off vertically from a position which is 90 degrees to a normal horizontal flight attitude. Examples of tail-sitters are the United States Navy projects with Lockheed and Convair which utilize a turboprop power plant, and the USAF project with Ryan Aeronautical Corporation utilizing turbojet power plants. Examples of the flat-riser are the Rolls-Royce "Flying Bedstead" and the Bell VTO aircraft. The basic design problem associated with any aircraft of this type becomes one of achieving in a single vehicle VTO and military performance capabilities. A possible solution to this problem has been proposed by A. V. Roe, Canada, Limited, in the form of their Project Y2 (Secret).

The report offers a greater insight into the world of the flying saucer than perhaps the military realizes. First, it suggests that man-made saucers were not a science-fiction-style pipe dream: the idea was both sound and feasible. Second, that the Air Force wanted to develop flying saucers as a weapon system demonstrates the seriousness with which the project was being undertaken. Third, and perhaps most significant of all, is the eye-opening reality that the Air Force had already established plans to have its flying saucer fleet on standby at military bases in the event of need at a time of crisis.

Countless reports are on file of UFOs seen in the vicinity of both Army and Air Force facilities. This is often seen as evidence that aliens are keeping a watchful eye on our burgeoning military technology. Maybe they are. But a more likely scenario is that the flying saucers are so widely seen near military bases because that is precisely from where they are operating!

Over and over, the report nearly screams out an obvious conclusion: nearly half a century ago, if not before, the cream of the Western scientific community was working with the U.S. military in an attempt to design, build, and deploy flying saucers.

There were, states the document, two versions of small research VTO aircraft, designated by the contractor as Project Y, a *tail-sitter*, and Project Y2, a *flat-riser*.

Early in the investigation, Project Y was rejected by the contractor in favor of the flat-riser. Apparently, the Project Y2 design incorporated a number of radical ideas in fundamental areas that had not then been thoroughly investigated.

Most significant of all was the original proposal for the construction of a large radial-flow gas turbine engine that, when covered, would form a flying wing with a circular form, "similar in appearance to a very large discus."

A wealth of thinking went into the craft's power source and cockpit.

The engine is designed to fly "edge on" to the wind instead of axially as is present practice on conventional aircraft design. An alternate version for a multiengine aircraft . . . would avoid concurrent development of the airframe and engine while providing the other essential characteristics of the vehicle. The cockpit is located at the center of the aircraft with the orientation of the cockpit determining the fore and after center-line of the aircraft as well as the normal direction of forward flight. The airframe, fuel cells, and the gas turbine power plant encircle the cockpit.

The take-off and landing capabilities of the vehicle gelled perfectly too with the characteristics that many witnesses to UFOs have reported on a wealth of occasions.

This aircraft is designed for vertical take-off and landings while in the horizontal flight attitude, i.e., a "flat-riser." Since this aircraft rises vertically from a horizontal position, it does not require a landing gear or auxiliary landing devices. The flat-riser flight take-off technique, the elimination of the landing gear and auxiliary landing devices, are brought about by the peripheral exhaust which produces a "powerful ground cushion effect." This is one of the fundamentals on which this new radical aircraft design is based. Since this airframe and engine will have a circular planform, the outer perimeter of the aircraft will be the exhaust of the engine and the thrust forces will be used for control of the aircraft. A unified control system must be designed which will produce the same aircraft responses irrespective of whether the aircraft is in hovering, transition, or forward flight. The circular planform may be modified to accommodate trim flaps of some nature if they are found to be necessary. The air intakes are placed in the inner circle on the upper surface of the aircraft for vertical take-off while additional air intakes are installed in the upper and lower forward facing surfaces for forward flight.

The report went on to note that a research vehicle was planned for production that would investigate stability, control, and performance before a multiengine operational aircraft or radial-flow single-engine aircraft was developed. This prototype configuration would also investigate certain fundamental areas concerning aircraft behavior.

The center location of the fuel cells allows for the use of the fuel as a coolant medium against aerodynamic heating for the cockpit. The mechanical engineering details should not present any unsolvable problems in the airframe design; however, the rotor assembly and exhaust control systems are considered major problems. The basic structural ribs of the airframe lend themselves readily to mass production since they are identical. Sixty ribs are proposed as the foundation of the airframe. These ribs "butted" to the outer surface of the fuel cells with the inner side of the fuel cells comprising the cockpit opening. For the multiengine version certain engineering problems may arise due to the complexity of controlling eight engines, eight fuel systems, eight lubricating systems, etc.

The aircraft, at rest, cannot use the bottom forward facing air intake; therefore, "take-off air is supplied through 30 square feet of door area in the top intake." This air is exhausted through exhaust nozzle (outer perimeter) of the aircraft and is directed downward. This downward ejection of the air produces a "ground cushion effect," which results in an additional thrust component for take-off and allows for a ground cushion to break the landing of the aircraft. The effect is present only when the exhaust air is distributed from the periphery of the aircraft (flat-risers). In forward flight, the air enters the plenum chamber through the forward facing air intakes in both the upper and lower surfaces of the aircraft. Engine exhaust gasses are carried around the exhauster duct and are expelled through the annular nozzle which is located on the upper and lower surfaces near the periphery, and through the backward facing nozzles which are located on both sides of the aircraft.

The proposed power plant for the single-engine research vehicle would essentially be a double-sided radial-flow turbojet engine. At the heart of it would be a large-diameter rotor disk that would utilize compressor air bleed as its only means of lubrication.

The compressor stators, diffuser, combustion tubes, and turbine nozzle guide vanes are designed as an integral part of the airframe. The rotating element of the conventional gas turbine engine, namely, the compressor rotor, connecting shaft and turbine wheel have been rearranged to a disc configuration. The compressor rotor blades are mounted vertically on the inner disc ring; the turbine wheel blades are mounted vertically on the outer disc ring, and the connecting disc ring is comparable to the conventional connecting shaft. This disc rotates on a double-sided air bearing mounted between the upper and lower combustion tubes. The combustion system consists of flame tubes distributed between the structural ribs of the aircraft. The engine pressure is contained between the outer skin and the rotor bearing plates with the latter structure being mounted between the combustion tubes. For take-off the intake air is brought through the top intakes to the first stage of the rotor and is compressed radially outwards through six stages giving a normal pressure ratio of 3 to 1 from the last compressor stage. The air is diffused and passes through the flame tubes, turbine inlet guide vanes, through the turbine wheel, and then through the exhaust nozzle which is the outer perimeter of the aircraft. During forward flight, the upper air intake ducts are closed and the forward facing air intakes are open. Due to the radial flow through the engine, the compressor blades and turbine blades are straight. Therefore, these parts may be more easily manufactured than for the conventional engine compressors and turbines. The proposed air bearing supporting the rotating element eliminates many of the problems which are imposed by mechanical type bearings. The large area of the bearing surface, approximately 100 square feet on both sides, is available to support the weight of the very large turbine rotor. The air supply for the flat bearing comes from "secondary air" in the combustion region while the supply for the vertical bearing comes from the rear of the last rotor stage of the compressor. Exhaust of the bearing air is controlled by a low pressure annulus and the main "exhauster" which utilized this air for cooling the turbine blade roots. A ground supply of compressed air applied to the air bearing will be used when starting the engine. In stopping the engine, the rotor will ground on self-lubricating bearing pads. The material used in the self-lubricating bearing pads will be cast iron or carbon which will provide good dry bearing surfaces on steel. These pads are not expected to suffer excessive wear or provide undue stopping torque on the turbine rotor. The multiengine version would utilize numerous small engines having low specific weights to provide the exhaust gases.

Probably the most complex challenge of the craft's design involved the vehicle's control systems.

The aircraft is controlled by regulating shutters which vary the amount of thrust through the annular nozzles (for pitch and roll control) and through the backward facing nozzles for yaw control located on the peripheral edge. The contractor claims that the use of this "jet control" at all times eliminates the difficulty associated with hinged control surfaces in supersonic flight. This statement on the part of the contractor is based on initial testing of the principle and much more data must be assembled before it can be completely accepted. A proposed method of achieving jet control utilizes the so-called "Coanda effect" whereby a jet stream is deflected through large angles by having a curved surface in contact with its edge at one side. Additional investigation into the mechanism required to utilize this effect must be accomplished in the early phases of this development. In the proposed aircraft thrust forces are used for control at all times. It is mandatory to use the thrust force for take-off and hovering flight since there are no aerodynamic forces available due to the lack of forward movement. In forward supersonic flight thrust forces are used in lieu of conventional hinged-type controls.

The performance estimated by the contractor was based on rather broad assumptions and has not as yet been investigated by a wind tunnel test program.

NOTE: The above estimate utilizes net thrusts and SFC which are based on the "simplifying assumption"—"Plain nozzles and 100 percent thrust recovery from the jet bending."

And there ends the report. But it may not be entirely coinciden-
tal that in precisely the same year that the project began, 1952, flying saucer reports filed through official channels in the United
States reached an all-time high. According to a CIA document on a
wave of UFO encounters over Washington, D.C., in the summer of
1952, "During 1952 alone, official reports totaled 250. Of the 1,500
reports, Air Force carries 20 percent as unexplained and of those received from January through July 1952 it carries 28 percent unexplained."

To what extent Silverbug was successfully put into operation and
how many UFO reports from the 1950s and onward can be directly
attributed to aircraft designed and possibly even built and flown as a
result of the Silverbug project is questionable. However, indications
are that the operation was a success and was constantly being improved upon. Only a few years later, just as the Avrocar was being
dismissed in official circles as a dismal failure, the U.S. military was
planning to build a nuclear-powered, battle-ready flying saucer that
it intended placing in near-Earth orbit.

The reality of these incredible plans can once again be validated
by examining now-declassified U.S. military documents. A report
dated October 1962 is titled "Environment Control Systems Selection for Manned Space Vehicles" and was prepared by North American Aviation Inc. for the Air Force Systems Command at
Wright-Patterson Air Force Base. Though much of the text is highly
technical, the description of the proposed flying saucer as the
"lenticular reentry vehicle" is extraordinary.

The overall weapon system concept results in a requirement
for three basic orbiting components. First, there is a requirement for a manned bombardment vehicle which houses the
basic control function in space. Secondly, a weapon cluster is
required. This is an unmanned weapon carrier which combines
and integrates several weapons into a common orbiting package to facilitate handling and servicing. The third requirement

is the weapon itself. The disc-shaped configuration was chosen for its greater usable volume for weapon storage and crew accommodations and for other advantages. It has a basic diameter of 40 feet and a gross launch weight of about 45,000 pounds. The vehicle functions as a manned orbital bombing system with an internal armament load of four winged reentry weapons and also acts as an orbital control and maintenance center for additional unmanned weapon clusters. The operational mission design is 6 weeks duration at a nominal orbital altitude of 300 nautical miles, with a crew of four men. Primarily because of its excellent surface area–volume–weight relationship, the lenticular shape has been chosen as its satellite-reentry configuration for the manned bomber. The basic disc shape is inherently unstable assuming a representative center of gravity location. However, control surfaces, flaps, and speed brakes suitably located and configurations tailoring can make the lenticular shape stable and, with other desirable characteristics, a very satisfactory manned reentry and landing configuration will evolve. The disc-shaped configuration with control surfaces on the aft portion of the vehicle eliminates the problem of high heating due to low shock interactions between conventional fuselage nose and wing leading-edge surfaces. This problem is common to winged body lifting vehicles. The manned bomber requires two separate power systems; one for the boost and reentry phases and another for the normal 6-week orbital operation. Unfortunately, it is not feasible to provide one system which can supply the energy for both requirements. Energy for the orbital operation can most feasibly be supplied from nuclear or solar sources. The nuclear reactor cannot be activated until the vehicle is in orbit, and on reentry, would probably be left in space to avoid the possible hazards associated with a hot reactor should a crash occur on landing.

That the U.S. Air Force had plans in the early 1960s to build flying saucers is illuminating enough in itself. That those same saucers
would be fully armed and battle-ready, would orbit the Earth at a
height of three hundred miles for up to six weeks, would be powered
by a nuclear reactor, and that all this information was successfully
hidden from the media and public alike for decades, is nothing
short of incredible. Note too the references to the way in which,
with a few modifications, the disc-shaped design made for a highly
desirable reentry vehicle from space. Bear in mind, also, that all of
this research was being undertaken at a time when the official
manned U.S. space program was still in its infancy.

At the very least the U.S. intelligence community was using the
UFO mystery as a convenient cover for its own aerospace activities.
An unclassified Central Intelligence Agency report titled "CIA's
Role in the Study of UFOs, 1947–90," written by CIA historian Ger-
ald Haines, makes no bones of that fact.

In November 1954, CIA had entered into the world of high
technology with its U-2 overhead reconnaissance project. Working with Lockheed's Advanced Development facility in Bur-
bank, California, known as the Skunk Works, and Kelly
Johnson, an eminent aeronautical engineer, the Agency by August 1955 was testing a high-altitude experimental aircraft—
the U-2. It could fly at 60,000 feet; in the mid-1950s, most
commercial airliners flew between 10,000 feet and 20,000
feet. Consequently, once the U-2 started test flights, commercial
pilots and air traffic controllers began reporting a large increase in UFO sightings. The early U-2s were silver (they were
later painted black) and reflected the rays from the sun, especially at sunrise and sunset. They often appeared as fiery objects to observers below. Air Force BLUE BOOK investigators
aware of the secret U-2 flights tried to explain away such sightings by linking them to natural phenomena such as ice crystals

and temperature inversions. By checking with the Agency's U-2 Project Staff in Washington, BLUE BOOK investigators were able to attribute many UFO sightings to U-2 flights. They were careful, however, not to reveal the true cause of the sighting to the public. According to later estimates from CIA officials who worked on the U-2 project and the OXCART (SR-71, or Blackbird) project, over half of all UFO reports from the late 1950s through the 1960s were accounted for by manned reconnaissance flights (namely the U-2) over the United States. This led the Air Force to make misleading and deceptive statements to the public in order to allay public fears and to protect an extraordinarily sensitive national security project. While perhaps justified, this deception added fuel to the later conspiracy theories and the cover up controversy of the 1970s. The percentage of what the Air Force considered unexplained UFO sightings fell to 5.9 percent in 1955 and to 4 percent in 1956.

So where does all this leave us? There can be little doubt that the Nazi war machine *was* seeking to perfect a flying-saucer-like craft in the closing stages of the Second World War. They may even have had some considerable success in this area. At the close of hostilities both the former Soviet Union and the U.S. government possibly got their hands on this burgeoning technology and began utilizing it for their own purposes. It appears that the FBI was largely kept out of the loop with respect to the ultrasecret U.S. military research project, but did come close to compromising the security surrounding it. Throughout the 1950s and 1960s U.S. scientists and military personnel designed, and possibly built and deployed, ever more advanced saucer-style vehicles; while at the same time the CIA kept a watchful eye on Soviet advances in this area.

Can the entire UFO mystery be explained away as a direct result of these decades-old projects? Or is this simply one facet of an even bigger mystery? To date, there appears to be no clear answer. However, the next time someone tells you that UFOs are flying out of the infamous Area 51 (a secure installation in Nevada that undertakes classified work for the U.S. military), tell them that they are probably correct. There is a distinct possibility, however, that those same UFOs are piloted not by little gray men from the other side of the galaxy but by large and burly men in standard-issue U.S. Air Force flight suits.

UNITED STATES DEPARTMENT OF JUSTICE

FEDERAL BUREAU OF INVESTIGATION

Denver, Colorado
April 26, 1960

Re: UNIDENTIFIED FLYING OBJECTS,
    INVESTIGATIVE SOCIETY;
    GEORGE W. VAN TASSEL

On April 17, 1960, a lecture was given by GEORGE
W. VAN TASSEL at Phipps Auditorium, City Park, Denver,
Colorado, which was advertised to be a lecture, movie film,
and discussion of unidentified flying objects. The audience
was comprised of a majority of older individuals and also
a majority of the audience was female. There were few
young people, although some family groups.

The program was sponsored by the Denver Unidentified Flying Objects Investigative Societies, one of which
meets monthly at the Jefferson County Bank, Lakewood,
Colorado, whose executive officer was the Master of Ceremonies.
The program consisted of a 45 minute movie which included
several shots of things purported to be flying saucers, and
then a number of interviews with people from all walks of
life regarding sightings they had made of such unidentified
flying objects. After the movie GEORGE W. VAN TASSEL gave a
lecture which was more of a religious-economics lecture
rather than one of unidentified flying objects.

VAN TASSEL stated that he had been in the "flying
game" for over 30 years and currently operates a private
Civil Aeronautics Authority approved airfield in California.
He said he has personally observed a good many sightings and
has talked to hundreds of people who have also seen flying
saucers. He said that he has also been visited by the people
from outer space and has taken up the cause of bringing the
facts of these people to the American people. He said it
is a crusade which he has undertaken because he is more or
less retired, his family is grown and gone from home, and
he feels he might be doing some good by this work.

PROPERTY OF FBI - This memorandum is loaned to you by the
FBI, and neither it nor its contents are to be distributed
outside the agency to which loaned.

62-83894-418

ENCLOSURE

*From the early 1950s until the mid-1960s the FBI carefully monitored a
number of people who claimed to have had face-to-face contact with
alien beings, as this FBI document of 1960, "Unidentified Flying
Objects, Investigative Society; George W. Van Tassel," shows.*

Six

COSMIC COMMIES

When people contemplate the possibility of a meeting between humans and an alien species, they tend to imagine that any visiting extraterrestrials are going to differ in appearance and character from ourselves.

One such view was presented by the science writer and author Edward Ashpole in 1995: "Any technological species visiting us from a far-away biosphere would not look like us. We are vertebrates, and vertebrates have a long history of evolution going back to a certain group of fishes. The bones which form the human skeleton can be traced back through that evolutionary history and are not going to be duplicated in another planetary biology. Statistically it would be impossible."[1]

Furthermore, different environments will likely produce quite different life-forms. In 1974, the authors Jack Stoneley and Anthony T. Lawton speculated on the likely variety: "The extreme heat and gaseous surface of a planet like Jupiter might produce a creature that would float beneath its own built-in balloon, feeding off organic compounds produced in electrical discharges in the upper atmosphere. The intelligences we may one day encounter could have two legs or two hundred; they might be flat or round, they may walk, swim, fly, roll, slide, crawl, hop, or squirm. They may be hairy or bald, transparent or solid. They may have one eye, a thousand eyes or, though rather unlikely, no eyes at all. They may even be just shapeless masses suspended in an atmosphere." [2]

For all the arguments that alien visitors to our planet would look, appropriately enough, like nothing on Earth, in the early 1950s numerous people throughout the world (and particularly within the United States) claimed contact with a breed of alien that purportedly looked very much like the human species. In many cases, those who maintained that they had met such beings asserted that the aliens were highly concerned by our warlike ways and our burgeoning nuclear arsenals. Thus was created the cult of the contactee. Many of these people gained massive publicity from their claims, wrote books, were in high demand on the lecture circuit—and even attracted the attention of the U.S. government.

Born March 12, 1910, in Jefferson County, Ohio, George Wellington Van Tassel claimed contact with humanlike extraterrestrial beings in August 1953 near his home in Yucca Valley, California. The full story surrounding Van Tassel's adventures with otherworldly creatures is truly strange, involving wild accounts of meetings with imaginatively named aliens, including Numa of Uni; Ah-Ming of Tarr; Rondolla of the Fourth Density; and Zolton, the Highest Authority in the Sector System of Vela. Why would someone making such wild claims become the subject of an extensive FBI surveillance file that lasted from 1954 until well into the 1960s?

Here is the story. According to the FBI's records, prior to moving to Yucca Valley in 1947, Van Tassel had worked for the Douglas Aircraft Corporation in Santa Monica, Hughes Aircraft, where he was employed as an assistant to Howard Hughes, Universal Airlines, and Lockheed.

Quite what prompted him to relocate to Yucca Valley is unclear. But, along with his wife and children, Van Tassel soon settled into his new, if somewhat unconventional, surroundings: his famous cave under Giant Rock—an area leased from the Government.

To the uninitiated, the thought of a family living in a cave situated beneath a sixty-foot-high rock ten miles from Joshua Tree, California, must seem more than a little strange and conjures up images of some prehistoric family struggling to live in less than friendly conditions.

Initially, day-to-day living was more than a little taxing for the Van Tassels, but, ever resourceful, the family soon began to make ends meet via an airstrip they rented—the Giant Rock Airport—and a small, but hospitable restaurant.

As time went on, Van Tassel began to improve the family's living facilities, and the cave became a friendly environment. It was fully furnished, equipped with electricity, its own water supply, an impressive library of books, and as the journalist Ed Ritter noted in 1954, "a comfortable living room where [Van Tassel] studies and entertains guests." There is nothing so far that would prompt the Federal Bureau of Investigation to take an interest in the affairs of George W. Van Tassel. But remember, this was the McCarthy era.

As a result of his alleged August 1953 encounter, Van Tassel had compiled the first issue of the *Proceedings of the College of Universal Wisdom*, an eight-page journal that served as a mouthpiece for not only Van Tassel but his cosmic communicators too. In the opening edition, Desca, like Rondolla, also of the Fourth Density, urged Van Tassel's followers (whose number would soon reach almost one thousand) to "remove the binding chains of limit on your minds, throw out the barriers of fear [and] dissipate the selfishness of individual desire to attain physical and material things."

In the edition of the *Proceedings* dated December 1, 1953, Van Tassel revealed that on November 6 a "message was received from the beings who operate the spacecraft," with orders from Ashtar, "the Commandant of Space Station Schare" (pronounced Share-ee), to contact the office of Air Force Intelligence at Wright-Patterson Air Force Base, Dayton, Ohio. He was to advise them,

"The present destructive plans formulated for offensive and defensive war are known to us in their entirety . . . the present trend toward destructive war will not be interfered with by us, unless the condition warrants our interference in order to secure this solar system. This is a friendly warning."

Were Van Tassel's contacts genuinely of alien origin? Were they merely the ravings of a deluded mind? *Or were they possibly a part of some sophisticated Communist-inspired intelligence operation designed to disrupt the internal security of the United States?* This possibility was certainly of concern to a Yucca Valley resident who, on August 5, 1954, wrote to the FBI suggesting that Van Tassel be investigated to determine if he was working as a Soviet spy. The identity of the woman who prompted the FBI to undertake its investigation of Van Tassel remains unknown. There is a distinct possibility, however, that she had access to Van Tassel's *Proceedings*. Moreover, copies of Van Tassel's *Proceedings* in the possession of the FBI from this period show that certain comments and entries in the documents had carefully been circled by someone who was clearly interested in Van Tassel's politics and his purported alien friends.

Concerned that Van Tassel might be a witting or unwitting player in a subversive Communist plot, the FBI was determined to ascertain the facts. On November 12, 1954, Major S. Avner of the Air Force's Office of Special Investigations (AFOSI) met with N. W. Philcox, who provided FBI liaison with the Air Force, to discuss the Van Tassel matter.

Three days later, Avner reestablished contact with Philcox, informing him that the Air Technical Intelligence Center (ATIC) at Wright-Patterson Air Force Base "has information on Van Tassel indicating that he has corresponded with them regarding flying saucers." Almost certainly this was a reference to the letter Van Tassel had written to ATIC at the request of the mysterious Ashtar, who it will be recalled offered a "friendly warning" with respect to plans formulated for offensive and defensive war. Consequently the Air

Force offered "to furnish the Bureau with more detailed information if it is so desired."

Whether or not the FBI accepted the Air Force's offer of "more detailed information" on Van Tassel is not known. But the FBI was more than capable of conducting its own investigations. One day after Major Avner of AFOSI spoke with Philcox, two special agents of the Los Angeles FBI office met with Van Tassel at his Giant Rock home. In a memorandum to FBI director J. Edgar Hoover dated November 16, 1954, the agents wrote:

Relative to spacemen and space craft, VAN TASSEL declared that a year ago last August, while sleeping out of doors with his wife in the Giant Rock area, and at about 2:00 A.M. he was awakened by a man from space. This individual spoke English and was dressed in a gray one piece suit similar to a sweat suit in that it did not have any buttons, pockets, and noticeable seams. This person, according to VAN TASSEL, invited him to inspect a space craft or flying saucer, which had landed on Giant Rock air strip. VAN TASSEL claimed the craft was bell shaped resembling a saucer. He further described the ship as approximately 35 feet in diameter and is now known as the scout type craft. Aboard this craft was located three other male individuals wearing the same type of dress and identical in every respect with earth people.

VAN TASSEL claims that the three individuals aboard the craft were mutes in that they could not talk. He claimed they conversed through thought transfers, and also operated the flight of the craft through thought control. He stated that the spokesman for the group claimed he could talk because he was trained by his family to speak. The spokesman stated that earth men are using too much metal in their everyday work and are fouling up radio frequencies and thought transfers because of this over use of metal. According to VAN TASSEL, these individuals came from Venus and are by no means hostile nor do they intend to harm this country or inhabitants in any manner. He declared they did not carry weapons, and the space craft was not armed. He mentioned that a field of force was located around the space craft which would prohibit anything known to earth men to penetrate. VAN TASSEL claims this craft departed from the earth after 20 minutes and has not been taken back since.

Van Tassel added that "through thought transfers with spacemen," he had been able to ascertain that a third world war was on the horizon, which was likely to be "large" and "destructive," that much of this correlated directly with certain biblical passages; that the war would not be "universal"; and that the "space people are peace loving and under no circumstances would enter or provoke a war." And to illustrate their benevolence toward humankind, the aliens, said Van Tassel, bestowed upon him some remarkable data, including information on how the human life span could be extended to anywhere between three hundred and fifteen hundred years. "This principle was not developed by Van Tassel," said the FBI.

Van Tassel then described his newsletter to the FBI agents:

In connection with his metaphysical religion and research, he publishes bimonthly a publication in the form of a booklet called PROCEEDINGS OF THE COLLEGE OF UNIVERSAL WISDOM, YUCCA VALLEY, CALIFORNIA. He declared this publication is free and has grown from an original mailing list of 250 to 1,000 copies. VAN TASSEL stated that he sends his publication to various individuals, Universities, and Government Agencies throughout the world. He declared this publication is forwarded to the Federal Bureau of Investigation at Washington, D.C. He stated that he has donated 10 acres of his ranch holdings to the college. He mentioned that many of the buildings will be made free of metal, which will be keeping within the request of the spacemen.

The FBI seemed particularly interested in who was funding Van Tassel's operations on such a grand scale.

He declared that for the most part he secures money for his needs of life, for the furtherance of his religion, research, and college through the generosity of certain individuals, number about 100. He failed to identify any of these people. He also mentioned that he derives income from his air strip and a very small restaurant which is located at Giant Rock.

VAN TASSEL voluntarily stated that he is not hiding anything nor is he doing anything against the laws of this country in his research at Giant Rock. He voluntarily mentioned that he is a loyal American and would be available at any time to assist the Bureau.

VAN TASSEL did not volunteer the names of any individuals whom he was soliciting for funds except his statement above that he sent his publications to various individuals, universities and Government agencies and also the Federal Bureau of Investigation in Washington, D.C.

At the conclusion of the interview, the two agents obtained various copies of Van Tassel's *Proceedings.* These were then dispatched to Washington for scrutiny and became the subject of a confidential report. In part, the report stated, "One of the pamphlets contains an article by Van Tassel claiming that Jesus Christ was born of space men and that the Star of Bethlehem was a space craft that stood by while Jesus was born."

Today, such claims are part and parcel of UFO lore and attract a great deal of interest and controversy. Fifty years ago, however, in some U.S. states, to postulate that Jesus Christ was of extraterrestrial descent would likely result in one's being admitted to a mental ward. And it is worth noting that Van Tassel's claims preceded the famed writer Erich Von Daniken's books on the issue of "ancient astronauts" by more than fifteen years. If nothing else, Van Tassel was a remarkable setter of trends.

As a result of his ever-growing reputation as someone with alleged intimate knowledge of alien intelligences, Van Tassel found himself increasingly in demand at public meetings and conventions, where he espoused at length on his dealings with the aliens, their intentions for humankind, and their philosophy as a whole.

On April 17, 1960, Van Tassel gave a lengthy speech at the Phipps Auditorium, Denver, Colorado, having been invited by the Denver Unidentified Flying Objects Investigate Society, whose "executive officer" acted as the master of ceremonies.

To ensure that the lecture was well attended, the society advertised it on local radio, and that, not surprisingly, caught the attention of the Denver FBI, who subsequently directed a special agent to attend and report back the details of Van Tassel's talk.

The following, comprehensive document on the lecture, some four pages in total, was generated by the FBI and is so detailed that a surreptitious tape recording may have been made to ensure that nothing was omitted.

The program consisted of a 45 minute movie which included several shots of things purported to be flying saucers, and then a number of interviews with people from all walks of life regarding sightings they had made of such unidentified flying objects. After the movie GEORGE W. VAN TASSEL gave a lecture which was more of a religious-economics lecture than one of unidentified flying objects.

VAN TASSEL stated that he had been in the "flying game" for over 30 years and currently operates a private Civil Aeronautics Authority approved airfield in California. He said he has personally observed a good many sightings and has talked to hundreds of people who have also seen flying saucers. He said that he has also been visited by the people from outer space and has taken up the cause of bringing the facts of these people to the American people. He said it is a crusade which he has undertaken because he is more or less retired, his family is grown and gone from home, and he feels he might be doing some good by this work.

Van Tassel then began a detailed examination of the highly contentious claim that there is a biblical link to the UFO mystery.

The major part of his lecture was devoted to explaining the occurrences in the Bible as they related to the space people. He said that the only mention of God in the Bible is in the beginning when the universe was being made. He said that after that all references are to "out of the sky" or "out of heaven."

He said that this is due to the fact that man, space people, was made by God [sic] and that in the beginning of the world the space people came to the earth and left animals here. These were the prehistoric animals which existed at a body temperature of 105 degrees; however a polar tilt occurred whereby the poles shifted and the tropical climates became covered with ice and vice versa.

Van Tassel then postulated that, to ensure life on Earth continued following the Ice Age, the aliens populated the planet with other species of animals, and that this led to the legend of Noah's Ark. Regardless of the veracity of this claim, it is notable that here is yet another example of a U.S. government agency having on file documents that refer to Noah's Ark. Van Tassel was by now in full flow and continued to reveal details of what he claimed to be the origin of humankind.

After the polar tilt the temperature to sustain life was 98.6 degrees, which was suitable for space people, so they established a colony and left only males here, intending to bring females at a latter date on supply ships. This is reflected in Adam not having a wife. He said that Adam was not an individual but a race of men.

[Van Tassel] said that this race then inter-married with "intelligent, upright walking animals," which race was EVE. Then when the space people came back in the supply ships they saw what had happened and did not land but ever since due to the origin of ADAM, they have watched over the people on Earth.

He said that this is in the Bible many times, such as MOSES receiving the Ten Commandments. He said the Ten Commandments are the laws of the space people and men on earth only give them lip service. Also, the manna from heaven was bread supplied by the space people.

He also stated that this can be seen from the native stories such as the Indians in America saying that corn and potatoes, unknown in Europe were brought here by a "flaming canoe." He said that this can be shown also by the old stories of Winged Chariots and Winged white Horses, which came from out of the sky.

He said that JESUS was born of MARY, who was a space person sent here already pregnant in order to show the earth people the proper way to live. He said the space people have watched over us through the years and have tried to help us. He said they have sent their agents to the earth and they appear just as we do; however, they have the power to know your thoughts just as JESUS did. He said this is their means of communication and many of the space people are mute, but they train a certain number of them to speak earth languages.

Bringing matters up-to-date, Van Tassel went on to proffer an ingenious explanation for so-called poltergeist and spectral phenomena.

Van Tassel said that the space people here on earth are equipped with a "crystal battery" which generates a magnetic field about them which bends light waves so that they, the space people, appear invisible. He said this has resulted in ghost stories, such as footsteps, doors opening, and other such phenomena.

Possibly the FBI's main concern with Van Tassel's wild claims was the effect that his warnings about atomic destruction would have on the American populace. The world of 1960 was very different from that of today, and under no circumstances could the Western alliance have been expected to relax its attitude toward the Soviet Union. If enough of Van Tassel's followers expressed a desire for an end to the arms race, this relatively minor figure might have mutated into a major national security problem. Van Tassel had reiterated the space people's interests at the Phipps Auditorium.

The space people are now gravely concerned with our atom bombs. He said that the explosions of these bombs have upset the earth's rotation and, as in the instance of the French bomb explosion in North Africa, have actually caused earthquakes. He said that the officials on earth are aware of this and this was the reason for the recent Geophysical Year in order to try to determine just what can be done. He said these explosions are forcing the earth toward another polar tilt, which will endanger all mankind. He said that the space people are prepared to evacuate those earth people who have abided by the "Golden Rule" when the polar tilt occurs, but will leave the rest to perish.

He advised that the space people have contacted the officials on earth and have advised them of their concern but this has not been made public. He also said that the radioactive fallout has become extremely dangerous and officials are worried but each power is so greedy of their own power they will not agree to make peace.

The FBI likely viewed Van Tassel as a troublemaker. After all, he was vehemently criticizing the U.S. Air Force's handling of the

UFO mystery. The Denver FBI office also made this known to the Air Force Office of Special Investigations at Lowry Air Force Base, Denver.

Van Tassel also spent some time saying that the US Air Force, who are [*sic*] responsible for investigations on unidentified flying objects, has suppressed information; and as they are responsible only to the Administration, not to the public, as elected officials are, they can get away with this. He said that also the Air Force is afraid that they will be outmoded and disbanded if such information gets out. The Administration's main concern in not making public any information is that the economy will be ruined, not because of any fear that would be engendered in the public. He said this is due to the number of scientific discoveries already made and that will be made which are labor saving and of almost permanency so that replacements would not be needed.

The covert FBI agent concluded his report:

Throughout his lecture, VAN TASSEL mentioned only the US economy and Government and the US Air Force. He did refer to the human race numerous times but all references to Government and economy could only be taken as meaning the US. One question put to him was whether sightings had been made in Russia or China. He answered this by saying sightings had been reported all over the world, but then specifically mentioned only the US, Australia, New Zealand and New Guinea. He also mentioned that he was not advocating or asking for any action on the part of the audience because he said evil has a way of destroying itself. He did say that he felt that the audience, of about 250 persons, were the only intelligent people in Denver and he knew they had not come out of curiosity but because they wanted to do the right thing. He said that they were above average in intelligence and when the critical time came, the world would need people such as this to think and guide.

Perhaps the most interesting aspect of Van Tassel's character was his love of all weird and wonderful electronic devices, the most famous being his imaginatively titled Integratron. With a name like that, the Integratron sounds as if it would have been perfectly suited to a 1950s science-fiction movie, blasting into oblivion marauding radioactive monsters. The truth, though, was quite different.

For years Van Tassel worked on his machine, the purpose of which, he said, was to try to enhance humankind's latent psychic powers and extend the human life span. Though his project never came to fruition, his reputation as someone with a deep fascination with advanced technology was not lost on his followers. Nor was it lost on the FBI.

In April 1965, rumors flew around the FBI office in Miami that Van Tassel had perfected a weapon that could make people blind. The production and utilization of this weapon was somehow related to an acquaintance of Van Tassel's who was described in FBI memoranda as "an ultra-rightist with tendency toward violence."

A two-page Teletype report to FBI headquarters, dated April 9, 1965, states:

A source, who has furnished reliable information in the past, and in addition has furnished information which could not be verified or corroborated, advised that a secret device, which can be carried on a person and used to blind people, has recently been perfected. This device, also referred to by [censored] as a weapon, formerly developed to keep others from seeing operator of weapon. [Censored] reports no other details regarding description and use of device. However, he said his information was second hand.

The source states that it has been determined the alleged device, was developed by GEORGE W. VAN TASSEL, Giant Rock,

Yucca Valley, California, who reportedly owns or operates an airport some 20 miles from Yucca Valley in the desert area.

Source stated VAN TASSEL claimed he worked over seven years in research and development of this device and the machine to make it. The weapon reportedly is of an electrical type, not further described. Any additional information can be obtained only by individuals who purchase the device and must be present at the time it is made.

Five days later, having examined the claims and counterclaims concerning Van Tassel's machine, the Miami FBI office determined that further investigation was unwarranted.

Because of Van Tassel's apparent mental condition, as evidenced by his statements and apparent beliefs concerning interplanetary travel by men from Venus, and in view of his other highly imaginative and incredible statements concerning space travel and population, it is believed that no further inquiries need be conducted by the Miami or Los Angeles Offices concerning Van Tassel.

Clearly, the FBI's interest in Van Tassel had waned. An April 12, 1965, FBI document refers to him as "an eccentric, self-ordained minister of a quasi-religious organization"; while a three-page document of that same year from the FBI at Los Angeles to Director Hoover comes straight to the point, describing him as a "mental case."

The final entry in the FBI's file on Van Tassel is a copy of a letter dated August 17, 1965, from a member of the American public to the Information Office of the Air Force's UFO study program, Project Blue Book. As was the case in 1954, the letter writer expressed concern that Van Tassel's claims were detrimental to the well-being of the United States: "In my opinion, it is quite subversive and in conflict with the interests of the United States the way this gentleman uses the demoralizing of religion and also his accusations against our Government."

The FBI took no action on this letter, and until his death on February 9, 1978, at the age of sixty-seven, George Wellington Van Tassel and the FBI never again crossed paths.

We could speculate endlessly upon Van Tassel's claims of alien contact. And while many of his purported extraterrestrial friends (Rondolla, Zolton, and Ah-Ming, in particular) sound as if they would have been more at home on a cheap science-fiction television series, similar accounts abound in the archives of the FBI.[3]

Declassified FBI records show that other so-called contactees had attracted the attention of the Bureau, including Truman Bethurum, George Hunt Williamson, Daniel Fry, and George Adamski. As with Van Tassel, many of their claims stretched credibility to its limit.

Truman Bethurum, for example, stated that he had liaised with humanlike aliens (although of smaller stature and of darker skin) from Clarion, a planet in our solar system hidden from Earth as a result of its orbit around the sun. Of all the contactees, Bethurum was perhaps the most envied among his colleagues, since during his alleged experience aboard a UFO he was introduced to its spectacularly attractive female captain, Aura Rhanes.

"Tops in shapelines and beauty" were the words that the lucky Bethurum used to describe Captain Aura in his book *Aboard a Flying Saucer*, a book that comes across like *Baywatch*-meets-*Star Trek*. Today we may find Bethurum's story to be little more than an amusing aside, but the FBI felt obligated to look into the man's account.

In December 1954, the Palm Springs Republican Club contacted the FBI, as its president had both spoken with Bethurum and read his then recently published book. "I am always skeptical and I have been wondering if he could be trying to put over any propaganda," stated the club president in a letter to J. Edgar Hoover.

"Although I would like to be of service," replied Hoover, "information in FBI files is confidential and available for official use only. I would like to point out also that this Bureau is strictly a fact-finding agency and does not make evaluations or draw conclusions as to the character or integrity of any individual, publication or organization."

Nevertheless, FBI files *do* reflect knowledge of Bethurum's activities: "In June, 1954, an inquiry was made by the Cincinnati Office concerning Bethurum and his flying disk lectures since that office had received a complaint similar to current correspondent's."

Although known to the FBI, Bethurum's activities were of less concern than those of Van Tassel. Bethurum was not as outwardly political as Van Tassel, and his dealings with Aura Rhanes bordered on the farcical. On several occasions in the middle of the night, the gorgeous Aura supposedly materialized in Bethurum's bedroom, which did not exactly please his wife, who later divorced him, evidently unable to compete with a woman of Aura's galactic charms.[4]

George Hunt Williamson, whose real name was Michel d'Obrenovic, had an equally strange tale to tell. Not only did he, too, write a book detailing his encounters—*The Saucers Speak*, cowritten with Alfred C. Bailey—he also imparted details to Edward J. Ruppelt, former head of Project Blue Book. As Ruppelt recalled in 1955, "George Williamson said the story started back in the summer of 1952 when he and a few other people who believed that flying saucers weren't hallucinations got together with a ham radio operator in Arizona. On the night of August 26, they were playing around with the radio receiver when they picked up a strange signal. They listened to the signal and soon found that it was international code coming in at a 'fantastically fast and powerful rate,' from a spaceship hovering off the earth."

Williamson's contacts continued until February 1953, and a wealth of technological data was imparted, after which time he was advised to go out and "spread the word" to like-minded persons.

An FBI document of June 2, 1961, took note of Williamson's activities:

Bufiles indicate that George Hunt Williamson [has] come to the Bureau's attention in the past in connection with allegations that flying disks exist. In 1954, Williamson was connected with a program to be presented in Cincinnati which was entitled "The Real Flying Saucer Story." [5]

Williamson retired from the saucer scene later in the 1960s.

In 1949, Daniel Fry was employed as an engineer with the Aerojet General Corporation at the White Sands Missile Range, New Mexico. On July 4 of that year Fry claimed that he had made initial contact with an extraterrestrial named A-lan, who "wants everyone in this world to understand the truth about our existence and how we can spiritually profit from the beneficence of extraterrestrial contact."

Six years later, Fry was referenced in FBI memoranda following an investigation of the Detroit Flying Saucer Club, which intended to have Fry speak at one of its meetings. As the club was codirected by a cousin of Fry's, the FBI was able to glean detailed information about Fry's claimed experiences, including his having flown in a saucer from Sandia Base to New York City in only thirty minutes. An FBI memorandum states:

FRY CLAIMS SAUCER CLUBS HAVE ACTUALLY RECEIVED MESSAGES FROM OUTER SPACE AND ALTHOUGH [HE] SAYS HE DOES NOT KNOW, HE FEELS THEY DO EXIST; HAVE BEEN SEEN BY MANY PEOPLE AND CLAIMS HE HAS SEEN THEM HIMSELF. HE FEELS THE PURPOSE OF CONTACTS WITH EARTH IS LIMITED AT THIS TIME TO PREPARING PEOPLE TO RECEIVE LANDINGS FROM OUTER SPACE. HE SAID THE SAUCERS ARE

FRIENDLY TO U.S. HE SAID MESSAGES RECEIVED INDICATE
ALL PLANETS BUT EARTH HAVE CONQUERED OUTER SPACE.
OUTER SPACE PEOPLE CONSIDER THOSE ON EARTH THE LOW-
EST FORM OF UNIVERSAL EXISTENCE.[6]

Other contactees were the subject of FBI files too. Heavily censored August 1954 memoranda refer to an unnamed woman who
claimed repeated contact with nonhuman entities in the mid-
1950s.

According to [censored] stated that there were two spaceships
from which she had been receiving messages. They were described as 150 miles wide, 200 miles in length, and 100 miles
in depth . . . these ships are designated M-4 and L-11 and they
also contain mother ships which measure approximately 150
to 200 feet in length. . . . There were approximately 5,000 of
these mother ships. . . . "Affa" is the Manager or the Commander of the ship M-4 which is from the planet Uranus and "Ponnar" is the Manager or the Commander of the ship L-11 which
is from the planet Hatann. . . .
    These contacts with "Affa" and "Ponnar" were for the pur-
pose of protecting our own earth from destruction caused by
the explosion of the atom bomb, hydrogen bomb, and wars of
various kinds which they, "Affa" and "Ponnar," say disrupt
the magnetic field of force which surrounds the earth. . . .
"Affa" and "Ponnar" are presently working the area of the
Pacific Ocean repairing "fault lines" which are in danger of
breaking.

The FBI also had a relationship with the man who will surely go
down in history as the definitive contactee: George Adamski. Born
in Poland on April 17, 1891, Adamski emigrated to the United
States with his family several years later and went on to become the
most widely supported—and ridiculed—of the contactees. The

story essentially begins on November 20, 1952, when along with six other people (George Hunt Williamson maintained that he was one of the six) Adamski allegedly witnessed the landing of a UFO in the California desert and subsequently made contact with its pilot.

FBI documentation, however, shows that Adamski's interest in UFOs preceded this by at least two years. The author Timothy Good has stated that Adamski claimed to have had otherworldly contacts as a child and to have later received instruction from them in Tibet, hence Adamski's 1936 book, *Wisdom of the Masters of the Far East*, published by The Royal Order of Tibet.

At the outset of its surveillance of George Adamski, the FBI was seemingly unaware of his early contacts, but a memorandum of May 28, 1952, references his 1950 experiences and also reveals some interesting facts that suggest the FBI considered Adamski, like Van Tassel, potentially subversive.

A study of the documentation shows that much of the FBI's initial data on Adamski came from a source (whose name the FBI declines to reveal) who imparted details to the San Diego office on September 5, 1950.

[Source] advised the San Diego Office that he first met Adamski about three months ago at the café which is named the Palomar Gardens Café, owned and operated by Adamski, at the road junction, five miles East of Rincon, California, at a point where the highway branches off leading to Mount Palomar Observatory.

[Source] became involved in a lengthy conversation with Adamski during which Adamski told them at great length of his findings of flying saucers and so forth. He told them of a spaceship which he said he saw between the earth and the moon, which he estimated to be approximately three miles in length, which was flying so fast that he had to take about eighty photographs before he could get three of them to turn out.

Adamski then revealed to the source his claimed knowledge of covert interaction between representatives of the U.S. government and the aliens.

According to [source] Adamski stated that the Federal Communications Commission, under the direction of the "Military Government" of the United States, has established communication with the people from other worlds, and has learned that they are so much more advanced than the inhabitants of this earth that they have deciphered the languages used here. Adamski stated that in this interplanetary communication, the Federal Communications Commission asked the inhabitants of the other planet concerning the type of government they had there and the reply indicated that it was very different from the democracy of the United States. Adamski stated that his answer was kept secret by the United States Government, but he added, "If you ask me they probably have a Communist form of government and our American government wouldn't release that kind of thing, naturally. That is a thing of the future—more advanced."

Adamski's comments that the aliens had a Communist type of government certainly caused raised eyebrows within the FBI. With the Cold War at its peak, this was without a doubt the foremost—if not the only—reason behind the FBI's continued surveillance of Adamski.

Adamski, during this conversation, made the prediction that Russia will dominate the world and we will then have an era of peace for 1,000 years. He stated that Russia already has the atom bomb and the hydrogen bomb and that the great earthquake which was reported behind the Iron Curtain recently was actually a hydrogen bomb explosion being tried out by the

Russians. Adamski states this "earthquake" broke seismograph machines and he added that no normal earthquake can do that.

Adamski stated that within the next twelve months, San Diego will be bombed. Adamski stated that it does not make any difference if the United States has more atom bombs than Russia inasmuch as Russia needs only ten atom bombs to cripple the United States by placing these simultaneously on such spots as Chicago and other vital centers of this country. The United States today is in the same state of deterioration as was the Roman empire prior to its collapse and it will fall just as the Roman empire did. The Government in this country is a corrupt form of government and capitalists are enslaving the poor.

The document continues in a similar vein. It's no wonder that, in the eyes of the FBI, Adamski was thereafter officially considered a "security matter."

In January 1953, Adamski was once again the subject of FBI interest when word got back to the San Diego office that "Adamski had in his possession a machine which could draw 'flying saucers' and airplanes down from the sky."

Despite his pro-Soviet statements of 1952, Adamski was concerned that the device, which supposedly operated on the principle of "cutting magnetic lines of force," could be used against U.S. aircraft. He requested a meeting with representatives of both the FBI and the Air Force's Office of Special Investigations, which took place on January 12, 1953.

At the outset, Adamski maintained that the machine was in fact the brainchild of another individual and that, despite what the FBI had been told, Adamski had yet to see it. But he knew enough about it and its operator to suggest that production of the device might not be in the best interests of the U.S. government, since the person concerned "was not entirely loyal." On this matter, Adamski seemingly cooperated to the full and supplied the FBI and the Air Force with enough data to allow a formal investigation of the machine's "inventor" to begin. Adamski also divulged details of his celebrated encounter of November 20, 1952, in the Californian desert.

At a point ten and two-tenths miles from Desert Center on the road to Parker and Needles, Arizona, [Adamski] made contact with a space craft and had talked to a space man. Adamski stated that he, [deleted] and his wife Mary, had been out in the desert and that he and the persons with him had seen the craft come down to the earth. Adamski stated that a small stairway in the bottom of the craft, which appeared to be a round disc, opened and a space man came down the steps. Adamski stated he believed there were other space men in the ship because the ship appeared translucent and he could see the shadows of the space men.

Adamski said that the alien was "over five feet in height, having long hair like a woman's and garbed in a suit similar to the space suits or web suits worn by the U.S. Air Force men."

Echoing the claims of George Van Tassel that the aliens were mute, Adamski related to the FBI and OSI agents that he conversed with the being by means of sign language, but felt that his mind was being "read." To back up this claim, Adamski stated that when he was about to take a photograph of the UFO, the alien "motioned" him to stop. Adamski told the agents that he took his photograph regardless. This did not apparently go down too well with the camera-shy space traveler, who snatched the incriminating evidence out of Adamski's hands and departed. Adamski's adventures were not over, however.

Adamski further advised that he had obtained plaster casts of the footprints of the space man and stated that the casts indi-

cated the footprints had designs on them similar to the signs of
the Zodiac.

On January 12, 1953, Adamski advised that on December
13, 1952, the space ship returned to the Palomar Gardens and
came low enough to drop the [film negative] which the space
man had taken from him, Adamski, and had then gone off over
the hill.

Adamski stated that when he had the negatives developed at
a photo shop in Escondido, California, that the negative that
the space man had taken from him contained writing which he
believed to be the writing of the space men. Adamski furnished
the writer with copies of the space writing and photographs of
the space ship.

Not everyone was convinced that the photographs were genuine,
however. One source informed the FBI that "the photographs were
taken by setting the camera lens at infinity, which would sharpen
the background of mountains and trees and blurs the saucer, which
was probably strung on a thin wire. [Source] advised that if the camera were set at infinity the wire would not show."

From March 23, 1953, onward, much of the FBI's dealings with
Adamski related to what was, or what was not, said by Adamski during a lecture he delivered to the Californian Lions Club on March
12 of that year. According to the San Diego FBI office, Adamski had
prefaced his talk by stating in effect that "his material had all been
cleared with the Federal Bureau of Investigation and Air Force Intelligence."

Certain that no such clearance had been afforded Adamski, representatives of both the FBI and the Air Force visited him at his
Palomar Gardens Café and "severely admonished" him for suggesting that his material had the blessings of both the FBI and Air Force.
They insisted that he sign an official document for both agencies to
the effect that his material did *not* have official clearance. With one
copy of the statement retained by Adamski, additional copies were

circulated to Hoover and the FBI offices in Dallas, Los Angeles, and Cleveland, since "these offices have received previous communications concerning [Adamski]."

On December 10, 1953, matters took a further downward turn for Adamski when a representative of the Los Angeles–based Better Business Bureau (BBB) turned up at the Los Angeles FBI office and advised that the BBB was investigating Adamski's 1953 book, *Flying Saucers Have Landed,* to determine if it was a fraud.

The BBB informed the FBI that to ascertain the facts, Adamski had been interviewed by one of its staff, and during the interview Adamski had produced a document "having a blue seal in the lower left corner, at the top of which appeared the names of three Government agents"—one from the FBI and two from the Air Force. Once again, the implication was that Adamski's material had the official clearance of both agencies.

"[The Better Business Bureau] is interested in whether or not this document is authentic and whether your organization is making an endorsement of [Adamski's] book," the FBI was asked.

The document was not authentic. Investigations undertaken by Special Agent Willis of the San Diego FBI revealed that the document Adamski had shown the Better Business Bureau was a self-doctored copy of the statement he had been obliged to sign for both the FBI and the Air Force months earlier. An FBI report of December 16, 1953, from Louis B. Nichols, head of the FBI's public relations department, to Clyde Tolson, records the events surrounding this massive blow to Adamski's credibility.

[Deleted] instructed Willis to call on Adamski at the Palomar Gardens Café, Valley Center, California. (This is located five miles east of Rincon, California, near the Mount Palomar Observatory.) Willis was told to have the San Diego agents, accompanied by representatives of OSI if they care to go along, call on Adamski and read the riot act in no uncertain terms pointing out he has used this document in a fraudulent, improper manner, that this Bureau has not endorsed, approved, or cleared his speeches or book, that he knows it, and the Bureau will simply not tolerate any further foolishness, misrepresentations, and falsity on his part. Willis was told to instruct the Agents to diplomatically retrieve, if possible, the document in issue from Adamski. Willis said he would do this and send in a report at once.

Despite threats of prosecution, the FBI took no further action against Adamski regarding the faked document. Yet Adamski's actions were foolish in the extreme and dealt a major blow to his credibility.

Documentation declassified by the FBI demonstrates that the FBI's interest in Adamski tailed off in the mid-1950s, only to revive briefly at the end of the decade.

In February 1959, Adamski toured New Zealand and gave a series of lectures before audiences in both Wellington and Auckland. This was evidently of some interest to the U.S. intelligence community, and his talks were sporadically monitored. For example, a one-page Foreign Service dispatch was sent from the American embassy in New Zealand to the Department of State in Washington, detailing the salient points of what Adamski had to say. Circulated to the FBI, the CIA, the Air Force, and the Navy, the document was titled " 'Flying Saucer' Expert Lecturing in New Zealand."

Mr. George ADAMSKI, the Californian "flying saucer expert" and author of the book *The Flying Saucers Have Landed* and others, has been visiting New Zealand for the last two weeks. He has given well-attended public lectures in Auckland and Wellington as well as meetings with smaller groups of "saucer" enthusiasts. In Wellington his lecture filled the 2,200 seats in the Town Hall. He was not permitted to charge for admission as the meeting was held on a Sunday night, but a "silver coin" collection was taken up and this would more than recoup his expenses.

Adamski's lectures appear to cover the usual mass of sighting reports, pseudo-scientific arguments in support of his theories and his previously well-publicized "contacts" with saucers and men from Venus. He is repeating his contention that men from other planets are living anonymously on the earth and, according to the press, said in Auckland that there may be as many as 40,000,000 of these in total. He is also making references to security restrictions and saying that the US authorities know a lot more than they will tell.

The report of Adamski's lecture in Wellington in *The Dominion* was flanked by an article by Dr. I. L. THOMPSON, Director of the Carter Observatory, vigorously refuting Adamski on a number of scientific points. However, the news report of the lecture called it "the best Sunday night's entertainment Wellington has seen for quite a time."

Interest in flying saucers in New Zealand seems to be roughly comparable to that in the United States. There is a small but active organization which enthusiasts have supported for some years. This organization publishes a small paper and receives and circulates stories of sightings. At the Adamski lecture in Wellington, approximately 40 members of the "Adamski Corresponding Society" wore blue ribbons and sat in reserved seats in the front row. Press reports suggest that Adamski probably is making no new converts to saucer credence in his current tour. His audiences have given forth with a certain amount of "incredulous murmuring" and are said to be totally unimpressed with his pictures of saucers.

Ten months later Adamski was again the subject of FBI interest when, as had been the case previously, a member of the American public contacted the Bureau to express concern that Adamski was promoting pro-Soviet ideas. .

[Censored] said that in recent weeks she and her husband had begun to wonder if Adamski is subtly spreading Russian propaganda. She said that, according to Adamski, the "space people" are much better people than those on earth; that they have told him the earth is in extreme danger from nuclear tests and that they must be stopped; that they have found peace under a system in which churches, schools, individual governments, money, and private property were abolished in favor of a central governing council, and nationalism and patriotism have been done away with; that the "space people" want nuclear tests stopped immediately and that never should people on earth fight; if attacked, they should lay down their arms and welcome their attackers.

[Censored] said the particular thing that first made her and her husband wonder about Adamski was a letter they received from him dated 10/12/59, in which it was hinted that the Russians receive help in their outer space programs from the "space people," and that the "space people" will not help any nation unless such nation has peaceful intent.

It occurred to them that the desires and recommendations of the "space people" whom Adamski quotes are quite similar to Russia's approach, particularly as to the ending of nuclear testing, and it was for this reason she decided to call the FBI.

A few scant documents aside, there ends the FBI's file on George Adamski. Up until the time of his death on April 23, 1965, Adamski continued to proclaim that his accounts of interaction with alien creatures were utterly genuine; and perhaps inevitably, nearly forty years on, the controversy continues.[7]

It would be tempting to believe that the FBI's surveillance of, and interest in, George Van Tassel, George Adamski, Truman Bethurum, George Hunt Williamson, and Daniel Fry was generated solely as a result of their claimed extraterrestrial contacts. However, Adamski's comments to the effect that "Russia will dominate the world," and Van Tassel's statements concerning atomic weaponry, lead to the almost inescapable conclusion that, in the 1950s era of Cold War anxiety, McCarthyism, and Reds-under-the-beds, official interest in the contactees resulted from the political nature of many of their assertions. As far as the FBI was concerned, the threat of Communism and the Soviets far outweighed that of alien beings from some far-flung corner of the galaxy.

Seven

THE REAL MEN IN BLACK

"The door banged really slowly but hard, like someone was hitting it with their fist instead of knocking, [and] when I opened it, there was this horrible little man about five feet tall. He was dressed in a black suit and tie and had a funny little black hat on. His face was really strange. he looked like someone with anorexia, you know? IIis cheeks were all gaunt; his eyes were dark and his skin was almost white.

"I didn't know what to do and just stared; it was really frightening. Then he suddenly gave me this horrible grin, and I could tell his lips had been colored, like with makeup or something. He took off his hat and had this really bad wig on. You know, he looked about sixty but the wig was jet-black.

"All he said was, 'We would ask you cease your studies.' I said, 'What?' Then he repeated it, exactly the same and I had to ask what he meant. 'The sky lights; always the sky lights,' he said. Then it dawned on me. I'd seen a UFO late at night about a week before when me and my husband had been driving home, and we both had a really weird dream after about some little men standing around our car on the edge of the woods.

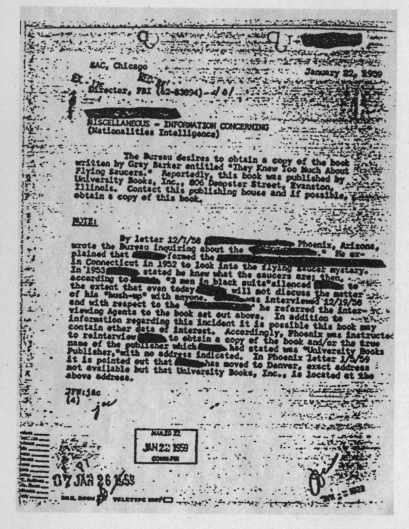

SAC, Chicago   January 22, 1959

Director, FBI (62-83894)-_/o/

MISCELLANEOUS - INFORMATION CONCERNING
(Nationalities Intelligence)

        The Bureau desires to obtain a copy of the book
written by Gray Barker entitled "They Knew Too Much About
Flying Saucers." Reportedly, this book was published by
University Books, Inc., 806 Dempster Street, Evanston,
Illinois. Contact this publishing house and if possible,
obtain a copy of this book.

NOTE:

        By letter 12/7/58 ██████████ ████████ Phoenix, Arizona,
wrote the Bureau inquiring about the ██████████. He explained that ██████ formed the ██████████████████████
in Connecticut in 1952 to look into the flying saucer mystery.
In 1953 ████████ stated he knew what the saucers are; then,
according to ██████ "3 men in black suits" silenced ██████ to
the extent that even today ██████ will not discuss the matter
of his "hush-up" with anyone. ██████ was interviewed 12/19/58
and with respect to the ██████████ he referred the inter-
viewing Agents to the book set out above. In addition to
information regarding this incident it is possible this book may
contain other data of interest. Accordingly, Phoenix was instructed
to reinterview ██████ to obtain a copy of the book and/or the true
name of the publisher which ██████ had stated was "University Books
Publisher," with no address indicated. In Phoenix letter 1/5/59
it is pointed out that ██████ has moved to Denver, exact address
not available but that University Books, Inc., is located at the
above address.

JFN:jac
(4)

                    MAILED 21
                    JAN 22 1959
                    COMM-FBI

07 JAN 26 1959

MAIL ROOM ☐ TELETYPE UNIT ☐

Official FBI records of 1959 on Gray Barker and Albert Bender, two
authors who were responsible for bringing to light the activities of the
Men in Black.

"Then he said something like 'Cease and dream easy.' I think that was it, and he gave me a really long stare like he was going to attack me, or something. But he just walked away down the drive. I started to feel dizzy and slammed the door. I just crawled to the bed and fell asleep for about three hours. But when I woke up, there was this horrible smell like burning rubber all through the house. We had to have the windows wide open for days and get the carpets and furniture cleaned to get rid of [the smell].

"It really shook me up, and apart from telling you, I haven't really talked to anyone—and I don't really want to." [1]

This account comes from a British woman who lives in a rural, English village near to Cannock Chase, a large, forested area in the central part of the country. It is a classic description of an encounter with what has popularly become known as a Man in Black.

Since the early 1950s the Men in Black (we use the plural as they are generally reported traveling in groups of two or three) have been a persistent part of UFO lore, as have their attempts to silence witnesses to UFO encounters. Not surprisingly, perhaps, accounts of Men in Black–style encounters abound in the files of a number of government and intelligence agencies.

While many of the cases herein cited seem to have a paranormal or otherworldly aspect, there are firm grounds for believing that the MIB are, in reality, covert operatives of the intelligence services of the United States and Great Britain. In support of our argument we cite various papers that have surfaced from the CIA, FBI, U.S. Air Force, and an elite division of Britain's Royal Air Force.

Typically, those who attract the attention of the Men in Black are either UFO researchers who perhaps have some sensitive information, or witnesses to UFO phenomena. More often than not the person concerned is visited at home by the MIB and warned not to discuss his or her experiences with outsiders.

Time after time the MIB are described as being dressed in black suits, black hats, black ties, and white shirts. They are often short, painfully thin, with slightly oriental or, on occasion, Spanish features. They also seem to have a tenuous grasp of the English language and are glaringly unaware of our most basic customs and conventions. The Spanish reference is particularly interesting since in November 1947 the FBI office at Pittsburgh was informed by a letter writer in Port Allegany that "the saucers reported as seen in various parts of the country, were actually from Spain . . . this had been ascertained by the Government in Washington, but it was not being made known."

One of the most learned scholars in the field of the Men in Black is John Keel. The author of numerous books on unexplained phenomena—including the celebrated title that became a hit film starring Richard Gere, *The Mothman Prophecies*—Keel has spent decades chronicling the accounts of MIB activity and presents a strong case for the reality of the mystery. Keel too has had his run-ins with one particular type of MIB that he terms "the cadavers."

"These are people who look like they've been dead a long time," says Keel. "Their clothes hang on them; their flesh is pasty white and they look like maybe somebody's dug them up from a cemetery. This cadaverous type has turned up in strange places: England, Sweden. [The writer and investigator] Brad Steiger saw one. I saw one in the early sixties. They're very elusive when you approach them and hurry away, [and] they do have a habit of turning up in UFO areas and following UFO investigators around."[2]

The Men in Black mystery really began in earnest back in 1952. That year, Albert K. Bender, a resident of Bridgeport, Connecticut, established a UFO investigative society known as the International Flying Saucer Bureau. Bender's group was warmly received by UFO researchers both in the United States and abroad and soon blossomed into an impressive body with a network of investigators.

A year later, without warning, Bender disbanded the IFSB, alluding to an unusual experience in which three men in black suits had visited him to discuss his UFO research. Supposedly, Bender had discovered the truth of the UFO mystery and the MIBs wished him to remain silent—which he did for a number of years—and to ensure that silence Bender was given the full, unexpurgated facts pertaining to an alleged alien mission on Earth.

One day, according to Bender, he was overcome by dizziness and retired to his bedroom. Suddenly he became aware of "three shadowy figures in the room. The figures became clearer. All of them were dressed in black clothes. They looked like clergymen, but wore hats similar to homburg style. The faces were not clearly discernible, for the hats partly hid and shaded them. Feelings of fear left me. The eyes of all three figures suddenly lit up like flashlight bulbs, and all these were focused upon me. They seemed to burn into my very soul as the pains above my eyes became almost unbearable. It was then I sensed that they were conveying a message to me by telepathy."

The three men did indeed convey a message, but such was Bender's terror that he stayed silent for years, conveying only the basic facts of the visit to a few trusted colleagues. Of those, one was Gray Barker, who went on to write the definitive exposé of the Men in Black in 1956, *They Knew Too Much About Flying Saucers.*

A full decade after he retired from the UFO scene, Bender's uncensored story surfaced in *Flying Saucers and the Three Men,* a bizarre book published privately by Gray Barker. It contained all manner of weirdness pertaining to Albert Bender's alleged experiences, including information on a "secret UFO base" in Antarctica; the MIB's mission to obtain a unique element from the earth's oceans; and demonology, the occult, spiritualism, and black magic. Put off by this material, many of the seminal UFO researchers in the United States largely ignored Bender's book when it was first published.

If Bender's account was isolated and one of a kind, there would be grounds for believing that his claims were simply the product of a disturbed mind. But quite literally hundreds of similar stories have surfaced across the planet. Indeed, there is official FBI documentation at our disposal that has a bearing on the Bender affair.

On August 28, 1953, Gray Barker was visited by an agent of the

FBI, who asked him a number of questions concerning Albert Bender's International Flying Saucer Bureau. Bender had forwarded to Barker a number of business cards that he had printed identifying Barker as "Chief Investigator" for the IFSB.

In his 1956 book, _They Knew Too Much About Flying Saucers_, Barker admitted having given "four or five [of the cards] to close friends, who still had them when I checked with them one week later." It was therefore something of a surprise when the FBI turned up on Barker's doorstep with one of the aforementioned business cards. "I have always been puzzled about how the Federal Bureau of Investigation got hold of one of them," Barker later said.

"What's this all about?" asked the agent. Somewhat nervously, Barker explained that the IFSB was simply an organization formed to investigate "flying saucer phenomena" and that the business cards were a means by which IFSB investigators could be identified.

The FBI man then asked Barker if he knew a certain individual (whose name Barker could not later recall) who lived in Florida. Barker replied that he did not. This prompted the agent to advise Barker that the man had suffered an epileptic fit and had been taken to the nearby St. Mary's Hospital. With his belongings was one of Barker's cards.

Satisfied that Barker was not acquainted with the man, the FBI agent thanked Barker and departed. "Then it struck me," recalled Barker. "How in the world had anyone from Florida come into possession of one of my business cards?"

Barker began to wonder if there really had been an epileptic man, or if this had simply been a ruse to allow the FBI to covertly check out Barker, Bender, and the IFSB. Barker voiced these concerns in a report to Bender, who wrote back, "I cannot for the life of me see why [the FBI] would be checking up. It certainly proves one thing—the government is more interested in the Saucers than we realize."[3]

Five years later, both Barker and Bender were once again the subject of FBI interest. On November 22, 1958, an inquiring citizen of Oklahoma City contacted J. Edgar Hoover about the FBI's treatment of UFO investigators.

Recently many rumors have been printed in UFO periodicals, concerning reports that Special Agents of the Federal Bureau of Investigation have discouraged certain saucer investigators, particularly Mr. Albert Bender of Bridgeport, Connecticut, from further research into the secret of these elusive discs. Since you are the Director of the FBI, I would like to know whether or not these reports are factual or whether they are just rumors.

Hoover's response was swift: "I am instructing a Special Agent of our Oklahoma City Office to contact you concerning the matter you mentioned." A note from Hoover to the special agent in charge at Oklahoma City added, "An agent of your office should contact [the letter writer] immediately and secure copies of or information concerning the periodicals described."

In a memorandum to Hoover on December 9, 1958, the Oklahoma office reported that the periodical in question was the *Saucerian Bulletin*, published by Gray Barker, in which it was stated that the three men responsible for silencing Albert Bender were from "the FBI, Air Force Intelligence, and the Central Intelligence Agency."

An FBI report of December 12 states:

Bender formed the International Flying Saucer Bureau in Bridgeport, Connecticut, in 1952 to look into the flying saucer mystery. In 1953 Bender allegedly stated that he knew what the saucers are. Then "three men in black suits" silenced Bender to the extent that even today Bender will not discuss the matter of his "hush-up" with anyone.

A month later, on January 22, 1959, Hoover was still hot on the trail of Barker and Bender.

The Bureau desires to obtain a copy of the book written by Gray Barker entitled "They Knew Too Much About Flying Saucers." Reportedly, this book was published by University Books, Inc . . . Illinois. Contact this publishing house and if possible, obtain a copy of this book.

Three weeks later a copy of Barker's book was in Hoover's hands, as were copies of Bender's *Space Review* magazine. The FBI subsequently noted that its files contained "no information pertaining to the hush-up of Bender." About his *Space Review* journal they noted, "This magazine contains numerous articles and squibs concerning the sighting of flying saucers throughout the world. It does not appear to have any security significance."

This would seem to imply that whoever Bender's mysterious visitors were, they were not FBI agents. It is curious, however, that nowhere in the released papers is there any mention of the FBI's 1953 interview with Gray Barker. Was this simply an off-the-record interview, or does the FBI have its reasons for not releasing its files on the matter? Another possibility is that Barker made it all up—it wouldn't be the only example.

On May 14, 1969, the FBI was in receipt of yet another letter from a member of the public who had latched onto the stories surrounding the Men in Black.

There currently are rumors over the grapevine and in print that suggest men with oriental features wearing dark clothes go around terrorizing people who have had close-up views of UFOs. It is also rumored these creatures have impersonated armed forces officers and FBI investigators. They are supposed to ride around in black or dark automobiles that either have old license tags or none at all. Several are reported to have attempted to run down witnesses of UFO sightings, made disturbing almost macabre phone calls, silenced several investigators who were supposed to have learned some dark secret about extra-terrestrial craft or mission plans and opened mail, tapped telephones and even taken pictures of several homes where UFO witnesses lived. Can you give me any information on such rumors?

Since both Albert Bender and Gray Barker were known to the FBI, and J. Edgar Hoover possessed a copy of Barker's book on the MIB, it is somewhat amusing to note that the FBI responded that it was completely ignorant of the Men in Black mystery and had no information in its possession that related to rumors of MIB activity.

In 1979, the Men in Black were still out there, still masquerading as representatives of the military. One researcher, Richard D. Seifried, recalls an incident during that year when two MIB were present at a UFO lecture in Ohio. According to Seifried, both were dressed in "very neat, dark suits, sported GI haircuts and what looked like Air Force regulation dress shoes."

At the end of the lecture Seifried and his friends left the hall and, while walking along a corridor toward the parking lot, saw the two men directly in front of them. "They rounded the corner," recalled Seifried. "Although we were probably no more than forty or fifty feet behind them, by the time we turned the corner the two men had disappeared . . . what they did was inhuman."[4]

Nothing about the MIB is straightforward. In fact, the Men in Black do not even always dress exclusively in black. In the 1960s, in particular, the MIB changed their tactics and, to ensure the silence of witnesses to UFO encounters, began to pass themselves off as military and governmental personnel. With reports mounting, even the U.S. Air Force was plunged into the MIB controversy, as shown by this widely circulated memo of March 1, 1967, from Lieutenant General Hewitt, Assistant Vice Chief of Staff of the Air Force.

Information, not verifiable, has reached HQ USAF that persons claiming to represent the Air Force or other Defense establishments have contacted citizens who have sighted unidentified flying objects. In one reported case an individual in civilian clothes, who represented himself as a member of NORAD, demanded and received photos belonging to a private citizen. In another, a person in an Air Force uniform approached local police and other citizens who had sighted a UFO, assembled them in a school room and told them that they did not see what they thought they saw and that they should not talk to anyone about the sighting. All military and civilian personnel and particularly Information Officers and UFO investigating Officers who hear of such reports should immediately notify their local OSI offices.

The CIA had been in a similar situation with MIB overtones in the mid-1950s. According to the report entitled "CIA's Role in the Study of UFOs, 1947–90," written by CIA historian Gerald Haines:

The Agency was also involved in two rather famous UFO cases in the 1950s, which helped contribute to a growing sense of public distrust of CIA with regard to UFOs. One focused on what was reported to have been a tape recording of a radio signal from a flying saucer; the other on reported photographs of a flying saucer. The "radio code" incident began innocently enough in 1955, when two elderly sisters in Chicago, Mildred and Marie Maier, reported in the *Journal of Space Flight* their experiences with UFOs, including the recording of a radio program in which an unidentified code was reportedly heard. The sisters taped the program and other ham radio operators also claimed to have heard the "space message." OSI became interested and asked the Scientific Contact Branch to obtain a copy of the recording. Field officers from the Contact Division (CD), one of whom was Dewelt Walker, made contact with the Maier sisters, who were "thrilled that the government was interested," and set up a time to meet with them. In trying to secure the tape recording, the Agency officers reported that they had stumbled upon a scene from *Arsenic and Old Lace*. "The only thing lacking was the elderberry wine," Walker cabled Headquarters. After reviewing the sisters' scrapbook of clippings from their days on the stage, the officers secured a copy of the recording. OSI analyzed the tape and found it was nothing more than Morse code from a U.S. radio station. The matter rested there until UFOlogist Leon Davidson talked with the Maier sisters in 1957. The sisters remembered they had talked with a Mr. Walker who said he was from the U.S. Air Force. Davidson then wrote to a Mr. Walker, believing him to be a U.S. Air Force Intelligence Officer from Wright-Patterson, to ask if the tape had been analyzed at ATIC. Dewelt Walker replied to Davidson that the tape had been forwarded to proper authorities for evaluation, and no information was available concerning the results. Not satisfied, and suspecting that Walker was really a CIA officer, Davidson next wrote DCI Allen Dulles demanding to learn what the coded message revealed and who Mr. Walker was. The Agency, wanting to keep Walker's identity as a CIA employee secret, replied that another agency of the government had analyzed the tape in question and that Davidson would be hearing from the Air Force. On 5 August, the Air Force wrote Davidson saying that Walker "was and is an Air Force Officer" and that the tape "was analyzed by another government organization." The Air Force letter confirmed that the recording contained only identifiable Morse code which came from a known U.S.-licensed radio station. Davidson wrote Dulles again. This time he wanted to know the identity of the Morse operator and of the agency that had conducted the analysis. CIA and the Air Force were now in a quandary. The Agency had previously denied that it had actually analyzed the tape. The Air Force had also denied analyzing the tape and claimed that Walker was an Air Force officer. CIA officers, under cover, contacted Davidson in Chicago and promised to get the code translation and the identification of the transmitter, if possible. In another attempt to pacify Davidson, a CIA officer, again under cover and wearing his Air Force uniform, contacted Davidson in New York City. The CIA officer explained that there was no super agency involved and that Air Force policy was not to disclose who was doing what. While seeming to accept this argument, Davidson nevertheless pressed for disclosure of the recording message and the source. The officer agreed to see what he could do. After checking with Headquarters, the CIA officer phoned Davidson to report that a thorough check had been made and, because the signal was of known U.S. origin, the tape and the notes made at the time had been destroyed to conserve file space. Incensed over what he perceived was a runaround, Davidson told the CIA officer that "he and his agency, whichever it was, were acting like Jimmy Hoffa and the Teamster Union in destroying records which might indict them." Believing that any more contact with Davidson would only encourage more speculation, the Contact Division washed its hands of the issue by reporting to the DCI and to ATIC that it would not respond to or try to contact Davidson again. Thus, a minor, rather bizarre incident, handled poorly by both CIA and the Air Force, turned into a major flap that added fuel to the growing mystery surrounding UFOs and CIA's role in their investigation.

This episode offers us more clues into the workings of the CIA and its relationship to the UFO and Men in Black mysteries than the Agency would perhaps prefer. First, that the CIA would take an interest in a relatively obscure case such as this demonstrates that all avenues were being pursued in monitoring breaking stories on unidentified flying objects. Second, the whole saga shows that the CIA was not above passing its agents off as employees of other agen-

cies in its attempts to gain possession of UFO data. That the two elderly Maier sisters had stumbled onto nothing more sinister than a
Morse code transmission is irrelevant. Clearly, CIA personnel
sought to obtain under covert and misleading circumstances what
was perceived initially to be UFO-related evidence. How often have
we now heard of Men in Black–style characters turning up on
people's doorsteps demanding evidence of UFO activity, only to
have the government agency the men allegedly work for assert that
it has no record of them? And this, of course, brings up another
question: How many similar MIB-like cases remain classified
within the archives of the CIA and the Air Force?

Further support in favor of the theory that at least some of the MIB
are intelligence personnel comes from the author and investigator
William L. Moore. According to Moore, in the United States at
least, the Men in Black are "really government people in disguise"
who originate with a "rather bizarre unit of Air Intelligence known
currently as the Air Force Special Activities Center."

Moore relates that the history of the AFSAC can be traced back
to the 1127th Field Activities Group—"an oddball unit, a compos-
ite of special intelligence groups. . . . The men of the 1127th were
con artists. Their job was to get people to talk." Recruited into the
group were "safe-crackers, cat burglars, lock-pickers . . . imperson-
ators, assorted masters of deception . . . and useful flakes of all
types," says Moore.[5]

But for firm proof that links the MIB mystery with the workings
of the military and the intelligence community, we have to turn our
attention to Great Britain.

On the evening of August 30, 1962, the world was about to
change drastically for Anne Henson. "At the time that this happened," Henson recalls, "I lived on a dairy farm and was still at
school; I was sixteen at the time. I actually moved back here with my
family some years ago and we run a nursery business now.

"It was the middle of the night and something must have woken me up because I sat up in my bed and I could see through the window what looked like a round ball of light in the sky; my room overlooked the Brendon Hills. It seemed to change color from red to green to yellow, and I could see a circle with rays of light coming from it.

"At first I thought it was a star, but it wasn't static. Then I thought that it must be a helicopter or something like that, but there was absolutely no sound from it. Well, it then began moving backwards and forwards and went from left to right. I was very intrigued by it because it was making fairly rapid movements. But it was the colors of the lights that attracted me first; they were nice bright colors. It would come towards me quite quickly and appeared to increase in size, and then reversed and moved sideways at a middle speed. But it always returned to its original position just above the hills.

"Over an hour or so, the light gradually receded until it was just like a pinprick of light. Well, I went to sleep, but the next night I wondered if it might be there again—and it was. This happened on a few occasions and I got quite used to seeing it when it was a clear night.

"To be honest," says Henson with a tinge of humor in her voice, "I got quite friendly with it, really. I didn't feel threatened by it, because although it came close to our farm, it didn't come *that* close. Now, when I'd seen it a few times, I decided that I would get a compass and graph paper and try to track where it was coming from because this was intriguing me. I thought: this is a bit different."

It was what happened when Henson approached officials that really set wheels in motion. "After I saw the light for a few times and tracked the movements of it, I contacted RAF Chivenor. I told them what I'd seen, and then I got a letter saying that my sighting was being looked at. Then this chap turned up at the house. . . .

"It was an evening when he arrived for the first time, and he pulled up in this old black car; and when he came in the house, he was wearing a black suit and tie. I would imagine that he was in his late thirties and I was most disappointed that he wasn't wearing a uniform. He announced himself as a Royal Air Force official and, of course, I took it as such. To me, he was an authority, put it like that. He actually came to visit me on several occasions. I assumed he was from RAF Chivenor; he didn't actually say so. I was a bit overawed that somebody was actually coming to see me.

"Altogether," says Henson, "he came on three nights. On the first night he came up to my bedroom and we sat there waiting for the clouds to clear. Unfortunately, that night and the next night he came, we couldn't see anything. So, he said that he would have to come back again. Now, on the third night, he saw it."

Did he have any opinion as to what the phenomenon was?

"No, none at all. He was just concentrating on looking at it. But he was very cagey. He wasn't very friendly, but he wasn't nasty either. But on this night he took some photos of the light. He didn't seem very surprised by what he saw. It was all very, very low-key, which I suppose is the way to play it if it was something unusual. If he'd have got excited, I'd have got excited.

"He then left and he took his camera and took my compass drawings and notes—and I never got them back. But before going he said that nobody else would believe what I'd seen and there was no point in me talking about it at school. At that age, you don't want to be laughed at—and my family had laughed at me, anyway."

Today, Henson is puzzled about her bizarre experience. "I thought originally that it was some military object, but then the Ministry of Defense said it was a planet; although that didn't explain the way it moved. Now, it all hinges on whether or not you believe in UFOs. I can't see why there shouldn't be life on other planets. And if there is, why shouldn't they come here to have a look at us?"

Anne Henson's case is a classic Men in Black encounter. It started with the sighting of a strange object and was followed by a visit from a dark-suited authority figure who warned her not to talk about what she had seen and confiscated her compass drawings and notes that displayed the movements of the phenomena she had observed.

But Henson's account differs in one striking aspect. Not only have the official files pertaining to her encounter surfaced into the public domain at the Public Record Office, Kew, but the MIB has been identified as an employee of the Special Investigation Section of an elite British Royal Air Force body known as the Provost and Security Services.

The work and duties of the P&SS center around the investigation of crime and disciplinary matters involving Royal Air Force personnel; security vetting; and the issuing of identity cards and permits. Far more significant, investigators attached to the P&SS are trained in the field of counterintelligence (CI). Such training is undertaken at the RAF Police School, and prospective candidates for counterintelligence work are required to take specialized courses in subjects such as computer security and surveillance. Before being considered for CI work, personnel have to attain the rank of corporal within the RAF Police; and after training, successful applicants can expect to be posted to a Royal Air Force station on CI duties to a P&SS unit.

CI investigators are responsible for issues affecting the security of the Royal Air Force, which includes the loss of classified documents, espionage cases, and the protection of royalty and VIPs when visiting RAF stations.

That an organization of this caliber would take a keen interest in the subject of UFOs is intriguing to say the least. The confidential report on Anne Henson's encounter prepared by Sergeant S. W. Scott of the P&SS's Special Investigation Section states:

MISS ANNE HENSON, aged 16, said that on 30th August, 1962 between 10:30 P.M. and 10:55 P.M. she opened the window of her room which faces N.N.E. and saw a diminishing star-like object with what appeared to be red and green coloured flames coming from it. It was slightly larger than the average star and appeared to be round. After about 2½ minutes it became very small and she could only see it with the aid of binoculars. She was quite sure that it was not the navigation lights of an aircraft because she had seen these many times and could recognize them immediately.

She did not look for it again until 17th October 1962, when she saw the object again which was partially obscured by fog. With the aid of binoculars she compared the object with several stars and noticed that the stars were silvery white whereas the object was red and green. Near to and above the object she noticed another exactly similar but smaller object. She noticed a difference in the colour of the original object which was now emitting green and orange flames in the same way as before.

MRS. C. HENSON, mother of ANNE HENSON, said that she had seen the object described by her daughter. She could offer no explanation as to the identity of the object but was of the opinion that it was not a star. She declined to make a written statement.

A visit was made on 1st November, 1962 when the sky was clear and all stars visible. MISS HENSON, however, said that the object was not in view on this particular night. Observations were maintained for one hour but nothing was seen.

MISS HENSON was asked to continue her observations and on the next occasion on which she saw the object or objects to compile a diagram showing its position in relation to the stars. This she agreed to do.

On 28th November, 1962, the next available opportunity, [the witnesses address] was again visited. However, although observations were maintained for 2 hours the sky remained obscured and nothing was seen. MISS HENSON was interviewed and said that she had seen the objects again on two occasions and although she had compiled a diagram she had omitted to note the date. She said that she would again watch for the objects noting times and dates and compile another diagram which she will forward by post to this Headquarters.

MISS HENSON reports unidentified aerial phenomena and

provides a diagram showing their position in relation to stars. The objects have not been seen by the Investigator who cannot therefore give an opinion as to their identity.

It is considered that MISS HENSON is a reasonable person, although at 16 years of age girls are inclined to be over-imaginative. However, MISS HENSON is supported by her mother, a person of about 50 years of age, who seems quite sincere. The matter should be brought to the notice of [the] Department at Air Ministry set up to investigate such phenomena.

A copy of Sergeant Scott's report was ultimately dispatched to an Air Force Intelligence office that concluded Anne Henson had simply misperceived a celestial body, such as a star or a planet. That may indeed have been the case; however, a far more important issue should be noted. As this affair reveals, there are now documented and verifiable cases where dark-suited officials *have* visited the homes of UFO witnesses, *have* warned them not to talk about their UFO encounters, and *have* confiscated data pertaining to the incident at issue. More importantly, in Britain at least, those same dark-suited visitors appear to originate from within an elite division of the Royal Air Force trained in counterintelligence and espionage operations. Interestingly, in many ways this parallels the claims of William L. Moore and his findings on the activities of the MIB in the United States.

It is also notable that shortly after the declassification of the documentation pertaining to Anne Henson's encounter, the document briefly vanished from the shelves of the Public Record Office amid rumors that it had been released in error by the Ministry of Defense. When questions about the nature of its disappearance were raised at a parliamentary level, however, the documentation quickly and quietly resurfaced at the PRO. Such is the controversy and sensitivity surrounding the MIB mystery.[6]

We do not try to pretend to have solved the riddle of the Men in Black. It must be said that some of the accounts veer toward the paranormal in nature. We do, however, believe that the Provost and Security Services, CIA, FBI, and U.S. Air Force records cited here indicate that at least *some* MIB encounters are the work of the world's intelligence agencies that have a vested interest in the complexities of the UFO puzzle. The question is, why?

Part Three

MIND GAMES

THE USE OF SUPERSTITIONS IN PSYCHOLOGICAL OPERATIONS
IN VIETNAM

PROBLEM:

    a. To devise guidelines for the exploitation of enemy vulnerabilities provided by superstitions and deeply-held traditional beliefs.

    b. To be aware of and accommodate those superstitions of friendly forces and populations that may have a bearing on military operations.

DISCUSSION:

    A strong superstition or a deeply-held belief shared by a substantial number of the enemy target audience can be used as a psychological weapon because it permits with some degree of probability the prediction of individual or group behavior under a given set of conditions. To use an enemy superstitic as a starting point for psychological operations, however, one must be sure of th conditions and control the stimuli that trigger the desired behavior.

    The first step in the manipulation of a superstition as an enemy vulnerability is its exact identification and detailed definition of its spread and intensity among the target audience. The second step is to insure friendl control of the stimuli and the capability to create a situation that will trigger the desired superstitious behavior. Both conditions must be met or the psyops effort will not yield the desired results; it might even backfire.

    As an illustration, one can cite the recent notion spread among combat troops in the First Corps area that VC and NVN troops were deathly afraid of the "Ace of Spades" as an omen of death. In consequence soldiers, turned psy-warriors with the assistance of playing card manufacturers, began leaving the ominous card in battle areas and on patrols into enemy-held territory. The notion was based on isolated instances of behavior among Montagnard tribes- men familiar from French days with the Western deck of cards. A subsequent survey determined that the ace of spades does not trigger substantial fear reactions among most Vietnamese because the various local playing cards have their own set of symbols, generally of Chinese derivation.

    Here then was an incorrect identification of a superstition coupled with a friendly capability to exploit the presumed condition. It did not work.

    For a correct identification of a superstition coupled with an inability to exploit same, one could postulate the case of an enemy dictator or ruling group with deeply-held beliefs in astrological predictions of the future. Unless the favored soothsayer can be motivated to say the desired things - an unlikely possibility - the accurate knowledge of this enemy weakness could not be turned to friendly advantage.

For decades the U.S. Army has taken an interest in the way in which superstitions, witchcraft, and sorcery can be employed as tools of warfare. This document, "The Use of Superstitions in Psychological Operations in Vietnam," was prepared for the Army in 1964.

Eight

WARFARE AND WITCHCRAFT

Of the many and varied tools of warfare that were employed on battlefields throughout the world in the twentieth century, few were as strange as those officially proposed for use by the U.S. Army in the mid-1960s. While the conventional weapons of war will always have their place, some within the military were at the time investigating truly groundbreaking and bizarre ways of defeating the enemy—including the use of witchcraft, vampires, sorcery, and magic.

As startling as this may sound, official documentation is available that supports this highly unusual and controversial scenario. But before examining these files, we need to first address one crucial matter: What was it that prompted the military to initiate such studies in the first place? To answer that question it becomes necessary to take a look at the life and career of one Edward Lansdale.

Major General Edward G. Lansdale was born in Detroit, Michigan, in 1908, the second of the four sons of Sarah Frances Philips of California and Henry Lansdale of Virginia. During the Second World War, Lansdale served with the Office of Strategic Services and was commissioned as a lieutenant in the U.S. Army in 1943, serving in various military intelligence assignments throughout the war. After several wartime promotions, in 1945 Lansdale was transferred to Headquarters Air Forces Western Pacific in the Philippines, where he became chief of the Intelligence Division and extended his tour until 1948.

During this period, Lansdale helped the Philippine Army rebuild its intelligence services, was responsible for the disposition of unresolved cases of large numbers of prisoners of war involving many nationalities, and conducted numerous studies to assist the U.S. and Philippine governments in learning the effects of the Second World War on the Philippines. He was commissioned a captain in the regular U.S. Air Force in 1947, with the temporary rank of major; and after leaving the Philippines in 1948, he served as an instructor at the Strategic Intelligence School, Lowry Air Force Base, Colorado, where he received a temporary promotion to lieutenant colonel in 1949.

In 1953 Lansdale became a member of General J. W. "Iron Mike" O'Daniell's mission to the French forces in Indochina, acting as an adviser on special counterguerrilla operations. After returning to further duties in the Philippines, he was transferred to Saigon, where he served until the end of 1956. During this period, Lansdale helped advise the Vietnamese armed forces and the Vietnamese government on numerous internal security problems, including the pacification campaigns of 1954–55, as well as psychological operations, intelligence, the integration of sect armies, civic action, and the refugee program.

In June 1957 after brief staff duty with USAF Headquarters, Lansdale was transferred to the Office of the Secretary of Defense, with duties as deputy assistant to the secretary of defense for special operations. Two years later, Lansdale served on the staff of the President's Committee on Military Assistance—the Draper Committee. He was given a temporary promotion to brigadier general in April 1960; and on February 24, 1961, he was appointed assistant to the secretary of defense, where his primary duties focused on attention to special operations of an extremely sensitive nature.

Among his decorations were the Distinguished Service Medal, awarded by the Air Force for his work in Indochina during 1954 to 1956; the National Security Medal, awarded by the National Security Council for his service in the Philippines during 1950 to 1953; the Philippines' Legion of Honor; and the Philippines' Medal of Military Merit.

Back in the 1950s, at the request of President Elpidio Quirino, Lansdale was transferred to the Philippines-based Joint United States Military Assistance Group (JUSMAG), to advise the intelligence services of the armed forces of the Philippines, which were then faced with a serious threat to national security posed by the Communist Huks. Ramon Magsaysay had just been appointed secretary of national defense and Lansdale was made liaison officer to Secretary Magsaysay for JUSMAG. The two became intimate friends, frequently visiting combat areas together. Lansdale helped the Philippine armed forces develop psychological operations, civic actions, and the rehabilitation of Huk prisoners.[1]

While involved in the campaign against the Huks, Lansdale helped create an ingenious military and intelligence operation that utilized, for psychological warfare purposes, a local and much feared legend: that of the terrifying Asuang vampire.

"To the superstitious," wrote Lansdale, "the Huk battleground was a haunted place filled with ghosts and eerie creatures. A combat psywar squad was brought in. It planted stories among town residents of an Asuang living on the hill where the Huks were based. Two nights later, after giving the stories time to make their way up to the hill camp, the psywar squad set up an ambush along the trail used by the Huks. When a Huk patrol came along the trail, the ambushers silently snatched the last man of the patrol, their move unseen in the dark night. They punctured his neck with two holes, vampire-fashion, held the body up by the heels, drained it of blood, and put the corpse back on the trail. When the Huks returned to look for the missing man and found their bloodless comrade, every member of the patrol believed that the Asuang had got him and that one of them would be next if they remained on that hill. When daylight came, the whole Huk squadron moved out of the vicinity." Lansdale died in 1987.[2]

Whether vampires are a physical reality or myth and fantasy is hardly the point. The Communist Huks certainly believed in the reality of the Asuang vampire, and this belief allowed U.S. and Philippine forces to gain strategic ground in their conflict with the Huks without even firing a shot.

Almost certainly, the significance of this incident was not lost on Pentagon strategists, since studies into the exploitation for military purposes of similar legends, superstitions, and fears of the supernatural were addressed by the U.S. Army on a variety of occasions in the years that followed.

For our purposes, we present two documents from the 1960s: "Witchcraft, Sorcery, Magic, and Other Psychological Phenomena, and Their Implications on Military and Paramilitary Operations in the Congo"; and "The Use of Superstitions in Psychological Operations in Vietnam." The former report was authored on August 8, 1964, by Paul Juredini and James R. Price, analysts attached to the Counterinsurgency Information Analysis Center of the Special Operations Research Office (SORO), which undertook work for the U.S. Army at the American University, Washington, D.C.; while the latter document surfaced from the military's Joint Public Affairs Office in 1967.

The first document begins by revealing the then current thinking on the part of the U.S. Army with respect to witchcraft, its use from an intelligence-based perspective, and the way in which a belief in such phenomena was being manipulated during the hostilities in the Republic of the Congo.

Rebel tribesmen are said to have been persuaded that they can be made magically impervious to Congolese army firepower. Their fear of the government has thus been diminished and, conversely, fear of the rebels has grown within army ranks.

The problem, therefore, which CINFAC was asked to explore is the role of supernatural or superstitious concepts in a counterinsurgency in the Congo. Any reply to this question involves consideration of several factors. It is necessary to examine the nature of general African beliefs about magic, insofar as this may be done on the basis of published studies. It is also necessary to gain some insight as to the roles played by magic in other African revolutionary upheavals. And finally, it is suggested that today's insurgency situation should not be studied in a vacuum, but should be considered as part of a continuum stemming from the pre-independence Belgian administration, the impact of Western culture upon African tribal systems, the circumstances of the birth of the Congo Republic, and the nature of the struggle for power within the Congo since 1960.

This opening section of the paper makes it abundantly clear that the Army was acutely aware of the way in which the use of witchcraft, sorcery, and magic was being exploited by Congolese rebels at the time and of the adverse effect that this was having on the country's armed forces. Undoubtedly, this was a matter of keen interest to American military planners. After all, if you can simply scare the enemy into surrendering, you can save a huge amount of both money and manpower.

The document continues in a similar vein and reveals that the Army had been largely able to determine that the process that led to an increased belief in, and fear of, the supernatural began at times of extreme stress and in a high-threat situation such as a war or regional conflict.

A review of the available literature indicates that in Africa, uprisings embodying supernatural practices have tended to occur generally whenever the continued physical safety or internal power structure of a tribe or tribes has been seriously threatened. Manifestations of witchcraft and sorcery in these in-

stances can be said to reflect, in part, a return to traditionalism. A tribe unites more readily when a threat is explainable
and solutions are propounded in terms of tribal common de-
nominators of belief. In order to determine the degree to which
such a generalization is applicable to the current situation in
the Congo, a brief recapitulation of certain aspects of recent
Congolese history will serve as a useful point of departure. The
tribal uprisings which have erupted in the Republic of the
Congo (Leopoldville) since its independence in 1960 can be
traced to situations which appeared to threaten the various
tribes both in terms of their physical well-being and their position within the structure of Congolese national society. With independence, these tribes found themselves lacking the basic
services which the colonial administration had provided—ali-
mentation, hygiene, medical care, schools, and physical security—while at the same time the future of the tribe and its
organization was being debated by the new government at
Leopoldville. By and large, however, it was the disruption in
government machinery which forced the younger members of
the tribes to seek the urban centers in an effort to improve
their situation, and pushed the older members back towards
traditionalism and its beliefs in magic and witchcraft.

The disintegration of the Congo was caused by two dominating
factors: the absence of groups that could replace the departing colonial administration and the power struggle that took place between
those Congolese political parties that favored centralism and those
that favored federalism. This conflict prevented any attempts by the
Congolese government to restore some semblance of administrative
order. Not until the bloody riots of January 5, 1959, did the Belgian
government realize that it would have to give freedom to the Congo
much sooner than it had envisioned.

In the ensuing agreements between Congolese representatives
and the Belgian government, provisions were made for the utiliza-

tion of Belgian colonial civil servants in their former capacities until Congolese replacements could be trained. Such agreements were never implemented, however. On July 8, 1960, eight days after independence, the Congolese National Army in the capital city of Leopoldville mutinied against its Belgian officers.

On July 12, Premier Patrice Lumumba called on the United Nations to eject the Belgian troops and help restore order. In the weeks following the arrival of UN forces, Lumumba's followers made repeated attempts to reimpose central government control on Katanga and Kasai. These attempts, and the high number of casualties resulting from them, precipitated a power struggle, and anarchy thus set in, providing Lumumba's followers with opportunities to set up their own political organizations. These were cast along tribal lines, and the trappings of tribalism, including manifestations of beliefs in both magic and witchcraft, began again to impinge upon the world of politics.

When the United Nations refused to accede to all of his demands, however, Lumumba turned against it and accepted the proffered assistance of the Communist Bloc countries, along with that of Ghana, Guinea, and the United Arab Republic. Communist machinations, and subsequent attempts by UN Ghanian troops to disarm the Congolese Army, prompted General Mobutu to remove Lumumba.

With this removal, the Belgians accepted the traditional boundaries of the chiefdoms, reemphasized the hereditary character of tribal chieftaincy, and made the chiefs responsible for population registration, public health, tax collection, security, and labor matters within the respective chiefdoms.

The next section of the document, titled "Supernatural Aspects of the Present Insurgency Situation," elaborates on the way in which belief in sorcery and witchcraft then became rife in the region and also how that belief became deeply ingrained into the day-to-day living of the citizens—to the extent that it was seen as an essential element of their society.

We began this discussion with an observation that threats to the concept or form of tribal structures in Africa tend to generate uprisings characterized by emphasis upon traditionalist elements in African life. The current uprisings in the Congo, and for that matter elsewhere in black Africa, gain impetus from the insurgent practice of employing magical procedures to convince tribal insurgents that no harm can be done to them by forces of the central government.

These tactics are effective, because in the Congo and elsewhere in black Africa beliefs in witchcraft, sorcery, magic, and other supernatural phenomenon are deeply rooted among the people. Although the manifestations of these beliefs vary widely according to tribal and cultural circumstances, magico-religious causes are usually cited to explain misfortunes of any kind, even those of clearly natural origin. If crops are blighted, if a hut caves in and kills its occupants, if the chief becomes unfriendly, or if sudden illness or death occurs, bewitching is usually given as the primary cause. The people may understand that in fact the house fell because termites ate away the foundations, but that it fell at the time it did was a result of witchcraft or sorcery. Witchcraft is also cited as a factor in personal disputes, especially where the relationship is inherently subject to tensions—as for example, in the relationship between husband and wife, or between co-wives. In these cases, not only physical or direct remedies, but occult remedies as well are considered necessary to counteract the evil influence.

A distinction drawn by Evans-Pritchard in his *Witchcraft, Oracles, and Magic Among the Azande* (Oxford University Press, 1937) which is helpful for purposes of study is that between witchcraft and sorcery. Although these two concepts often overlap, especially in application (the same person may be thought to practice sorcery as well as witchcraft), they do represent two distinct theories of supernatural behavior which are shared by practically all African tribal societies. A sorcerer is one who is thought to practice evil magic against others.

Interestingly, the authors considered sorcery a valid and demonstrably real tool that served a very real purpose for those who practiced it.

The techniques of sorcery may be learned by anyone, and are usually based upon the use of various organic or vegetable compounds called "medicines" which, when prepared according to stringent ritualistic requirements, are believed to acquire magical properties enabling them to work the will of the sorcerer. The reciprocal to the concept of sorcery, or the practice of evil magic, is the concept of the use of magical rites or medicines for socially-approved purposes. These include everything from the protection of personal safety, to improvement of soil fertility, to success at the hunt or in battle. In short, "good" magic may be invoked to stimulate good results in any phase of the life cycle. Again, strict and proper ritual must be observed in the preparation of the necessary medicines, and these rituals—which include taboo observance, verbal formulae, etc.—are idiosyncratic to particular tribes, and even differing schools of thought within the same tribe or sub-tribe.

The authors then discussed the definition of witchcraft and its use from a historical perspective in the Congo.

Witchcraft, on the other hand, is said to be an inborn trait which enables its possessor to harm other people merely by wishing to do so. "Medicines" play no part in true bewitching operations. Some tribes believe that witchcraft power is activated by feelings of hostility or envy even without conscious decision on the part of the witch—or even without the witch's knowing that he contains witchcraft power within him. In the Congo, belief that the witchcraft power was embodied as a physical substance in the belly was so widespread that the Belgian authorities had to ban the practice of tribal elders' performing autopsies upon the bodies of suspected witches. In 1924 the colonial administration also banned use of the poison ordeal—the other universally accepted method of screening suspected witches. Ritually-prepared poison was administered to suspects in the belief that the innocent would survive and the guilty perish.

European influences on African supernatural belief systems, which extended back into the latter stages of the nineteenth century, were not bypassed either. This amply demonstrates how deeply Juredini and Price had researched their subject matter.

Although Africa's infrastructure of supernatural beliefs and practices has been subjected to concentrated assault by Europeans—primarily missionaries—for as many as five hundred years in some areas, few lasting inroads have been made against ingrained traditions. In the Congo, practically all education since 1878 has been in the hands of various Catholic and Protestant missionary groups. Missionary activities have succeeded in establishing rather substantial church organizations and church membership, but closer examination reveals that to the extent that Christian and other European influences have taken root in the Congo, they have also often been modified so as to merge with, not supersede, the traditional foundations of the country and its people. Europeanized Congolese may carry amulets and charms, consult oracles about the advisability of business transactions, and observe other rituals learned in childhood. Others hold both traditional and Christian funeral ceremonies. Institutionally, many syncretic sects—often pseudo-Christian—stand between Christianity and tradition, started by prophets who believed they were divinely inspired. Most began as messianic cults but developed nationalistic and anti-European characteristics along the way.

Ironically, the influence of Western society upon long-established belief systems in the Congo only seemed to harden the acceptance of—and reliance upon—occult-based practices.

Among the people, there is little evidence that traditional beliefs in witchcraft, sorcery, and magic have been diminished by Western influences. The evidence is rather that the practice of secret magical rites is on the increase. History indicates that beliefs in witches and magic die hard in all societies. And because of Africa's particular cultural setting, it is unlikely that these beliefs will disappear other than as a result of generations of careful and gradual education in the Western mold. Western education is not, however, an immediate solution. In Africa beliefs in magic and witchcraft are used to explain ultimate causations—the existence and origin of fortune and misfortune. Western secular education does not provide unequivocal answers to questions of such a fundamental nature. Western institutions have, as a matter of fact, served in some ways to increase tensions and anxieties in African societies, especially as these relate to superstitious beliefs and practices. The control of witches and sorcerers is of paramount importance to people who believe in magic. Yet the imposition of political systems of a Western type upon African tribes has resulted in the elimination of the most efficacious witch-control measure—the poison ordeal. In addition, the execution of convicted witches and sorcerers is no longer allowed. As a result, many Africans feel that Western political systems such as the modern state have aligned themselves on the side of evil because from their standpoint the "civilized" elimination of traditional control measures works to protect witches and sorcerers from retaliation by their innocent victims. The African man-in-the-bush is, therefore, much more at the mercy of those who wish to harm him by supernatural means than ever before. He thus tends to rely more and more upon the witch-doctor* who, in the absence of the poison ordeal and other drastic sanctions, provides the main source of protection from evil.

---

*The term *witch-doctor* is used in the popular sense for the convenience of the reader. A more precise [*sic*] but less familiar term would be majico-religious practitioner, since the practices attributed to witch-doctors neither necessarily include, nor are confined to witchcraft per se, but may include sorcery and other forms of magic as well.

The final section of the document, titled "Counterinsurgency Analysis," addresses whether the belief in sorcery and witchcraft should be utilized for strategic, military purposes, and if so how. The authors, however, were careful to point out both the benefits and the potential downside that undertaking such actions might invoke.

In the context of the current insurgency situations in Kivu and Katanga, where insurgents rely upon "medicines" and ritualistic observances to protect them from firepower, the suggestion to devise and employ magical practices in counterinsurgency operations is obvious and tempting. Before adopting this course of action, however, the U.S. counterinsurgency planner should give serious consideration to several pertinent factors:

In the event that the U.S. role, if any, in the Congo will be of an advisory character, the advisors must rely upon the extent of their influence upon Congolese counterparts. U.S. policy recommendations must, therefore, be acceptable to Congolese leaders. The Congolese leadership class is driven almost exclusively from a small elite group who, having obtained Western education under the Belgians, have become "Europeanized" (a concept virtually equivalent to "civilized") to the extent that they are known as evolues. Kasavubu, Lumumba, Kalonji, Adoula, Mobutu, and Tshombe are all evolues and as such are fiercely proud of their "civilized" status and image. These evolues can be expected to resist any association with policies which might reflect endorsement of "uncivilized" behavior, even though they themselves might be to some extent dependent upon secret charms or other superstitious beliefs or practices.

The report stresses that while beliefs in witchcraft, sorcery, and magic were endemic throughout sub-Saharan Africa, those beliefs varied considerably in detail according to tribe or subtribe. Literally, one man's charm was another man's poison, depending upon particular tribal beliefs. It followed, therefore, that the counterinsurgency planner—if he or she desired to exploit the psychological potential of superstition—had to be able to compile and analyze a large quantity of specific and detailed information embracing the entire spectrum of superstitious beliefs and other values of the specific ethnic group concerned. This tended to relegate the use of magic to limited tactical objectives rather than broad strategic concepts or solutions to fundamental problems, stated the report.

By the same token, however, the prevalence of superstitious beliefs in Africa suggests that the counterinsurgency planner requires considerable information about these beliefs for intelligence and counterintelligence purposes alone. A sound understanding of magical concepts, practices, and mannerisms is necessary for defensive purposes should they play any role or importance in an insurgency situation. Knowledge of the specific uses of charms, medicines, bodily scarification, and the like, will help to identify membership in a particular cult, or will enable patterns of activity to be defined. Failing complete and detailed information of this type, both operational and counterintelligence planning will be unrealistic. Unfortunately, such information may not be quickly acquired about the more than 200 reported tribes in the Congo, but must be painstakingly gathered and evaluated over a long period of time. Detailed studies of supernatural beliefs of specific tribes are limited. The secrecy inherent in most magical rituals presents a formidable obstacle to the outside investigator, whether he may be a scientist or an intelligence agent.

And finally, the tactics employed to counter current insurgencies in various parts of the Congo must be evaluated in terms not only of their immediate effectiveness against the short-term military problem, but in terms also of their positive or negative influence upon the long-range problem of establishing a viable political system.

But what if local superstitions were successfully exploited from a military perspective? The authors argued convincingly that this could lead to a far from desirable scenario and the creation of a government dependent on the use of magic.

It cannot be denied that the exploitation of superstitious beliefs by insurgent leaders is a double-edged weapon. Fear of magic and witchcraft can be reversed and used with telling effects against the insurgents. If reliable and detailed operational intelligence can be gathered, counterinsurgency planners will be able to concoct "medicines" and other devices within the superstitious framework of the target group, with which to neutralize and overpower the magic spells cast by insurgent witch-doctors. These procedures could well involve a continuing duel of thrust and parry, because the witch-doctors could also be counted on to devise counter-counter measures, and so forth. But there is little doubt that counter-magic tactics properly conceived and imaginatively executed could be quite effective in achieving short-run victories. A broader question is whether the exploitation of superstition in this fashion is not also a triple-edged weapon, in that superstition itself, rather than the central government, may become, in the long-run, the main beneficiary. Since tribalism and superstition, so closely related to each other, have provided a fertile seedbed for political instability in the Congo, and measures which enhance the divisive and destructive aspects of tribalism simply lay additional obstacles in the already cluttered path toward Congolese nationhood. Should the central government successfully use occult methods to defeat a movement based upon such methods, the very concepts of sorcery and magic which lend impetus to the insurgencies of the moment may gain strength and acquire even greater trouble-making potential for the future. In other words, the more successful the counterinsurgency campaign, if that campaign is based upon a counter-magic approach, the more ominous the outlook for the future. Any thesis that an insurgency inspired or sustained by magical concepts may be defeated more easily and at less cost and trouble by employing counter-magic is therefore questionable on these grounds.

The authors stressed the historical abundance of examples where sorcery and warfare had crossed paths:

Nor does the current situation in the Congo represent anything new in the history of insurgency insofar as the use of magical practices is concerned. History is replete with instances wherein uprisings have been reinforced by magic spells. The T'ai P'ing rebellion in China was led by a man who represented himself as the younger brother of Jesus Christ. The Boxer cultists believed that they could cause cannon to fall apart at great distances by psycho-kinetic means. Those who took the Mau Mau oaths in Kenya were taught that oath violation would be instantly lethal. African history contains numerous other examples or similar phenomena (the "Maji-Maji" rebellion in

Tanganyika, the Makomobe uprising in Portuguese East Africa, etc.). Current problems in the Congo as well as the Lumpa uprising in Northern Rhodesia today exemplify the same superstitious manifestations.

Any study of historical examples of uprisings supported by superstitious practices, however, will reveal that vigorous military counter-measures of a conventional nature have produced optimum results in suppressing the insurgency. If there are substantial political or economic motives behind the uprisings, these naturally must be taken into account. The reference here is to military tactics and their effects against magic.

It appeared to the authors, however, that belief systems in "black Africa" were relatively easy to influence and modify—something that would have been of keen interest to military strategists.

Despite the ingrained quality of superstition throughout black Africa, there is a certain core of pragmatism immediately applicable to the present problem. The history of messianic movements and especially those movements whose primary function is the detection and/or neutralization of witchcraft and sorcery reveals that Africans easily recognize and accept concrete proof of the ineffectiveness of a particular magical rite or charm. Such recognition and acceptance in no way affect the basic pattern of belief in magic. The opposite is in fact true, as is proven by the continuing succession of short-lived anti-witchcraft cults throughout Africa. Africans are quite prepared to admit that they have been fooled by a particular practitioner or cult. The pattern then is to reject the "false" cult and accept one which, until events prove otherwise, is the "real thing." The same type of mental processes seem to apply to witch-doctors themselves. Informed opinion is that most witch-doctors believe themselves as individuals to be clever charlatans, since they are aware that they really have no magic power. But an individual witch-doctor is also likely to believe that he alone is a charlatan and that his colleagues do indeed have magical abilities.

For all the problems that the beliefs in superstitions and witch-craft in the Congo posed, the authors believed that the situation could be rectified with relative ease by disciplined, well-led troops.

In the Congo, as elsewhere in black Africa, there is every reason to believe that disciplined troops, proficient in marksmanship, and led by competent officers, can handily dispel most notions of magical invulnerability. It is quite true that the raising of such a force may pose more problems in the Congo than in some other areas, but the problem is by no means insoluble. The elite gendarmerie organized by the Belgians to offset the ill-disciplined Force Publique gendarmerie is an example of what can be done in the Congo. The same concept of the gendarmerie was employed, together with foreign mercenaries, by Moise Tshombe in the Katanga secessionist movement. Tshombe's forces were generally conceded to be highly effective, and were suppressed only with great difficulty by the United Nations.

The immediate military problems related to the Congo's fundamental problems of instability and chaos appear more susceptible to lasting solution by conventional methods than by reliance upon purely psychological or occult phenomena whose values are limited to support functions in tactical situations and whose implementation is fraught with long-run risks. Drawing upon the Belgian experience as well as that of Tshombe in Katanga, it would appear that a more flexible approach to the military problem is to be found in the concept of elite troops: troops which are carefully trained and disciplined, and which are well-commanded. Unit morale and the confidence engendered by good training, knowledge of weaponry, and, above all, dynamic and competent leadership, can go far to counteract superstitious fears.

U.S. military interest in this particular field continued unabated. A document titled "Vietnam: PSYOP Directive: The Use of Superstitions in Psychological Operations in Vietnám," and dated May 10, 1967, states that the author was following U.S. mission psychological policy and guidelines and the document was to be implemented by all U.S. elements in Vietnam. The problem was twofold: to devise guidelines for the exploitation of enemy vulnerabilities provided by superstitions and deeply held traditional beliefs; and to be aware of and accommodate those superstitions of friendly forces and populations that could have had a bearing on military operations. Obviously, the U.S. military considered the manipulation of controversial and supernatural belief systems to be an ongoing and valid weapon of war in the mid-1960s.

A strong superstition or a deeply-held belief shared by a substantial number of the enemy target audience can be used as a psychological weapon because it permits with some degree of probability the prediction of individual or group behavior under a given set of conditions. To use an enemy superstition as a starting point for psychological operations, however, one must be sure of the conditions and control the stimuli that trigger the desired behavior.

The first step in the manipulation of a superstition, asserted the author, is to exactly identify it and detail its spread and intensity. The second step is to insure "friendly control of the stimuli" and have the capacity to create a situation that would trigger the desired superstitious behavior. Both conditions must be met or the effect might even backfire. An example of how such an operation could indeed backfire was provided:

As an illustration, one can cite the recent notion spread among combat troops in the First Corps area that VC and NVN troops were deathly afraid of the "Ace of Spades" as an omen of death. In consequence soldiers, turned psy-warriors with the assistance of playing card manufacturers, began leaving the ominous card in battle areas and on patrols into enemy-held territory. The notion was based on isolated instances of behavior among Montagnard tribesmen familiar from French days with the Western deck of cards. A subsequent survey determined that the ace of spades does not trigger substantial fear reactions among most Vietnamese because the various local playing cards have their own set of symbols, generally of Chinese derivation. Here then was an incorrect identification of a superstition coupled with a friendly capability to exploit the presumed condition. It did not work.

For a correct identification of a superstition coupled with an inability to exploit same, one could postulate the case of an enemy dictator or ruling group with deeply-held beliefs in astrological predictions of the future. Unless the favored soothsayer can be motivated to say the desired things—an unlikely possibility—the accurate knowledge of this enemy weakness could not be turned to friendly advantage.

In a minor key, psyops use of the venerated figure of Tran Hung Dao, victor in 1285 over the Golden Horde led by Kublai Khan's Chinese vassal, satisfies both requirements. We know the supernatural qualities with which the heroic figure of Tran Hung Dao is endowed in the popular mind, and the GVN has the capability of invoking him in patriotic appeals aimed against the invaders (see JUSPAO Poster #1271) which are among the most popular produced in the psyops field to date.

The report then turns its attention to the way in which the use of, and belief in, superstitions during the Vietnam War led to cata-

strophic results. The author quotes from a First Corps after-action
report:

As we started on the patrol we heard a lot of noise as the men
walked. The advisor, who was brand new, stopped them and
found handing around their necks, dangling from their belt or
in their pockets objects of stone, wood and metal. The noise
would have surely revealed our position, so the advisor collected all the amulets and sent them back to the camp area.
This proved to be a bad mistake. Before we had penetrated
deeply into the forest we had lost half the men. The other half
would have been better off lost, because they believed it was
their time to die. They had been deprived of the protection of
the good spirits. Needless to say, we came back without accom-
plishing our mission.

The author comments on this report: "An experienced advisor
would have balanced the noise factor against the morale effect of
depriving the soldiers of their magical protection. A compromise
could possibly have been found in wrapping the amulets in some
sound absorbing material."

A stern warning was offered to anyone contemplating the use of
this unusual brand of psychological warfare:

In summary, the manipulation of superstitions is a delicate affair. Tampering with deeply-held beliefs, seeking to turn them
to your advantage means in effect playing God and it should
only be attempted if one can get away with it and the game is
indeed worth the candle. Failure can lead to ridicule, charges of
clumsiness and callousness that can blacken the reputation of
psychological operations in general. It is a weapon to be employed selectively and with utmost skill and deftness. There
can be no excuse for failure.

The document ends with a six-point conclusion:

1. To exploit enemy superstitions, psyops personnel must be certain that:
   a. The superstition or belief is real and powerful.
   b. They have the capability of manipulating it to achieve results favorable to the friendly forces.

2. As a corollary, the psyops effort must insure that the audience against which a superstition campaign is launched is sufficiently homogeneous in their beliefs to be susceptible to this kind of manipulation. Superstitions vary widely, for example, among city and country people and the inhabitants of different regions of the same country, both in kind and in degree of intensity.

3. Would-be superstition manipulators must be prepared to face a credibility test if their efforts are traced to the source. Additionally, the triggering device of the superstition response must seem entirely credible to the target audience. As an example, many Vietnamese, particularly in rural areas, are provoked into a fear response if startled at night by the hoot of an owl or the call of a crow. These are considered death omens. The response will not occur, however, if the sound can be detected in any way as originating from an artificial source, such as a loudspeaker.

4. A psyops operator's desire to take advantage of manipulating enemy superstitions surreptitiously must be balanced against the counterproductive effects of possible failure and exposure of the attempt by the mass media. The U.S. image and the effectiveness of future psyops might lose more than the commander might hope to gain by successful execution of the plan.

5. In summary, enemy superstition manipulation should not be lightly employed by field psyops personnel. Proposals to make appeals based on superstitions or otherwise manipulate

target audience beliefs will be forwarded in each case to JUS-PAO and/or MACPD through the respective channels of their originators. They will be carefully analyzed there in the light of the considerations spelled out in this guidance. No psyops campaign in the area of superstition manipulation will be undertaken without JUSPAO/MACPD approval.

6. Where the superstitions of friendly forces and populations are concerned, psyops personnel will assist commanders as required or called upon in devising indoctrination materials familiarizing troops with these beliefs and counseling respect for and sensitivity to local beliefs and traditions.[3]

If such practices and studies continue on the part of the U.S. Army in the post–9-11 era, then undoubtedly the comments and assertions remain as valid in today's climate of terror as they were on the day that they were written.

These documents clearly show that the U.S. government and military have for decades held a deep-rooted interest in determining the ways in which all manner of superstitions, witchcraft, and sorcery can be exploited for psychological warfare purposes. Much of that research stems from the phenomenally successful—and ingeniously unconventional—methods employed against the Huk rebels in the Philippines in the early 1950s and cited by the late Major General Edward G. Landsdale. Until now, who would ever have seriously imagined that the twilight world inhabited by vampires, witch doctors, and sorcerers would one day have crossed paths with U.S. Army strategists and even the assistant secretary of defense of the United States?

Nine

ANIMALS AND ESPIONAGE

The U.S. Defense Intelligence Agency, created in 1961 by Defense Secretary Robert McNamara, brought together the military intelligence branches of the U.S. Army, Navy, and Air Force. Currently, the DIA satisfies the foreign intelligence and counterintelligence requirements of the secretary of defense, the Joint Chiefs of Staff, and various components of the Department of Defense and provides the military intelligence contribution to national intelligence. In other words, the DIA is a highly respected and vital component of the U.S. government and the intelligence world.

An examination of files that the DIA has declassified under the terms of the Freedom of Information Act reveals that, in the Cold War environment of the 1970s, the agency spent considerable time researching the existence (or otherwise) of extrasensory perception and psychic phenomena. Not only that, the DIA was predominantly troubled by one particularly nightmarish and nagging scenario: that the Soviets would succeed in utilizing ESP as a tool of espionage and the secrets of the Pentagon, the CIA, and just about everyone else would be blown wide open for Kremlin and KGB psychic penetration.

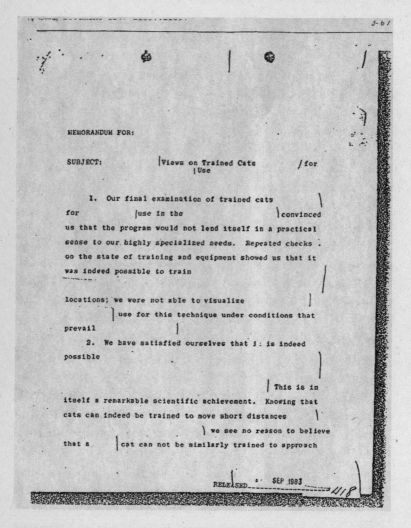

MEMORANDUM FOR:

SUBJECT: |Views on Trained Cats   / for
                           | Use

    1. Our final examination of trained cats
for |use in the   \convinced
us that the program would not lend itself in a practical
sense to our highly specialized needs. Repeated checks .
on the state of training and equipment showed us that it
was indeed possible to train

locations; we were not able to visualize
              | use for this technique under conditions that
prevail |
    2. We have satisfied ourselves that i: is indeed
possible

                                        | This is in
itself a remarkable scientific achievement. Knowing that
cats can indeed be trained to move short distances   \
                           \ we see no reason to believe
that a |cat can not be similarly trained to approach

A heavily censored CIA document from the mid-1960s on the Agency's
attempts to create a robotic cat for use in spying operations. It is titled
"Views on Trained Cats."

Acting on this concern, the DIA (along with the CIA and the Army) began to seriously address the issue of whether the powers of the mind would one day prove superior to—or at least the equal of—conventional tools of espionage and warfare. As a result of its intensive study of Soviet research into psychic phenomena for espionage purposes, the DIA learned of some of the notable advances made by both Russian and Czechoslovakian scientists whose attention was focused on the links between psychic phenomena and the animal kingdom.

In a September 1975 document, "Soviet and Czechoslovakian Parapsychology Research," the DIA reveals that Soviet research into psychic powers in animals began decades previously and focused on possible mind-to-mind contact between human beings and dogs. One section of the document is titled "Telepathy in Animals."

Soviet research on telepathy in animals in the 1920s and 1930s was devoted largely to proving that telepathy between man and animals did indeed exist. A good example of the early Soviet approach was research conducted by V. I. M. Bekhterev of Leningrad University, in collaboration with a circus performer, V. L. Durov. Bekhterev reported that Durov's trained dogs successfully solved arithmetic problems and identified or retrieved objects solely on the basis of their trainer's mental suggestion. The results of these tests were controversial, since the dogs' performances were good when Durov was present and supplied the "suggestions," but deteriorated markedly when he was absent and another individual attempted to mentally control them.

If telepathy is a real phenomenon, as the DIA suspected, Durov might indeed have succeeded in generating a mind-to-mind link with his dogs. That the results should have deteriorated markedly when Durov was absent, however, leaves his results open to question.

The DIA continued:

Bekhterev's original objective was to demonstrate that telepathy between man and animals was mediated by some form of electromagnetic radiation (EMR), but by 1937, he and other Soviet parapsychologists had concluded that no known form of EMR was the carrier of thought transmission. The EMR theory of information transfer is still unresolved by the Soviets, but is still the major basis underlying much of their research.

Three decades after Bekheterev's original research, the Soviets were still working hard to make advances in this intriguing area.

In 1962 B. S. Kazhinskiy advanced the theory that animals are capable of visual and aural perception and reflex understanding of the behaviour of other animals or humans. He postulated that this ability resulted from the capacity of one animal to detect (via its nervous system), analyse, and synthesise signal-stimuli given off by another animal. According to Kazhinskiy, the signals were transmitted in the form of a "bioradiational sight ray" and analysed by the percipient animal as a result of its Pavlovian conditioning. The term "bioradiational rays" is still used by some Soviet and Czech parapsychologists to refer to focusing and concentration of biological energy by the brain and the optical neural channels.

If Kazhinskiy's research into visual and aural perception was, and still is, considered valid, then it offers the possibility that the entire animal kingdom of our planet may somehow have the ability to utilize highly advanced mental tools that, largely, elude human beings.

The 1975 DIA paper next turns its attention to then contemporary research undertaken by the Soviets.

Present day Soviet and Czech parapsychology research with animals is devoted almost exclusively to investigation of sources of biological energy involved in physiological processes, the interactions of such energy with external fields, and the effects of externally generated fields on animal physiology. Reference to telepathy in the sense of communications by transmission of total, conceptual, mental formulations is seldom made.

Believing that they were on the verge of a major breakthrough, the Soviets channeled much of their effort into a project that was being undertaken at a major Russian university.

A significant advance toward identification of the EMR source of biological energy transfer was gained from recent research conducted at the University of Novosibirsk. Scientists there investigated the release of energy during cell division and during cellular damage and repair resulting from viral infection or toxic chemicals. In over 5000 experiments with cell cultures and animal organs it was shown that damaged cells radiated some form of energy and that the energy released was capable of causing damage in adjacent control preparations of organs or cells. Further investigation revealed that a uniform pattern, code, or rhythm of radiation was emitted by normal cells. This pattern was disturbed when cellular damage occurred, becoming quite irregular. It was also found that the patterns were transmitted from experimental to control preparations only when the cells or organs were cultured in quartz containers. Since quartz transmits ultraviolet (UV) radiation and standard laboratory glassware does not, the Soviets concluded that UV radiation mediated cellular information transfer. The researchers subsequently correlated given irregularities of emission with specific diseases and are now attempting to develop techniques for diagnosis and therapy by monitoring and altering cellular radiation codes.

The DIA also learned that two decades of research undertaken in Czechoslovakia had led to some startling results on "energy transfer" between biological tissue samples.

Czechoslovakian research on energy transfer between animal muscle preparations from animals to man, and from man to man, has also demonstrated EMR as the vehicle of biological energy transfer. In experiments conducted between 1948 and 1968 at the Okres Institute of Public Health, Kutna Hora, Czechoslovakia, Dr. Jiri Bradna demonstrated contactless transfer (myotransfer) of stimuli between frog neuromuscular preparations. Bradna placed identical preparations side by side; stimulation of one preparation with electric pulses at frequencies between 10 and 30 pulses per second caused contraction and a recorded electromyographic response in the other. In other experiments, stimulation of muscle preparations influenced the oscillations of a pendulum and increased the muscle tension of a human subject. Bradna obtained objective proof that energy in the very high frequency (vhf) range mediated the stimulus transmission. He also demonstrated that myotransfer could be blocked with ferrous metal filters and aluminium, could be deformed with magnets, ferrites and other conductors, could be reflected and transmitted over waveguides, and shielded with grids. Bradna concluded that primary perceptual and informational pathways between animals are based on metabolic processes at the macromolecular level and that the magnitude of energy transfer depends on muscular adenosine triphosphate (ATP) energy release.

Of particular interest to the DIA was the research of Dr. Bradna that bore on the potential for altering or influencing human behavior.

Bradna has reported successful application of myotransfer in physiotherapy. It has been found to be effective for both indi-

viduals and groups. In the latter case, the summation of stimuli has been shown to enhance the neuromuscular responses of
individuals within the group. Bradna feels that such stimuli influence the herd of animals and may also be a factor in altering
human behavior under conditions of isolation or overcrowding.

Declassified files of the DIA show that Soviet scientists postulated numerous theories to try to explain extrasensory perception
and psychic phenomena in animals. According to the DIA, a Dr.
Y. A. Kholodov had

investigated the effects of a constant magnetic field (CMF) on
rabbits. Whole-body exposures to fields between 30 and 2000
oersteds resulted in nonspecific exchanges in the electroencephalogram but no other directly measurable physiological
responses. Kholodov showed that weak magnetic as well as
other externally generated radiation fields have a direct effect
on nerve tissue, and for this reason he feels that natural and
artificial fields in man's environment may have an influence on
health and behavior via the nervous system and the hypothalamus. Kholodov's research is representative of current Soviet
efforts to explain paranormal phenomena on the basis of
known physical and biological parameters.

Conversely, another Soviet scientist, A. S. Presman, felt that biological energy and information exchange between living organisms
was the result of electromagnetic field (EMF) interactions between
individuals or between the individual and the environment.

Presman and other Soviet scientists have recorded EMF's from
man, frogs, and insects of various species at ranges from several centimeters to several meters from the body surface. The
frequencies of the EMF's were found to correspond to various
biorhythms of organs, rhythms of movement and acoustic sig-

nals and bioelectric rhythms. Presman thinks that in groups of animals, electromagnetic oscillations are synchronized by frequency matching and that the cumulative intensity may grow in proportion to the square of the number of individuals. Such cumulative emission is also thought to be possible as the result of synchronization of the emissions of many cells in animals in a highly excited state. Presman, like Kholodov, feels that the effects of sub-threshold stimuli are mediated through the hypothalamic region of the midbrain. The hypothalamus regulates diverse physiological processes in the organism (pulse, body temperature, oxygen consumption, carbon dioxide liberation, urine volume, urine nitrogen concentration, etc.) and these are the functions most commonly disturbed by changes in EMF's.

Presman also speculated on the reason for the apparent widespread telepathic abilities in animals versus the lack of such abilities in human beings.

Presman believes that electromagnetic signalling is universal between animals, but not between humans who may have lost the capability for such communication as a result of evolution and the development of verbal and artificial communication channels. He does not rule out the possibility that "spontaneous telepathy" may occasionally occur, but regards such occurrences as rare cases of atavism. Consequently, he regards man as the least suitable animal for studying electromagnetic communication.

The DIA also noted that, by 1975, Soviet research into ESP in animals had been modified and now encompassed a whole new range of disciplines and terminology.

It is important that the increased degree of sophistication which has occurred in Soviet ESP or telepathy research since

1960 be understood. At present the terms "ESP" and "telepathy" are seldom used. It is possible that the newer terms "biocommunication" and "psychotronics" will vanish in the near future only to be replaced by conventional high-energy physics terminology, or term such as "interpersonal subconscious reactions" or "mention" forces. In any event, the classical ESP experiments with animals are no longer of interest in the USSR. The typical Vasilev experimentation from 1920 to 1955 has been replaced with sophisticated research protocols which study complex interactions between man, animals and plants.

The file also addresses an intriguing Soviet naval experiment that occurred in the mid-1950s and that, at least fifteen years later, was still classified by Soviet authorities. Despite the secrecy surrounding the event, the DIA gleaned enough data to suggest that Soviet scientists were researching what happens at the moment of death, the nature of death, and the possibility of an after-life in animals.

Dr. Pavel Naumov, conducted animal biocommunication studies between a submerged Soviet Navy submarine and a shore research station: these tests involved a mother rabbit and her newborn litter and occurred around 1956, three years prior to the USS Nautilus disclosure. [Note from the authors: this is a reference to an ESP study allegedly undertaken by the U.S. Navy in 1960.] According to Naumov, Soviet scientists placed the baby rabbits aboard the submarine. They kept the mother rabbit in a laboratory on shore where they implanted electrodes (EEG?) in her brain. When the submarine was submerged, assistants killed the rabbits one by one. At each precise moment of death, the mother rabbit's brain produced detectable and recordable reactions. As late as 1970 the precise protocol and results of this test described by Naumov were believed to be classified. Many examples can be found in Soviet literature with dogs, bears, birds, insects and fish in conjunction with basic psychotronic research. The Pavlov Institute in Moscow may have been involved in animal telepathy until 1970.

Did the Soviet Navy's experiments of 1956 stumble upon the secrets of life after death in the animal kingdom? That the mother rabbit's brain produced, detected, and recorded reactions at the precise moment that her offspring were killed is both eye-opening and not a little disturbing. One is also prompted to ask, did the results of this experiment indicate the existence of some form of soul in the animal world? We know nothing more as the Soviets immediately and effectively classified their findings.

In the light of these DIA documents, it is conceivable that the U.S. military and intelligence communities were looking to determine if animals could possibly play a viable role in the world of espionage.

Almost thirty years have now passed since the Defence Intelligence Agency began its research into the world of ESP in animals. Do those studies continue? Are our animal friends capable of mind-to-mind contact of a type that we can only dream of? Has the existence of an animal-based soul been determined? Or has the whole matter been disregarded by American intelligence and filed away as one of the more bizarre aspects of its Cold War research and investigations? To date, those are questions that we cannot answer fully. However, even if further files on this fascinating subject do not ultimately surface, the DIA records in our possession thus far provide a unique glimpse into a strange—and, at times, almost magical—world that, until now, none would ever have dreamed would have attracted the attention of U.S. espionage agents and Pentagon generals.

Although not paranormal in nature, the following two accounts are certainly strange enough to merit our consideration and detail the way in which the worlds of spying and the animal kingdom have occasionally crossed paths.

Information has come to light showing that, in the 1970s, the British Security Service MI5, the equivalent of the USA's Federal Bureau of Investigation, gave serious thought to using a team of highly trained gerbils to uncover terrorists and spies. The details of the plan were disclosed in 2001 by Sir Stephen Lander, director-general of the Security Service, who was speaking at a conference at the London-based Public Record Office.

The proposed operation was largely modeled on the proven ability of gerbils to locate an otherwise undetectable increase in adrenaline levels in the scent of human sweat. According to Lander, the Israelis were the first to put the idea into practice: at security checkpoints at Tel Aviv Airport, a strategically placed fan would direct the scent of a suspect's sweat toward a cage of the gerbils.

In a scenario more than reminiscent of Pavlov's dogs, the gerbils were trained to activate a lever if they detected an increased adrenaline level in the subject, receiving food as a reward. However, according to Sir Stephen Lander, the system was never actively put into practice by MI5 — primarily because the Israelis were forced to abandon the idea after they determined that the gerbils were unable to differentiate between terrorists and passengers who were scared of flying. Sir Stephen also revealed that MI5 archives contained a whole volume on this particularly ingenious idea, which was, he added, based on 1970s research undertaken initially by the Royal Canadian Mounted Police.[1]

For the animal espionage story to beat all others, and one that sounds straight out of the world of science fiction, we have to turn our attention to the Central Intelligence Agency. Declassified memoranda from the CIA's Directorate of Science and Technology reveal that in the 1960s the Agency attempted to probe the darkest secrets of the Kremlin by turning cats into what could arguably be termed walking bugging machines. In one particular experiment conducted at the height of the Cold War, a cat—dubbed Acoustic Kitty—was wired up for use as a biological eavesdropping machine. CIA scientists, the files make clear, were hoping that the animal—

which was surgically altered to accommodate transmitting and control devices—would be able to listen to secret conversations from such locations as park benches and dustbins.

According to Victor Marchetti, a former CIA officer, "They slit the cat open, put batteries in him, wired him up. The tail was used as an antenna. They made a monstrosity. They tested him and tested him. They found he would walk off the job when he got hungry, so they put another wire in to override that." Not only that, but the operation was a financial disaster too, costing the American taxpayer more than $10 million. Then the real disaster occurred, says Marchetti. "They took it out to a park and put him out of the van, and a taxi comes and runs him over. There they were, sitting in the van with all those dials, and the cat was dead." [2]

Ten

MIND WARS

In 1977, Dr. Kenneth A. Kress, an engineer with the CIA's Office of Technical Services, prepared a document called "Parapsychology in Intelligence" for the Agency. This details the Agency's involvement in what could arguably be termed "psychic spying" and remained exempt from disclosure for nearly twenty years.

Among other highlights, the document demonstrates that the American government's interest in aspects of paranormal phenomena dates back to the Second World War. The document also reveals that the CIA researched the intelligence-gathering value of extrasensory perception (ESP) as far back as 1961 and perhaps even earlier. It also makes clear that the Agency had some very real successes in the field and the way in which the military and other branches of the intelligence community became embroiled in the controversy.

The document begins by explaining the nature of the CIA's investigations of parapsychology, the potentials and pitfalls that the Agency found when it immersed itself in the murky world of psychic phenomena and much more. Most notably, the report states, "Tantalizing but incomplete data have been generated by CIA-

The second possibility is mentioned only because the experiment was not controlled to discount the possibility that ███ could talk to other people.

SG1J

██████ commented that he was seeing a lot of things this second day that he hadn't seen the previous day. In fact, he mentioned seeing several landmark-type objects that simply did not exist at URDF-3. One explanation of this discrepancy could be that if he mentioned enough specific objects, he would surely hit on one object that is actually present. This could explain the inconsistency between:

> 1) his most positive evidence of the experiment - a
>   sketch of a rail-mounted gantry crane, and
> 2) the large number of objects he sees that, in
>   reality, are simply not present at URDF-3.

SG1J

This discrepancy between what ███ sees and what is really there certainly would make it difficult for the eventual user of his remote-viewing data since he would not know how to differentiate the fact from the fiction. At this SG1J stage of the experiment, the data is inconclusive to validate ██████ capability of remote viewing.

SG1J

██████ was shown a sketch of a perspective of the Operations Area at URDF-3 on the third day and was told that this was a sketch of the actual target. ██████ said he recognized the area but claimed that only one of the four headframes was present now. That was wrong, but his most damaging statements had to do with his interpretation of Building 1 (the underground building) at URDF-3. With the sketch as a reference, he "saw" the four main surface protrusions of Building 1 as four separate above-ground buildings sitting atop a concrete apron. He was asked specifically whether these four buildings he saw might really be the surface elements of an underground building. He failed either to pick up the lead or to remotely view correctly because he said, "No, that's a concrete apron, and there's nothing subterranean right in that particular area." This statement was his most negative evidence yet and tends to discredit his ability to remotely view URDF-3.

An extract from one of the CIA's many files on psychic spying from the early 1970s.

sponsored research. These data show, among other things, that on occasion unexplained results of genuine intelligence significance occur."

The CIA's prime interest in parapsychology was for intelligence collection. Stressing that he himself was involved with many aspects of such investigations, Kress added that the document was not aimed at historical completeness but at recording both interesting and possibly useful data and opinions for those who might have to evaluate intelligence-related aspects of parapsychology. Kress continues:

The Agency took the initiative by sponsoring serious parapsychological research, but circumstances, biases, and fear of ridicule prevented CIA from completing a scientific investigation of parapsychology and its relevance to national security. During this research period, CIA was buffeted with investigations concerning illegalities and improprieties of all sorts. This situation, perhaps properly so, raised the sensitivity of CIA's involvement in unusual activities. The "Proxmire Effect," where the fear that certain Government research contracts would be claimed to be ill-founded and held up for scorn, was another factor precluding CIA from sensitive areas of research.

Reactions to parapsychology are generally extremely positive or negative, with with few in between. As Kress explained, parapsychological data, almost by definition, are elusive and unexplained. When one adds a history replete with proven frauds, many people instantly reject the subject, saying, in effect, "I would not believe this even if it were true." Others, said Kress, who must have had personal "conversion" experiences, tend to be equally convinced that one unexplained success establishes a phenomenon. These prejudices, he noted, tend to make it difficult to evaluate parapsychology both carefully and scientifically.

Indeed, the documentation carefully asserted that the CIA was not saying that parapsychology was a proven intelligence tool. Rather, the assertion was that the evaluation was not yet complete and more research was needed, and that attention was being confined to psychokinesis and remote viewing. Psychokinesis is the purported ability of a person to interact with a machine or other object by unexplained means. Remote viewing is akin to clairvoyance in that a person claims to sense information about a site or person removed from a known sensory link.

U.S. government interest in parapsychology apparently dates back decades and extended to the highest levels of the Department of Defense.

Anecdotal reports of extrasensory perception (ESP) capabilities have reached U.S. national security agencies at least since World War II, when Hitler was said to rely on astrologers and seers. Suggestions for military applications of ESP continued to be received after World War II. For example, in 1952 the Department of Defense was lectured on the possible usefulness of extrasensory perception in psychological warfare. Over the years, reports continued to accumulate. In 1961, the reports induced one of the earliest U.S. government parapsychology investigations when the chief of CIA's Office of Technical Service (then the Technical Services Division) became interested in the claims of ESP. Technical project officers soon contacted Stephen I. Abrams, the Director of the Parapsychological Laboratory, Oxford University, England. Under the auspices of Project ULTRA, Abrams prepared a review article which claimed ESP was demonstrated but not understood or controllable. The report was read with interest but produced no further action for another decade.

Two laser physicists, Dr. Russell Targ and Dr. Harold E. Puthoff, reawakened CIA research in parapsychology. Targ, said the report, had been interested in parapsychology for most of his adult life. As an experimentalist, he was interested in scientific observations of parapsychology. Puthoff became interested in the field in the early 1970s. He was a theoretician who was exploring new fields of research after extensive work in quantum electronics.

In April of 1972, Targ met with CIA personnel from the Office of Strategic Intelligence (OSI) specifically to discuss paranormal phenomena. He revealed that he had contacts with people who purported to have both viewed and documented a number of Soviet investigations of psychokinesis.

Films of Soviets moving inanimate objects by "mental powers" were made available to analysts from OSI. They, in turn, contacted personnel from the Office of Research and Development (ORD) and OTS. An ORD Project Officer then visited Targ who had recently joined the Stanford Research Institute (SRI). Targ proposed that some psychokinetic verification investigations could be done at SRI in conjunction with Puthoff.

These proposals were quickly followed by a laboratory demonstration after Targ and Puthoff located a man who apparently had psychokinetic abilities. He was taken on a surprise visit to a superconducting, shielded magnetometer being used in high-energy-particle experiments involving quarks by Dr. A. Hebbard of the Stanford University Physics Department. The quark experiment required that the magnetometer be as well shielded as technology would allow.

But when the man focused his attention on the interior of the magnetometer, the output signal was visibly disturbed, indicating a change in the internal magnetic field. Several other correlations of his mental efforts with signal variations were observed. The report points out that these variations were never seen before or after the visit. The event was summarized and transmitted to the Agency in the form of a letter to an OSI analyst and as discussions with OTS and ORD officers. That led the CIA to address parapsychology with renewed vigor.

The Office of Technical Services took the first action. With the approval of the same manager who supported the ESP studies a decade previously, an OTS project officer contracted for a demonstration with the previously mentioned man for a few days in August, 1972. During this demonstration, the subject was asked to describe objects hidden out of sight by the CIA personnel. The subject did well. The descriptions were so startlingly accurate that the OTD and ORD representatives suggested that the work be continued and expanded. The same Director of OTS reviewed the data, approved another $2,500 work order, and encouraged the development of a more complete research plan.

Interestingly, the initial studies brought forward a whole range of seemingly paranormal skills on the part of the test subjects. Concerns were expressed about the value of the studies, however.

The Office of Technical Services funded a $50,000 expanded effort in parapsychology. The expanded investigation included tests of several abilities of both the original subject and a new one. Curious data began to appear; the paranormal abilities seemed individualistic. For example, one subject, by mental effort, apparently caused an increase in the temperature measured by a thermistor; the action could not be duplicated by the second subject. The second subject was able to reproduce, with impressive accuracy, information inside sealed envelopes. Under identical conditions, the first subject could reproduce nothing. Perhaps even more disturbing, repeating the same experiment with the same subject did not yield consistent results. I began to have serious feelings of being involved with a fraud.

Nevertheless, official Agency interest in parapsychology continued. But some within the CIA considered the whole subject too sensitive and potentially embarrassing to merit large-scale research.

Approximately halfway through this project, the SRI contractors were invited to review their results. After careful consideration of the security and sensitivity factors, the results were shared and discussed with selected Agency personnel during that and subsequent meetings. In February, 1973, the most recent data were reviewed; thereafter, several ORD officers showed definite interest in contributing their own expertise and office funding.

The possibility of a joint OTS/ORD program continued to develop. The Office of Research and Development sent new Project Officers to SRI during February, 1973, and the reports which were brought back convinced ORD to become involved. Interest was translated into action when ORD requested an increase in the scope of the effort and transferred funds to OTS. About this time, a third sensitive subject, Pat Price, became available at SRI, and the remote viewing experiments in which a subject describes his impressions of remote objects or locations began in earnest. The possibility that such useful abilities were real motivated all concerned to move ahead quickly.

The contract required additional management review before it could be continued or its scope increased. The initial review went from OTS and ORD to Mr. William Colby, then the DDO. On 24 April, Mr. Colby decided that the Executive Management Committee should pass judgment on this potentially sensitive project. By the middle of May, 1973, the approval request went through the Management Committee. An approval memorandum was written for the signature of the DCI, then Dr. James Schlesinger. Mr. Colby took the memorandum to the DCI a few days later. I was soon told not to increase the scope of the project and not to anticipate any follow-on in this area. The project was too sensitive and potentially embarrassing. It should be tabled. It is interesting to note that OTS was then being investigated for involvement in the Watergate affair, and that in May, 1973, the DCI issued a memorandum to all CIA employees requesting the reporting of any activities that may have been illegal and improper. As Project Officer, clearly my sense of timing had not been guided by useful paranormal abilities!

Despite this setback, CIA involvement—albeit not strictly at an official level—continued with the Stanford Research Institute and generated potentially important results for U.S. national security, specifically with respect to the protection of secure governmental facilities.

During the summer of 1973, SRI continued working informally with an OSI officer on a remote viewing experiment which eventually stimulated more CIA-sponsored investigations of parapsychology. The target was a vacation property in the eastern United States. The experiment began with the passing of nothing more than the geographic coordinates of the vacation property to the SRI physicists who, in turn, passed them to the two subjects, one of whom was Pat Price. No maps were permitted, and the subjects were asked to give an immediate response of what they remotely viewed at these coordinates. The subject came back with descriptions which were apparent misses. They both talked about a military-like facility. Nevertheless, a striking correlation of the two independent descriptions was noted. The correlation caused the OSI officer to drive to the site and investigate in more detail.

To the surprise of the OSI officer, Price had discovered a sensitive government installation that belonged to the National Security Agency a few miles from the vacation property. This discovery led to

Price's being asked to provide information concerning the interior workings of this site. The evaluation of Price's results was, as usual, mixed.

Pat Price, who had no military or intelligence background, provided a list of project titles associated with current and past activities including one of extreme sensitivity. Also, the codename of the site was provided. Other information concerning the physical layout of the site was accurate. Some information, such as the names of the people at the site, proved incorrect. These experiments took several months to be analyzed and reviewed within the Agency.

Price's ability to provide code names, accurate data on the layout of the installation, and even activities of extreme sensitivity, however, proved to be a major turning point for the project.

Now Mr. Colby was DCI, and the new directors of OTS and ORD were favorably impressed by the data. In the fall of 1973, a Statement of Work was outlined, and SRI was asked to propose another program. A jointly funded ORD and OTS program was begun in February, 1974. The author again was the Project Officer. The project proceeded on the premise that the phenomena existed; the objective was to develop and utilize them.

The ORD funds were devoted to basic studies such as the identification of measurable physiological or psychological characteristics of psychic individuals, and the establishment of experimental protocols for validating paranormal abilities. The OTS funds were to evaluate the operational utility of psychic subjects without regard to the detailed understanding of paranormal functioning. If the paranormal functioning was sufficiently reproducible, we were confident applications would be found.

Before long, however, problems surfaced. The tasks in the basic research area proved to be far more extensive than both time and available funding would allow. The contractors thought that a compromise should be reached by doing all of the tasks with less completeness. Meanwhile the ORD scientists argued vigorously that with such a controversial and emotive subject fewer but far more rigorous results would be of greater and more significant value.

And as the document elaborated, the rigor of the research became a serious issue between the ORD project officers and SRI, with Kress generally taking a position between the righteousness of the contractor and the indignation of the researchers. As an example of the kinds of disputes that developed over the basic research, consider the evaluation of the significance of data from the "ESP teaching machine" experiments. This machine

was a four-state electronic random number generator used to test for paranormal abilities. SRI claimed the machine randomly cycled through four states, and the subject indicates the current machine state by pressing a button. The state of the machine and the subject's choice were recorded for later analysis. A subject "guessing" should, on the average, be correct 25 percent of the time. SRI had a subject who averaged a statistically very significant 29 percent for more than 2,500 trials.

I requested a review of the experiment and analysis, and two ORD officers quickly and skeptically responded. They first argued that the ESP machine was possibly not random. They further argued the subjects probably learned the nonrandom machine patterns and thereby produced higher scores. During this review, it was noted that whether the machine was random or not, the data taken during the experiment could be analyzed to determine actual machine statistics. The machine randomness was then unimportant, because the subject's performance could then be compared with actual machine performance. The ORD Project Officers, however, did not believe it would be worth the effort to do the extra analysis of the actual data.

I disagreed. I had the Office of Joint Computer Services redo the data analysis. The conclusion was that during the experiment "no evidence of nonrandomness was discovered" and there was "no solid reason *how* he was able to be so successful." I further ordered the subject retested. He averaged more than 28 percent during another 2,500 trials. This information was given in written and oral form to the ORD Project Officers, who maintained there must be yet another flaw in the experiment or analysis, but it was not worth finding. Because of more pressing demands, the issue could not be pursued to a more definite conclusion.

This situation was complicated when the directorships of both the ORD and the OTS changed hands at this time and potential disarray was looming. Since neither director had any background or experience in paranormal research, the new director of ORD reviewed the parapsychology project and subsequently expressed reservations. Kress personally requested a meeting in which the director stated that while he could not accept the reality of paranormal functioning, he understood his own bias and could simply follow the advice of his staff.

The ORD Project Officers were feeling their own frustrations and uncertainties concerning the work and now had to face this unusual kind of skepticism of their new Director. The skepticism about the believability of the phenomenon and quality of the basic research adversely affected the opinions of many people in OTS. Support for the project was vanishing rapidly.

As a result of the mounting pressures that faced the team, the first real intelligence-collection operation using parapsychology as the primary tool was attempted on a facility in the Soviet Union.

The target was the Semipalatinsk Unidentified Research and Development Facility-3 (URDF-3, formerly known as PNUTS). The experimental collection would use our best subject, Pat Price. From experience it was obvious that Price produced bad data as well as good. Borrowing from classical communications theory concepts, this "noisy channel" of information could nevertheless be useful if it were characterized. An elaborate protocol was designed which would accomplish two characterization measurements. First, we needed assurance the channel was collecting useful data. I reviewed the photos of URDF-3 and chose two features which, if Price described them, would show the channel at least partially working. Referring to Figure 1a, these features were the tall crane and the four structures resembling oil well derricks.

The CIA personnel tasked with examining the potential usefulness of parapsychology agreed that if Price accurately described the crane and derricks, the Agency would be prepared to have him sign a secrecy agreement, making him witting, and collect more relevant intelligence details. Secondly, after a working channel was thus established, a signal-to-noise or quality characterization was required. This would be accomplished by periodic tests of the channel—that is, periodically Price would be asked to describe features of URDF-3 that were known. The accuracy of these descriptions would be used to estimate the quality of the data that the CIA had no obvious way of verifying.

Later, at SRI, Price was briefed by Targ and Puthoff. Since Targ and Puthoff presumably knew nothing about URDF-3, this protocol guarded against cueing and/or telepathy. Initially Price was given only the geographic coordinates, a world atlas map marked with the approximate location of URDF-3, and told it was a Soviet RD&E test site. Overnight, he produced the drawing on the bottom right of Figure 1b. Price further mentioned that this was a "damned big crane" because he saw a person walk by and he only came up to the axles on the wheels. This performance caught my attention; but with two more days of work, we never heard about the derricks. Eventually, a decision was needed. Because the crane was so impressive, my branch chief and I decided the derricks description requirement should be relaxed and we should continue.

When the decision was made to make Price witting, I decided to test him. My branch chief and I sat in a conference room while Targ and Puthoff brought a smiling Pat Price into the room. I was introduced as the sponsor, and I immediately asked Price if he knew me. Yes. Name? Ken Kress. Occupation? Works for CIA.

Since Price was then a covert employee, noted Kress, this response had some significant meaning. After having Price sign a secrecy agreement, and after some discussions, Kress confronted him again and rolled out a large version of a figure and asked if he had viewed this site. When Price replied in the affirmative, Kress asked why he had not seen the four derricks. Price answered that he would check.

Price closed his eyes, put on his glasses (he "sees" better that way) and in a few seconds answered: "I didn't see them because they are not there any more." Since my data were three or four months old, there was no rejoinder to the implied accusation that my data were not good. We proceeded and completed a voluminous data package.

In a few weeks, the latest URDF-3 reconnaissance was checked. Two derricks were partially disassembled, but basically all four were visible. In general, most of Price's data were wrong or could not be evaluated. He did, nevertheless, produce some amazing descriptions, like buildings then under construction, spherical tank sections, and the crane in Figure 1b. Two analysts, a photo interpreter at IAS and a nuclear analyst at Los Alamos Scientific Laboratories agreed that Price's description of the crane was accurate; the nuclear analyst wrote that "one: he, the subject, actually saw it through remote viewing, or two: he was informed what to draw by someone knowledgeable of URDF-3." But, again, since there was so much bad information mixed in with the good, the overall result was not considered useful. As proof of remote viewing, the data are at best inconclusive. The ORD officers concluded that since there were no control experiments to compare with, the data were nothing but lucky guessing.

The extent to which such phenomena could be considered real, the issue of lucky guessing by the participant, and the general skepticism that permeated the CIA led even Kress to wonder about the validity of the operation.

I began to doubt my own objectivity in evaluating the significance of paranormal abilities to intelligence collection. It was clear that the SRI contractors were claiming success while ORD advisors were saying the experiments were not meaningful because of poor experimental design. As a check on myself, I asked for a critique of the investigation from a disinterested consultant, a theoretical physicist with broad intellectual background. His first task was to evaluate the field of parapsychology without knowledge of the CIA data. After he had completed this critique, I asked him to acquaint himself with the CIA data and then to reassess the field. The first investigation produced genuine interest in paranormal functioning as a valid research area. After being acquainted with CIA data, his conclusion was, "a large body of reliable experimental evidence points to the inescapable conclusion that extrasensory perception does exist as a real phenomenon, albeit characterized by rarity and lack of reliability." This judgment by a competent scien-

tist gave impetus to continue serious inquiry into parapsychology.

As a result of the general skepticism and mixed results of the various operational experiments, however, a final challenge was issued
by the OTS management to do something of genuine operational
significance. Price was chosen, and suggestions were solicited, and
acted upon, from personnel in both OTS and the Deputy Directorate of Operations.

The interiors of two foreign embassies were known to the audio
teams who had made entries several years previously. Price
was to visit these embassies by his remote viewing capability,
locate the code rooms, and come up with information that
might allow a member of the audio team to determine whether
Price was likely to be of operational use in subsequent operations. Price was given operationally acceptable data such as
the exterior photographs and the geographical coordinates of
the embassies.

In both cases, Price correctly located the code rooms and produced copious data, including the correct location of interior doors
and colors of marble stairs and fireplaces. As usual, however, much
was also vague and incorrect. Nevertheless, the officer involved
concluded that this technique—whatever it was—offered definite
operational possibilities.

This result was reviewed within OTS and the DDO, and various
suggestions for potential follow-on activities were formulated.
This package of requirements, plus the final results of the current contract, were reviewed at several meetings within OTS
and ORD. The results of those meetings are as follows:

1. According to the ORD Project Officers, the research was
not productive or even competent; therefore, research support

to SRI was dropped. The Director of OTS felt the OTS charter would not support research; therefore, all Agency funding in paranormal research stopped.

2. Because of the mixed results, the operational utility of the capability was considered questionable but deserved further testing.

3. To achieve better security, all the operations-oriented testing with the contractor was stopped, and a personal services contract with Price was started.

4. Since I was judged to be a positively biased advocate of paranormal functioning, the testing and evaluation of Price would be transferred to a more pragmatic OTS operations psychologist.

The year 1974 saw a notable advance made with respect to the targeting of potentially hostile nations. The advance would be marred by tragedy, however. The OTS psychologist began his new responsibilities and chose to complete an unfinished DDO requirement.

The origin of the requirement went back to the fall of 1974 when several OTS engineers became aware of the parapsychology project in OTS and had volunteered to attempt remote viewing. They passed initial remote viewing tests at SRI with some apparent successes. To test these OTS insiders further, I chose a suggested requirement to obtain information about a Libyan site described only by its geographic coordinates. The OTS engineers described a new construction which could be an SA-5 missile training site. The Libyan Desk officer was immediately impressed. He then revealed to me that an agent had reported essentially the same story. More coordinates were quickly furnished but were put aside by me.

The second set of Libyan geographic coordinates was passed by the OTS psychologist to Price. A report describing a guerrilla training site was quickly returned. It contained a map-like drawing of the complex. Price described a related underwater sabotage training facility site several hundred kilometers away on the sea coast. This information was passed to the Libyan Desk. Some data were evaluated immediately, some were evaluated only after ordering special reconnaissance. The underwater sabotage training facility description was similar to a collateral agent's report. The Libyan Desk officer quickly escalated the requirement to what was going on inside those buildings, the plans and intentions, etc. The second requirements list was passed to Pat Price. Price died of a heart attack a few days later, and the program stopped. There have been no further CIA-sponsored intelligence collection tests.

While Price's death was a terrible shock, some also suspect it may have been sinister too. One who suspects this is British remote-viewing researcher Tim Rifat. "It was alleged at the time that the Soviets poisoned Price," says Rifat. "It would have been a top priority for the KGB to eliminate Price as his phenomenal remote-viewing abilities would have posed a significant danger to the USSR's paranormal warfare buildup. He may also have been the victim of an elite group of Russian psi-warriors trained to remotely kill enemies of the Soviet Union."[1]

While this may sound extreme, paranormal research in the former Soviet Union at the time in question *did* include studies designed to affect heart rhythms in human beings (see the next chapter). Was Pat Price the victim of a Soviet-sponsored "mind murder" or was this simply one of life's tragedies? We will probably never know.

In the post-1974 era, according to the available documentation at least, CIA involvement in this field was minimal, but studies pertaining to Soviet research into parapsychology were undertaken and reached the office of CIA director and future U.S. president George Bush. Nevertheless, interest appeared to be waning.

Since July, 1975, there has been only modest CIA and Intelligence Community Staff interest in parapsychology. The Office of Scientific Intelligence completed a study about Soviet military and KGB applied parapsychology. During November of 1976, Director George Bush became aware that official Soviets were visiting and questioning Puthoff and Targ at SRI about their work in parapsychology. Mr. Bush requested and received a briefing on CIA's investigations into parapsychology. Before there was any official reaction, he left the Agency. Various intelligence community groups, such as the Human Resources Subcommittee on R&D, have exhaustively reviewed parapsychology in CIA, DOD, and the open research, but have failed to conclude whether parapsychology is or is not a worthwhile area for further investigation. Several proposals from SRI and other contractors were received by CIA but none were accepted. There are no current plans for CIA to fund parapsychology investigations.

In a remarkable postscript, the paper revealed that the CIA was not the only arm of the U.S. intelligence community with an interest in determining if psychic phenomena could be a useful tool for espionage.

At this point, I have traced the action and reaction of various elements of CIA to what is certainly an unconventional and highly controversial subject. Also of interest are the concurrent reactions of other agencies to parapsychology. In August, 1973, parapsychology was discussed with several members of DIA. The DIA people were basically interested in the Soviet activities in this area, and expressed considerable interest in our own fledgling results. Numerous meetings have occurred during the past several years. DIA remains interested on a low priority basis.

The Defense Intelligence Agency's findings on parapsychology make for astounding reading (see the next chapter). The document continues and reveals that a fascinating discovery had been made by U.S. Army forces fighting in the Vietnam War.

The Army Materiel Command learned of CIA interest in the paranormal. We discovered the Army interest was generated by data which emerged from Vietnam. Apparently certain individuals called point men, who led patrols into hostile territory, had far fewer casualties from booby traps and ambushes than the average. These point men, needless to say, had a loyal following of men and, in general, greatly helped the morale of their troops under a brutal, stressful situation. The Army gave extensive physical and psychological tests to a group of unusually successful point men and came to no conclusion other than perhaps that paranormal capabilities may be the explanation! The Army was most interested in CIA results and wanted to stay closely informed. After a few more follow-up meetings, the Army Materiel Command was never heard from again.

The reaction to CIA interest in this field was less favorable elsewhere within U.S. intelligence, however.

The Defense Advanced Research Projects Agency (DARPA) reported that they had not only a showing of interest but a hostile response as well to the subject area. At one time, we felt we had the strong interest of some people at DARPA to discuss our data. The SRI contractors and I went to a briefing where we had a several-hour confrontation with an assemblage of hostile DARPA people who had been convened especially to debunk our results. After a long, inconclusive, emotional discussion, we left. Contacts with DARPA stopped for several years.

In addition to the DIA, the Army, and the Defense Advanced Research Projects Agency, both the Navy and the Air Force became players in the world of the paranormal.

The Navy reviewed part of the work and became interested. Some groups developed strong interest, and minor funding was provided to SRI by Navy to replicate one of SRI's earlier experiments under more controlled conditions. The experiment was replicated. Then the Navy asked SRI to repeat the same experiment under different conditions. An effect was observed, but it was not the same as the previous observations. About this same time, the Navy became very concerned about this research being "mind warfare"–related. Funding was stopped.

The active funding for parapsychology now has shifted to the Air Force's Foreign Technology Division with the addition of modest testing being completed by another group at DARPA. These investigations are not yet completed, but a second phase is funded by the Air Force. The Air Force project is attempting to evaluate whether signals and communications can be sent and received by paranormal functioning. Also aircraft and missile intelligence which can be verified is being gathered and evaluated. To date the results are more consistent than those seen during the CIA research, but still they are mixed. Some simple experiments seemed very impressive and conclusive. The more complex experiments are difficult to assess.

In closing, the document turns its attention to the way in which—by 1977—the media and the public had learned of aspects of U.S. government research into psychic phenomena and the benefits and hazards that this revelation offered the intelligence community.

In the non-government world an explosion of interest in unclassified parapsychology research occurred after the first publication of CIA-sponsored projects. Books have been written, prestigious professional societies have had sessions on parapsychology, and several national news reports have been broadcast and printed. Director Turner revealed publicly that CIA has had operational interest in parapsychology. The open publication of these investigations is generally healthy and helpful. It shows a reduction of associated emotionalism and bias. These publications will also stimulate other scientific investigations into parapsychology.

There is a less positive aspect to open interest and publications. Before adequate assessment was made by CIA and others, we may have allowed some important national security information out into the public domain. It is my opinion that, as it relates to intelligence, sufficient understanding and assessment of parapsychology has not been achieved. There are observations, such as the original magnetic experiments at Stanford University, the OSI remote viewing, the OTS–code room experiments, and others done for the Department of Defense, that defy explanation. Coincidence is not likely, and fraud has not been discovered. The implication of these data cannot be determined until the assessment is done.

If what the report says is true, then why is it that the collective phenomena remained so controversial and lacking in official government support?

This state of affairs occurs because of the elementary understanding of parapsychology and because of the peculiarities of the intelligence and military organizations which have attempted the assessments. There is no fundamental understanding of the mechanisms of paranormal functioning, and the reproducibility remains poor. The research and experiments have successfully demonstrated abilities but have not explained them nor made them reproducible. Past and current support of parapsychology comes from applications-oriented intelligence and military agencies. The people managing such agencies demand quick and relevant results. The intelligence and military agencies, therefore, press for results before there is sufficient experimental reproducibility or understanding of the physical mechanisms. Unless there is a major break-through in understanding, the situation is not likely to change as long as applications-oriented agencies are funding parapsy-chology. Agencies must commit long-term basic research funds and learn to confine attention to testing only abilities which at least appear reproducible enough to be used to augment other hard collection techniques (example: use parapsychology to help target hard intelligence collection techniques and deter-mine if the take is thereby increased). Parapsychology, like other technical issues, can then rise or fall on its merits and not stumble over bureaucratic charters and conjectures pro-posed by people who are irrevocably on one side or the other in the controversial area.

There ends the remarkable document. But to what extent—if in-deed any—has CIA interest and direct involvement in these partic-ularly controversial areas of intelligence-gathering continued and been expanded upon since 1977? In 1995, a CIA-sponsored report titled "An Evaluation of the Remote-Viewing Program—Research and Operational Applications" was produced by the American In-stitutes for Research. In essence, the report concluded that, from an intelligence-gathering perspective, remote viewing and related phe-nomena were largely useless. And there the matter rests—at least as far as the CIA is publicly concerned.

Not everyone agrees with that conclusion, however. "The CIA wanted a negative psi report and controlled the data access so that such a result would be a foregone conclusion," says W. Adam Man-delbaum, a former U.S. intelligence officer. "The AIR report was U.S.-intelligence-purchased disinformation intentionally formulated to misrepresent the true state of remote-viewing research, and the true operational utility of the phenomenon."[2]

Does the CIA continue to covertly investigate and utilize parapsychological phenomena for intelligence-gathering purposes? Or has the subject been dismissed from the minds of Agency personnel? Taking into account the intense secrecy and the hall of mirrors that surrounds all aspects of the CIA's work, one would almost have to be psychic to answer that question.

DST-1810S-202-78

DEFENSE INTELLIGENCE AGENCY

PARAPHYSICS R&D—WARSAW PACT (U)

PREPARED BY
U.S. AIR FORCE
AIR FORCE SYSTEMS COMMAND
FOREIGN TECHNOLOGY DIVISION

In 1978, the Defense Intelligence Agency was deeply involved in investigating the extent to which psychic research was being undertaken in the Soviet Union, as this report, "Paraphysics R&D—Warsaw Pact," makes clear.

Eleven

PSYCHIC SOVIETS

Three years after its report on extrasensory perception in animals was written, the Defense Intelligence Agency was still taking an interest in the powers of the mind. In 1978, the Foreign Technology Division (FTD) at Wright-Patterson Air Force Base, Ohio, prepared a document titled "Paraphysics R&D — Warsaw Pact" for the DIA. It provided up-to-date information on how the Soviets were looking at ESP and psychic phenomena as potential tools of warfare.

The lineage of the FTD can be traced back to the Technical Data Laboratory, established in 1942. During the Second World War, the laboratory evaluated captured German and Japanese documents, aircraft, and related equipment. After its formal inception in 1945, the FTD became the principal U.S. Air Force agency responsible for estimating the technological threat of potential adversaries as well as assessing the characteristics and performance of foreign aerospace weapons. Its mission was to acquire, collect, analyze, produce, and disseminate foreign aerospace scientific and technical (S&T) intelligence. The FTD was also required to conduct an integrated analysis program to meet the requirements of the U.S. Air Force Systems Command (AFSC), the AF Assistant Chief of Staff, Intelligence, and the Defense Intelligence Agency.

In its report to the DIA, the FTD defined paraphysics as "the investigation of unusual (paranormal) mental functioning" and noted the various types and their terminology.

An older term commonly used in relation to such phenomena is extrasensory perception (ESP), which includes telepathy and clairvoyance. Telepathy refers to apparent mind-mind communication ability without sensory means; clairvoyance refers to apparent mental ability to obtain information without known sensory means and without mediation through other people. Another general term in current use is "remote viewing" which is similar to general ESP but usually refers to a specific ability (i.e. describing remote geographic locations). An older term in general use is psychokinesis (PK), which refers to apparent mental influencing of configuration or motion of material objects. Certain mental states also appear to influence material properties or biological processes (in people and organisms) and seem to have elements of ESP or psychokinesis. These apparent interactions are also considered part of paraphysics or psychoenergetics research.

The Foreign Technology Division explained that most of these data were difficult to adequately evaluate and stressed that the available information was limited. Coupled with this was the huge diversity within Soviet academic circles on the nature and scope of their studies into the powers of the mind. Thus the FTD elected to focus its investigations on the findings of individual researchers rather than class the whole range of topics under one, unified banner.

The two most credible individuals who had secured positive results in paraphysics research were I. M. Kogan, a professor at the Moscow Higher Technical School, and G. A. Sergeyev of the Institute of Physiology at Leningrad.

Of all the data available, Kogan's experiments, which began in 1965, appear to be the best documented and controlled. Kogan's emphasis is on information theory aspects of telepathy, and his initial theoretical goal was to show that electromagnetic theory is not necessarily incompatible with apparent telepathic phenomena. During 1966–1970, he published results of some of his successful experiments in the USSR technical journal *Radio Engineering*. In 1969, some of the results were summarized in a paper "The Information Aspects of Telepathy," for a symposium on ESP at UCLA. Although he has released no data since 1970, he is definitely known to be still involved in extensive research and experimentation. The types of experiments reported include short-distance telepathic suggestion of "mental orders" and transmission (or perception) of single digits, and short- and long-distance telepathic transmission (or perception) of simple objects.

The potential utilization of "short-distance telepathic" research was of particular interest to the FTD.

The early short-distance experiments may have been performed to verify some of the research conducted by L. L. Vasil'yev in the 1920's and 1930's and used a hypnotic state as well as normal consciousness. Some experiments were also conducted in shielded rooms. Kogan was sufficiently satisfied that the results were far greater than expected by chance and that further research was warranted. For example, in one experiment involving selection of one of ten cards numbered one through ten, with "indicator" (sender) in a separate room, the "percipient" (subject, or receiver) selected 13 correct cards in 26 attempts.

The FTD noted that Kogan had secured some startling successes in mind-to-mind communication.

Kogan's long-distance experiments have been between Moscow and Leningrad, Moscow and Novosibirsk, and Moscow and Tomsk. In each of these experiments, the percipient's description could be matched correctly to three or four of the six intended targets. Kogan also demonstrated a basic communication application in one of the Moscow-Novosibirsk experiments. Two simple but contrasting objects were chosen to represent the Morse code; a three-letter word was then selected (unknown to percipient) and the appropriate series of "dots" and "dashes" were identified for this word. The percipient (in Novosibirsk) subsequently identified the correct sequence of target objects (and therefore Morse code symbols), and the intended three-letter word could be reconstructed. Perhaps the most meaningful experiment in terms of evaluation and apparent potential in a communication mode was performed in 1967. This involved attempts at transmission of randomly selected digits between 0 and 9. Distance between "sender" and "receiver" was varied from several meters to several kilometers. Reported results, as attested to by at least five members of the All-Union Technical Society of Radio Technology and Communications. . . . A. S. Popov (the Popov Society), indicates 105 of 135 numbers were described (received) correctly by the receiver. The article states this to be 78% correct; however, this is a significant understatement since it does not reflect the overall probability of such an occurrence. In fact, in terms of probability, this would have to qualify as the most statistically significant result ever reported in psychic literature.

The FTD advised the DIA that Kogan's research might have potential intelligence-related benefits.

It also appears that with planned redundancy, a similar approach could yield highly reliable results, perhaps sufficient for certain application attempts. For example, each of the numbers 0–9 could correlate to specific instructions or messages, and in this way basic "messages" could be transmitted to or received from remote locations (space, submarine, etc.). Kogan has made frequent reference to such applications and very likely considers them to be reasonable objectives. Kogan may also be investigating the possibility of a person other than the intended receiver to perceive the target objects. In the 1967 Moscow-Leningrad experiment, a second receiver, in Leningrad, did describe very accurately the target intended by the sender in Moscow. It is not known, however, if the sender was aware of the additional person involved in the experiment. However, this type of experiment has probably been repeated by Kogan, perhaps with additional receivers not known to the sender, or with receivers attempting to obtain information from a person without his knowledge (i.e. an unwitting "sender"). Kogan is also known to be experimenting with "targets" concealed in metal containers, although results are not known. Such experiments could have intelligence potential, although extent of such involvement, or interest, by Kogan is unknown.

The FTD then turned its attention toward the equally groundbreaking research of G. A. Sergeyev.

G. A. Sergeyev at the Ukhtomskii Physiological Institute in Leningrad, has published a few experimental results on telepathic investigations. In one of these experiments he claims to have observed a synchronization of certain electroencephalogram (EEG) patterns between sender and receiver when the sender was observing flashing lights (different frequency for each eye). The EEG pattern in the intended receiver was apparently unique enough for easy recognition and could be utilized in a "code" sense. Although his telepathic-type experiments are difficult to evaluate, there may be some degree of validity to them. Other researchers, in the US and Canada, have also noted the possibility of correlations in EEG patterns between sender and receiver in telepathic experiments under certain conditions.

The FTD had uncovered a substantial body of data similar to Sergeyev's and Kogan's from experiments undertaken by a host of other research scientists—some of which had alarming potentials. Stressing that while most of these investigators appeared to pursue their work part-time and were probably not associated with any formalized laboratory program, the FTD asserted that their research should be taken seriously and a study of its findings could prove to be invaluable. One example was the investigations reported by Larissa V. Vilenskaya.

She has been conducting research with E. K. Naumov (who is not currently active) and now appears to be involved with a variety of her own investigations. One aspect is her study of a phenomena initially referred to as "skin vision" or, more recently, "dermo-optics." This relates to an apparent ability of some people to identify colors of concealed "targets" simply by touching the opaque outer covering. Although initial experiments on dermo-optic phenomena were open to severe criticism mainly due to lack of proper experimental control, later experiments appear to have overcome some of these criticisms.

Humans were not the only subjects of Soviet psychic research.

Another Moscow researcher, V. N. Pushkin, has performed investigations on psychoenergetic processes involving apparent interaction with organic matter such as plants. One experiment reported recently involved apparent correlations in responses from a polygraph that was attached to a plant and emotional states induced in a hypnotized person. The experiment was repeated several times, it was checked for electrical interference, and was run under null conditions. Although no firm evaluation can be made, Pushkin does appear to be a respected researcher and he may in fact have observed some type of valid interaction.

The FTD then focused its studies on Gennadiy Aleksandrovich Sergeyev, doctor of technical services at the Institute of Physiology, Leningrad. Sergeyev's work lends weight to the theory that the heart attack of CIA remote viewer Pat Price in 1975 may indeed have had sinister overtones.

Sergeyev has investigated psychoenergetic effects of people with psychokinetic abilities (i.e. [Nina] Kulagina) on other people and on biological specimens. In one experimental series, frog hearts were placed in an appropriate solution, and Kulagina attempted to influence their activity. Sergeyev claims that normally frog hearts remain active in solution up to 1.5–2 hours after removal from the frog. In the first of the experiments the electrocardiogram (EKG) indicated activity ceased about 7 minutes after Kulagina began concentration on *"stopping the heart."* The heart had been in a ceramic container. In the second experiment, with the heart in a metallic container, heart activity ceased after 22 minutes. In both these experiments, Kulagina was 1.5 meters from the "target" hearts. Sergeyev measured weak electric and magnetic fields at the target heart that correlated with some of Kulagina's physiological activity. This may have been responsible for the effect noted on heart activity. In another experiment, Kulagina attempted to increase the heart rate of a skeptical physician. Electroencephalogram, electrocardiogram, and other parameters were measured in both. Abrupt changes in these parameters were noted in both people within 1 minute after the experiment began. After 5 minutes, Sergeyev judged the heart activity of the physician had reached dangerous levels, and the experiment was terminated. Subsequent analysis indicated a definite synchronous effect was noted between certain heart parameters for both the physician and Kulagina.

The FTD then revealed what it described as the most unusual psychoenergetic phenomena, the apparent ability of certain individuals to influence matter via mental volition. According to the FTD's findings, a form of energy transfer, which appears to be generated or regulated by mental activity, may be the basic source for such effects. The nature of this energy transfer and its interaction mechanism was being investigated by various researchers throughout the world. This apparent interaction of mind with inanimate material is usually referred to as psychokinesis and is associated with unexplainable motion or configuration changes, the FTD added.

One of the most fascinating mysteries investigated by the FTD that could conceivably have had vital and welcome intelligence-related applications was, the DIA learned, reported at the Third International Psychotronics conference by G. P. Krokhalev, a psychiatrist from Perm.

His experiments involve attempts to have "mental images" appear on photographic film. He claims to have recorded this effect under controlled conditions. As an example, a person who could visualize images well, even to the point of hallucinating, was able to specify the image beforehand that was later observed on the film. Although much of his work appears to be very nonprofessional, his later experiments with the apparent recording of mental imagery appear reasonably well controlled. However, no firm evaluation can be made of his experimental procedure or results at this time. Other researchers, such as L. Vilenskaya, have apparently observed some of Krokhalev's experiments and judged them valid. This form of

apparent psychoenergetic-type process is not new to parapsychological researchers. Krokhalev's investigations appear similar to those reported in the US by Dr. J. Eisenbud, who is a
psychiatrist at the University of Colorado Medical School. Dr.
Eisenbud conducted extensive controlled investigations into
the alleged ability of a subject, Ted Serios, who appeared to
cause specific images to appear on films when under intense
concentration. Eisenbud's recent work appears to be valid but
is subject to the same evaluation difficulty as most all investigations involving such phenomena. Since the early 1960's,
USSR researchers have expressed an interest in Eisenbud's
work, along with all the other forms of apparent psychoenergetic processes. There has also been recent evidence of similar
research, apparently with positive results, in a Japanese research laboratory. Sergeyev also noted Nina Kulagina appeared
to cause some type of observable effect at times on unexposed
photographic film during an attempted psychoenergetic experiment, even though there was no intent for any effect. This effect has also been noted by other researchers, though few
attempts to induce specific images have been made.

But how, why, and under what specific circumstances did research into these many and truly bizarre phenomena begin in the
Soviet Union?

Investigation of paranormal mental phenomena generally
began during the latter part of the 1800's in various countries,
including the Soviet Union. Initially, only a few independent researchers pursued such study, since paranormal phenomena
were usually associated with superstition, mystical, or occult
beliefs. The first indication of specific USSR interest in investigations into paranormal phenomena from a specific viewpoint
was around 1875, several years before the first attempt at
such study was formalized by establishment of the British So-

ciety of Psychical Research. This early USSR effort was initiated by D. I. Mendeleyev who submitted proposals for such study to the Physical Society of St. Petersburg (Leningrad University). He also pursued his own private investigations and continued to urge that the topic in general should be examined on a thorough scientific basis. Several other USSR investigators also began study of paranormal phenomena around this time.

The Soviet public, stated the FTD, had in general always appeared to be open to mystical-type phenomena, an openness that was somewhat officially acknowledged by Czar Nicholas II and his family's association with the highly controversial Rasputin.

Nevertheless, said the FTD, after 1917, open interest in psychic-type phenomena was largely suppressed since Marxism excluded anything associated with nonmaterialistic issues. On the other hand, the revolution also initially appeared to generate a desire for new knowledge, even in unconventional directions.

In 1919, V. M. Bekhterev, a noted physiologist at the Institute of Brain Research of the University of Leningrad, began investigations into unusual psychological and physiological effects associated with the hypnotic state, including cases of apparent telepathic experiences. Pavlov had also made reference to unusual abilities sometimes observed in animals and man and was open to such investigations. Bekhterev organized a special group (Commission for the Study of Mental Suggestion) to continue and elaborate on his early work. L. L. Vasil'yev, a research physiologist who joined this institute in 1921, was part of the commission. Vasil'yev's initial work was on effects of magnetic fields on psychological states; eventually he became the prime researcher in the area termed "mental suggestion."

Thirty-five years later, Vasil'yev's research was still continuing and he was about to be thrust onto the world's stage.

In 1956, Vasil'yev began corresponding with the French researcher, R. Warcollier, and apparently received updates on worldwide parapsychological studies. Subsequently, he wrote a book for the popular press, *Mysterious Phenomena of the Human Psyche*, which was published in 1959 in Moscow. This book discussed a variety of subliminal sensory influences from known Pavlovian concepts. Vasil'yev extrapolated some of these to account for possible telepathic phenomena (with the cortex of the brain viewed as an electromagnetic signal generator) and emphasized the view that paranormal abilities in general would eventually be explained on a purely physical basis. This modified approach, emphasizing "yet-to-be-discovered" physical explanations, apparently was necessary to avoid Marxist ideological conflict as well as to gain interest and support of scientists in conventional disciplines.

The publication of Vasil'yev's book, said the FTD, led other researchers to publish their articles and books, including one B. B. Kazhinskiy, described as an electrical engineer, whose book *Biological Radio Communication* appeared in 1962. The surfacing of paranormal phenomena issues in the Soviet press, remarked the FTD, appeared to be one of Vasil'yev's aims; in this he was certainly successful.

The FTD then turned its attention to Soviet research from 1960 to 1970.

Shortly after Vasil'yev's first publication, the issue of telepathy became hotly debated by many in the Soviet Union. Some chose to attack the protocol of Vasil'yev's experiments; some attacked such phenomena as contradictory to either Marxist theory or scientific principles, while others felt the phenomena did not contradict either Marx or science. In 1965, I. M. Kogan, a Doctor of Technical Sciences at Moscow Higher Technical School, was appointed as chairman of a special group to study

problems of telepathy in affiliation with the Moscow section of
the Popov Society. This group was called the Section of Bioin-
formation. E. K. Naumov was also involved in early phases of
this group's activities. In June 1968 Naumov also chaired a
parapsychology conference in Moscow which was open to Western researchers. However, Pravda carried a very critical article on parapsychology, especially on alleged psychokinesis
abilities. The basis for this criticism was centered on the show-
manship aspects of some psychic subjects and on various explanations that seemed to challenge strict Marxism. Reference
was also made to a telepathy experiment in May 1968 involving Kogan, Mirza, and others, which apparently failed. This
experiment had been given much advance publicity by the popular magazine *Literary Gazette*. Publicity and resulting pressure were considered by the experimenters to be key reason
[sic] for the failure and may have led to a more cautious attitude in publicity of all future activity. Kogan and his group,
nevertheless, continued to express great confidence in the validity of earlier experiments that were judged successful.
Kogan had previously indicated that his experiments did not
work all the time, and that on the average only about one half
of the experiments are considered successful.

Friction began to surface in the working relationship between
Naumov and Kogan at the turn of the 1970s.

It became apparent that Naumov's objectives were coming into
increasing conflict with Kogan. Naumov may also have been
too uncritical in his experiments, and postulated concepts or
models for paranormal phenomena that Kogan felt were
un-Marxist. In addition, Naumov was also known to associate
with people of questionable political orientation and was
openly critical of Kogan, accusing him of being too conserva-

tive. Kogan eventually began to break with Naumov, which may have contributed to Naumov's decline as a serious researcher. In 1974, Naumov was arrested by the KGB and sentenced for over a year to [a] labor camp in Siberia. The official KGB charge against him was taking fees for a lecture he gave on parapsychology. Research he initiated was probably discontinued.

The FTD found Kogan's situation suspicious.

Although Kogan has openly expressed his concern about premature release of experimental data, and no doubt the effect of pressure on experiments due to excessive publicity became clear from the 1967 failure (Moscow-Kerch experiment), it is nevertheless unusual that Kogan would not have published since 1970. This lack of publication, in light of his on-going involvement in psychoenergetic research, is highly suggestive that aspects of his research are classified and that he may be receiving direct government support.

It was not just Russian-based research that the FTD saw fit to examine. The document also details similar research being undertaken in other Warsaw Pact countries, including Czechoslovakia, Bulgaria, and Poland. In the early 1960s considerable publicity appeared in Czechoslovakia following psychokinesis experiments undertaken in the Physics Department at the University of Hradec in Prague. The FTD took note of this.

The investigations centered on the alleged ability of R. Pavlita, a factory department chief, and his daughter to cause movement of light metal foil by mental concentration. The foil, mounted in a sealed container, could apparently be made to start or stop rotating in specific directions. After 2 years of periodic testing, the experimenters concluded results were not sufficient for a scientific paper. However, in informal discussion, they felt some unusual and unexplainable effects occurred that could be an example of psychokinesis. Unfortunately, the popular press greatly exaggerated these "unofficial remarks," and the publicity apparently led to a discontinuation of formal research with Pavlita at that time. Dr. M. Ryzl also investigated Pavlita and was unable to find convincing evidence of psychokinetic ability. Apparently, considerable difficulty was encountered in separating ordinary energy transfer (such as body electrostatics or thermal radiation) from what might be considered paranormal effects.

In Bulgaria, the bulk of the research that was considered valid and worthy of both examination and commentary by the FTD had been undertaken by a Sofia-based researcher, G. Lozanov, whose work began in the 1940s.

Later, in the mid-1960's, Lozanov performed other experiments with blind people and noted some had an ability to distinguish differences in colors, and some could also describe drawings by "touch." In these experiments, the targets were underneath glass. These were similar to Soviet investigations generally referred to as "dermo-optics," and may be a form of clairvoyance. Dr. Lozanov also claims some of these blind subjects (usually children) improved their performance through training and practice. Around this time, a government-funded facility was created for the study and development of an accelerated learning method developed by Lozanov and included the study of parapsychological phenomena. This was called the Institute of Suggestology and was claimed by Lozanov to have a staff of about 30. Some of their investigations were with people who apparently had proven paranormal abilities. Lozanov is very active, making many public appearances to discuss his accelerated learning techniques and paranormal phenomena in general. His work appears to be well accepted and he has stated that an open climate exists in Bulgaria for such investigations. Apparently, folklore that contains accounts of such phenomena has helped create this openness.

Parapsychology research in Poland also revealed amazing advances.

Investigations were performed by several European researchers during the 1920's and 1930's on the abilities of Stefen Ossowiecki, a well-known Polish psychic. These investigations all concluded Ossowiecki displayed highly unusual abilities of a clairvoyant nature, including the ability to describe objects and written material sealed in lead containers and opaque envelopes. His achievements with numerous controlled tests of this type and his public psychic activities became well known; this publicity contributed to an openness toward paranormal phenomena in the general population. Recently, another Polish psychic from Warsaw, C. Klimuszko, has been receiving considerable publicity. He apparently has abilities similar to Ossowiecki (who died in 1944) and has been tested by the Psychotronic Section of the Polish Cybernetic Association. Specifics of such tests are not available, although they are claimed to confirm his abilities. L. Stefanski, a researcher from Warsaw, has also studied Klimuszko and claims he has the ability to obtain accurate information on lost or missing people. Stefanski believes hypnosis is necessary to develop and enhance paranormal perception, and apparently employs techniques similar to Kafka and Ryzl (the Czech researchers). He has also apparently had success with people who had not previously displayed any psychic aptitude. Another researcher, Dr. S. Manczarski, a physics professor, is also active in research, although specifics are unknown. Most of his work appears to be theoretically oriented.

While the FTD found no indication of an extensive research effort in Poland, there appeared to be at least a few dedicated researchers and people with reliable abilities, natural or developed. The backing of such investigations by the Polish Cybernetics Society, said the FTD, would probably generate additional investigations and research in the future.

The FTD had some intriguing ideas and theories about how these phenomena worked. Based on systematic evaluation of the research of a number of individuals and organizations, the FTD discussed the most promising theoretical models, beginning with the electromagnetic model.

[A] possible transmission mode considered by some researchers involves naturally occurring low frequency waves. Similar natural or induced frequencies in the brain could conceivably react or interfere with these natural frequencies in such a way as to cause specific interference patterns to be scattered throughout the earth-ionosphere. Such patterns, if detected, could stimulate or trigger corresponding patterns (or images) in others who have similar sensitivity and shared experiences. In this sense, the "modified" signal would only need to cause an association and need not represent precise data. In this model, information transfer could occur with appropriate learning or conditioning, even for complex targets. Alternatively, increasing exposure time (i.e. time available for a paranormal task) could also improve quality and accuracy of telepathic or clairvoyant impressions.

The FTD next considered a quantum physics model to explain psychic functioning.

One aspect of this can be expressed by the Einstein-Podeski-Rosen (EPR) paradox which basically states that elementary particles with the same quantum characteristics are bound together; a change in one causes a similar simultaneous change in the other regardless of distance between them. This concept of quantum level correlation, or coupling, can lead to several interpretations and models that could be consistent with psychic process.

A. Dubrov, a Moscow physicist, had proposed a model for paranormal perception based on a gravity-type interaction, the DIA was advised by the FTD.

In this concept, he considers it theoretically possible for aggregates of biological molecules that are in a loosely bound state (liquid crystal state) to create very weak quasi-gravitational field effects. This would result, in his view, from variations in gravitational attraction forces arising from changes in relative molecular spacing. Dubrov suspects that high strain conditions, such as muscular contraction, cell division, or neuron activity in the brain, could create such quasi-gravitational waves of sufficient strength for distant interaction.

The FTD discovered that this particular theory was also supported by Gennadiy Sergeyev of the Institute of Physiology at Leningrad.

Sergeyev has expressed similar views and has adopted Dubrov's concepts into his own theoretical work. Sergeyev considers the brain to be of a "paracrystal" nature which can emit (and absorb) a wide variety of electromagnetic radiation, including gravitational effects.

Nevertheless, the FTD added that this approach was highly speculative and could lead to several theoretical objections. But it could not be eliminated as a possibility.

The FTD then addressed an equally controversial possibility: holography.

This model considers the brain to have characteristics like a hologram, similar to conventional ideas of holography in laser physics. This hologram-like attribute is compatible with observed data on how memory appears to be distributed throughout the brain, and on observed data involving learning and learning disorders, imagination, perception, altered states of consciousness, and other aspects of brain functioning. This holographic model is easily adaptable to psychic processes, since this concept considers a basic hologram to potentially exist throughout the universe. This would be similar to the idea of a gravitational field extended to infinity. In any hologram, a small portion can reproduce data similar to the original, although not as accurately. In this sense, specific remote information exists throughout such a hologram and can somehow be accessed by appropriate "paranormal" processes in the brain. This model in essence views the brain as a hologram, interpreting a holographic universe.

Although the FTD conceded that none of the possibilities presented a clear answer to the mystery of how paranormal phenomena could accurately be defined, they asserted that the various concepts might serve as a bridge toward a meaningful dialogue in a variety of research areas.

A multidisciplinary research approach that eventually may clarify key theoretical issues appears to be emerging in the USSR and on a worldwide basis. It is certainly recognized that paranormal processes are not openly accepted in many areas. As is true for any emerging area of study, initial difficulties are great, language and terminology barriers exist, and resistance in established areas of research is high. In an area as complicated as paraphysics (especially psychic functioning), such difficulties can be expected. Yet these difficulties may not necessarily impact on eventual applications. An application emphasis is apparent in the work of many Warsaw Pact researchers and should pose a greater concern than their ability (or inability) to formulate appropriate theoretical models. It may well be that pursuit of application modes may be required before the most appropriate theoretical models are developed. Insight gained from possible application achievements may also clarify theoretical directions.

One of the more surprising areas that the FTD touched upon in its report to the DIA on psychic research was that of religion.

By some interpretations, the domain of paraphysics intersects in large measure with that of religion. On one hand, the appearance of a "supernatural" quality to some of the claimed phenomena has led some critics to conclude that belief in paranormal phenomena necessarily leads to acceptance of such religious concepts as a "soul" or of extra-physical entities such as spirits. For the officially atheist political and scientific community of the Soviet Union, that perception mandates opposition to paraphysics. On the other hand, religious believers have also sometimes had difficulty accepting the legitimacy of paraphysics, since many of the phenomena subtended by paraphysics have historically been linked to the forces of evil, or the devil. Thus, for believer and nonbeliever alike, paraphysics has raised philosophical questions which have stood in the way of its acceptance.

Certainly, the area that most concerned the FTD was how psychic phenomena could be utilized by an enemy as a weapon of warfare.

Like other areas of applied technology which may have military application, Soviet perceptions of Western research and development status have considerable impact on the level of official support given to paraphysics research. The original impetus for the Soviet government to establish Vasil'yev's laboratory at Leningrad State University seems to have been the common belief that the US Navy had conducted successful experiments in telepathy with a submerged submarine (the Nautilus experiments). Certainly Vasil'yev himself made several pointed references to that supposed test in his works, even though it has been claimed that he later recognized them as a hoax. It should also be noted that the Soviet government's official interest in paraphysics carries certain other risks in the international arena. The Chinese have used paraphysics research in a virulent attack against the Soviet Union, claiming that government interest was a reflection of the need of the revisionist regime for internal supports and an indicator of the departure of the Soviet regime from the paths of Leninist doctrine. While it is unclear that this avenue of attack has had any noticeable effect on international affairs, paraphysics now has been identified as a potential propaganda weapon.

But precisely how much funding was being channeled into psychic research by Soviet authorities during this period? The FTD had a few ideas.

In one form or another, the estimate of 12–20 million rubles (or dollars) has survived for at least the last decade and recurs as a current estimate routinely, despite the fact that no one knows, or is saying, how it was originally derived. In its report on Soviet government funding for paraphysics research, the RAND Corporation found that available knowledge of the level of Soviet involvement in paraphysics provides "prima facie evidence that the figure of 12 to 20 million rubles is, if anything, grossly inflated." Although the present study identifies a considerably larger number of persons in the Soviet Union and Warsaw Pact than were known to the RAND analysts, there is as yet no reason to disagree with their assessment. Official support for paraphysics in the Soviet Union and Warsaw Pact countries is highly variable over time, and changes markedly in response to changes in the political and scientific environment, as well as to Soviet perceptions of the corresponding degree of official support for paraphysics in the West. Although it is clear that there is at least some official support of a high-risk basis for paraphysics, the current magnitude of such research in the Soviet Union probably does not exceed a few hundred thousand rubles annually in the prime areas. The total subvention of research in the related areas of paraphysics/biophysics is somewhat greater, but the total research effort in all such fields appears never to have reached the inflated levels sometimes claimed for them.

Having looked at the historical aspects, military applications, and theoretical aspects of paranormal phenomena in the Soviet Union, the FTD then reached its conclusions.

Paranormal communication potential has already been demonstrated by USSR researchers. The experiments performed by Kogan's group in 1967 with single digits are the most statistically significant ever reported. Communication application is a known USSR research goal, and additional research toward this goal is known to have occurred during the past decade. It is also known that gifted people are identified from the general population and that training techniques are pursued for enhancing paranormal perception. Specific experiments can be expected in the near future (if not already accomplished) from submarines, space of command and control locations to demonstrate practical use. Scope of research in paranormal phenomena in other Warsaw Pact countries is not as extensive or as credible as in the USSR. However, trends have been noted that indicate a growing interest that will probably lead to new research efforts there as well. Although such research is receiving growing acceptance and support, it must be recognized significant applications or breakthroughs do not necessarily require large facilities or groups. Therefore, assessing actual achievements will remain as a serious intelligence problem.

The research undertaken by the U.S. Air Force's Foreign Technology Division in 1978 proves beyond any shadow of doubt that both it and the DIA were deeply interested in determining the extent of Soviet research in the field of parapsychology at the time.

Although the U.S. intelligence community is reluctant to openly and officially embrace psychic phenomena, on November 11, 2001, the British *Sunday Times* newspaper revealed that the Federal Bureau of Investigation had approached Transdimensional Systems, a company that employs fourteen remote viewers, as people with such psychic skills are termed in intelligence circles, with a view to predicting likely targets of future terrorist attacks. Officially, the FBI refused to comment on or confirm this, but conceded that investigators have been told to "think out of the box." A quarter of a century after "Paraphysics R&D—Warsaw Pact" was written, it seems that the worlds of the psychic and the spy continue to cross paths.

Twelve

THE DOWSING DETECTIVES

One of the strangest skills and talents allegedly possessed by humans is water-divining, or dowsing as it is usually known. Though the ability of the dowser to locate water by nonconventional means is looked upon with suspicion in some quarters, for many it is an age-old tradition that remains as relevant and vital today as it was centuries ago. Not only that, the skill has attracted the attention of some quite unlikely parties—including the government of the Soviet Union, the U.S. intelligence community, a British police force, and a department of the British government that played a key role in the battle against the Nazis during the Second World War.

The subject of dowsing is well covered in a formerly classified document titled "Paraphysics R&D—Warsaw Pact," prepared in 1978 for the U.S. Defense Intelligence Agency by the Air Force.

In its traditional form, dowsing refers to location of underground water or other geological anomaly by an operator holding a forked stick and walking over the target area. Deflection or rotation of the stick indicates the presence of the anomaly

(U) One of the obstacles standing in the way of universal scientific acceptance of dowsing-BPE is the lack of a convincing body of experimental data to explain the information carrier and receptor mechanism. Although there is at least one East European report which insists that the information is carried through acoustic action of free water molecules on the inner ear,[17] most East European researchers believe that the information carrier acts through magnetic or electromagnetic waves or fields. The body of experimental evidence for an electromagnetic carrier is extensive, if not exactly clear. Some researchers feel that the shape and composition of the dowsing rod are not important,[18] while others claim that the rod can be tuned, by its shape, composition, or the addition of capacitors, to selectively indicate any of a wide variety of materials.[19-23] At least one researcher claims that the information carrier can be transmitted for some distance by an ungrounded electrical conductor.[24] Even while dismissing the role of the rod itself, a prominent Czech researcher cites experimental data that tend to confirm the electromagnetic hypothesis. Jiri Bradna claims that, "myotensiometry proved that the effect of water and metals changed the muscles' resting and action tonus even without holding the dowsing rod,"[25] and suggests that this finding might help to explain the correlation between illnesses and place of residence noted elsewhere in the literature. He further states the muscles of the forearm both radiate and are sensitive to electromagnetic waves in the 40 and 68 MHz range, "as well as other harmonic frequencies."[26] Other prominent researchers feel that the carrier is most likely in the 1-10 Hz range.[27]

(U) As seems to be true in other areas of paraphysics research, the presence of an artificial magnetic field seems to affect BPE performance, although a static electric field seems to have no such effect.[28]

(U) Whatever the information carrier channel or sensory mechanism, a significant portion of the population can show the effect. The exact percentage of the population remains in some doubt; one researcher "assumes" that 3% of all persons possess BPE sensitivity,[29] while another report puts the number at 20-30%.[30] Yet another indicates that there is a high correlation between hypnotizability and sensitivity to BPE, but also indicates that hypnotizing the subjects did not increase their sensitivity.[31] In any event, it is clear that BPE sensitivity is not merely the province of a select few persons.

3. Ideomotor Response (U)

(U) The ideological need of the Communist countries to express all paraphysics observations in materialist terms has led to an unfortunate grouping of two different phenomena under a single name: the biophysical effect (BPE). As the preceding discussion indicates, BPE has been applied to sensorimotor response to subliminal cues from the external environment (dowsing). In addition, one group of Romanian researchers has applied the same term to ideomotor response to subconscious ideation; in this case, the so-called Wedding Ring Test.

(U) Subliminal Ideomotor Response (SIR) as used here refers to muscular activity caused by the subconscious mind in response to an explicit or implicit question put to the subject. In its traditional form, it is carried out by suspending a light, dense object (typically, a wedding ring) from a thread held in the hand by the thumb and forefinger. After assigning meaning to various forms of motion of the suspended object,* the subject can be asked questions, and the response will indicate the answer as it is known to the subconscious mind. Often this method allows the subject to answer questions for which the conscious mind does not believe there is an answer available, or believes an answer different from that resident in the unconscious.

---

*(U) For example: forward and back set to mean yes; side-to-side to mean no; circular motion to mean unknown. The arbitrary meanings thus set are then tested by asking questions to which the answer is unequivocally known. Obviously, any possible response with a simple choice answer (yes/no, boy/girl) can be asked if the subject properly assigns the meaning of a muscular response in the subconscious.

The governments of the United Kingdom, the United States, and the Soviet Union have all displayed an interest in the skill of dowsing. An example can be seen in a still partly classified document prepared by the U.S. Air Force's Foreign Technology Division in 1978.

sought after. The dowser has the feeling that the rod is twisting by itself, and that he cannot prevent its deflection. Actually, the deflection of the dowsing rod is caused by the subconscious reaction of the muscles, and it takes a moment for the rod to assume a new position. The magnitude of the rod's deflection depends on the ratio of the tension of the individual muscle groups that hold the dowsing rod.

One of the obstacles standing in the way of universal scientific acceptance of dowsing-BPE [Bio-Physical Effect] is the lack of a convincing body of experimental data to explain the information carrier and receptor mechanism. Although there is at least one East European report which insists that the information is carried through acoustic action of free water molecules on the inner ear, most East European researchers believe that the information carrier acts through magnetic or electromagnetic waves or fields. The body of experimental evidence for an electromagnetic carrier is extensive, if not exactly clear. Some researchers feel that the shape and composition of the dowsing rod are not important, while others claim that the rod can be tuned, by its shape, composition, or the addition of capacitors, to selectively indicate any of a wide variety of materials. At least one researcher claims that the information carrier can be transmitted for some distance by an ungrounded electrical conductor. Even while dismissing the role of the rod itself, a prominent Czech researcher cites experimental data that tend to confirm the electromagnetic hypothesis. Jiri Bradna claims that, "myotensiometry proved that the effect of water and metals changed the muscles' resting and action tonus even without holding the dowsing rod," and suggests that this finding might help to explain the correlation between illnesses and place of residence noted elsewhere in the literature. He further states the muscles of the forearm both radiate and are sensitive to electromagnetic waves in the 40 and 68 MHz range, "as well as other harmonic frequencies."

One reason for U.S. interest in the subject was the official interest in dowsing in the Soviet Union.

From the late 1930's until after the end of the Stalinist period, virtually no paraphysics research was conducted in the Soviet Union; certainly none was reported. The sole exception to this was in dowsing, which was allowed to continue throughout the entire Stalinist regime. The researchers assisted by defining their field in materialist terms. The "biophysical effect" certainly sounds more respectable and less threatening to a party functionary than does "water witching." (The invention of the term was like a scientific breakthrough.) Even more important, by demonstrating their ability to locate water and other needed natural resources during the period of forced collectivization and industrialization, the dowsers were able to meet the most severe test of ideological legitimacy of the time: utility. For its part, therefore, the regime allowed dowsing activities to exist, if not exactly flourish.

With undeniable evidence in hand showing that interest in dowsing has extended from the Pentagon to the Kremlin, let us now examine a specific case of official interest in dowsing, one that took place in wartime Britain. The story began on May 19, 1941, when one Sergeant J. Hall of the Warwickshire Police Force submitted the following report to his superior officer, Superintendent A. Woodward. The report, titled "Enemy Air Raid Incident St. Mary's Common, Warwick, 17th May, 1941," would eventually make its way through official channels.

I have the honour to report that at 0615 hours on Saturday, 17th May, 1941, I was on duty at Warwick Police Station, when Edward Harold Morris, 28 Rosefield Street, Leamington Spa, reported that, he had reason to believe that two of his workmen, James Hiatt, 20, Mill Street, Warwick and Harry Marston, 21, Linen Street, Warwick, employed at the Warwick Aviation Co., Saltisford, Warwick, had been struck and buried by the explosion of the bombs which fell on St. Mary's Common, Warwick, at 0130 hours on the same date.

It appears that the two men concerned had left their place of employment, a few minutes before the bombs fell, in order to visit the home of Harry Marston to see if his wife was all right as she is of rather nervous disposition. The route taken by these men would take them past the scene of the Incident and as they never reached home or returned to the place of their employment, the foreman became alarmed and reported the matter.

I immediately visited the scene of the Incident in company with P.C. 193, Walker and P.C. 319, Terry and with the assistance of employees of the Warwick Aviation Co., commenced digging operations.

After satisfying myself that the men were missing, I sent in a Situation Report for the assistance of a Rescue Squad which subsequently arrived and commenced operations.

Approximately 0830 hours on the same date, I was at the scene talking to George Pettifer, 38, Newburgh Crescent, Warwick, who was the foreman in the [sic] charge of the Rescue Squad, when I noticed P.C. 319, Terry coming from a nearby thicket fashioning a forked stick with a pen-knife. Knowing that P.C. Terry had had previous experience of divining, I kept him under observation. Wrapping what appeared to me to be an handkerchief around one of the forks, P.C. Terry commenced to walk over the bomb craters. About 30 seconds later he came to a standstill and I noticed that the forked stick which he was holding had commenced to wriggle very violently and from my observations I could see that he had great difficulty in holding it.

P.C. Terry eventually released his hold on the stick and I could see that he was suffering from a severe nervous strain.

He pointed to a particular portion of heaped soil near to one of the craters and said: "They are under there." Digging operations were immediately commenced and a quarter of an hour later the bodies of both men were recovered. J. Hall, Sergt. 226.

The report was of sufficient interest that, on May 22, 1941, the Regional Headquarters of the Police Force at Birmingham forwarded a copy to Sir George Gater of the British government's Ministry of Home Security. Police Constable Philip Terry, whose skills had led to the high-level exchange between the police force and the Ministry of Home Security, also filed his own report, which added some important and hitherto unreported aspects to the affair.

After we had been working for some time I suggested to P.C. Walker that I might be able to locate the men by means of divining if I had some of their clothing. P.C. Walker then sent for some of their clothing and I went and cut a forked stick out of a privet bush. I then held the stick and a cap belonging to one of the men, Mr. Marston, in my hands and walked over the craters and mounds of earth. Through the reactions received I then indicated a spot where I thought the bodies were lying. Work was immediately commenced at this spot and the bodies were located.

As far as divining of human bodies is concerned I have not had much experience, but I am fairly experienced in water divining. A few years ago, before joining the Police Force, I went to various parts of the country, mostly in my home district, for the purpose of finding water supplies. I was engaged by the Shipston-on-Stour Rural District Council on several occasions. This included the finding of the present water supply at my home in Ilmington.

An extract from the daily report of the chief constable of Warwickshire Police on May 31, 1941, revealed that "incidents of a somewhat similar nature occurred in this Constabulary district at Bishops Itchington, near Sutham on the 24th Nov. 1935 [and] Barford, near Warwick, on 5th–7th July, 1936." Although the Warwickshire Police Force apparently employed dowsers as a part of its work when circumstances dictated, not everyone was convinced of the veracity of dowsing. A handwritten note in the police dowsing files from a Professor Thomas, who was connected to the Ministry of Home Security, contains a word of warning.

I recommend that no official action should be taken. The use or otherwise of dowsing is a matter of much controversy, and though psychological explanations can be offered to cover some cases, the location of bodies under debris can hardly be due to more than a "hunch" on the part of the dowser.

Was the professor correct or were the events of May 17, 1941 (and those of November 1935 and July 1936), evidence of something more unusual having occurred? Due to the difference of opinions, the controversy continued unabated. In a June 15, 1941, memorandum titled "Corpse Divining," one Professor W. E. Curtis, also of the government's Ministry of Home Security, wrote to a colleague, Dr. R. E. Stradling, who had become embroiled in the events.

I saw Supt. Woodward on 12th June and visited the scene of the incident with Sergt. Hall and P.C. Terry.

There were two contiguous craters, each some 20ft. across, on the edge of St. Mary's Common. The line joining their centers was roughly perpendicular to a footpath along which the men would have come from the works, and this footpath was nearly tangential to the outer lip of one of the craters. Before enquiring where the bodies were found, I concluded that the most likely place would be on the short length, some 10 ft., of footpath buried under the crater lip. This was rendered more probable in view of the fact that a ¾ moon would be just rising at the time, so that the men would have had no difficulty in keeping to the path. There was no shelter of any kind within 50 ft., where there was a house, and they would therefore be likely to throw themselves down where they were. The bodies were in fact found within a few feet of the spot which the above considerations indicated as the most probable.

Professor Curtis was highly skeptical of the whole situation, and his argument *was* well founded and *did* establish a logical, down-to-earth explanation for P.C. Terry's supposed dowsing skills. Curtis concluded in a similar vein:

I feel therefore that this cannot be regarded as a very convincing case of "dowsing," since there are several other factors present, any or all of which may have influenced P.C. Terry subconsciously. Nevertheless, I am sure that he, Sergt. Hall and Supt. Woodward are entirely convinced of the genuineness of the occurrence. P.C. Terry himself, I gathered, is a little scared of these manifestations, and is certainly not out to turn them to his advantage. He has only once previously tried to locate a body (in a river), but failed, although another dowser succeeded, using a copper wire and a handkerchief belonging to the deceased. The latter is what gave him the idea of sending for a cap belonging to one of the men, although he frankly admits he has no idea whether it did any good.

Nevertheless, Professor Curtis was open-minded enough to recommend that P.C. Terry's alleged skills not be dismissed outright— as he noted in his closing words to Dr. Stradling: "I am not inclined to recommend further action, except that if an opportunity should occur for a further test of P.C. Terry's alleged powers, it should certainly be taken. An artificial test could of course be arranged, but I

feel that the results would probably be negative without being conclusive."

Needless to say, a further opportunity *did* present itself. On July
1, 1941, Police Constable Terry was involved in the hunt for yet another missing person, and again he turned to dowsing. In a remarkable three-page memorandum to the chief constable, Inspector
W. Drakeley of the Warwick Police Force wrote:

I have the honour to report that on Tuesday, 1st July, 1941, information was received at Warwick Police Station that several
articles of male clothing had been found on the river bank at a
point about mid-way between Barford Hill, Barford, and Longbridge Farm, Borough of Warwick, and in consequence it was
feared that one LEWIS GEORGE BLUCK, aged 45 years, a wood
cutter, of Oxhill, near Kineton, had been drowned.

Inspector Drakeley was inclined to believe that a genuinely unexplained phenomenon was at work.

I went to the scene accompanied by P.C. 319, Terry, of Warwick
Borough, who has had previous experience of the recovery of
bodies by means of divining.

As the initial information disclosed, I found on the east bank
of the River Avon at a point about mid-way between Barford
Hill and Longbridge Farm, several articles of a man's clothing,
and a track was plainly visible through the long grass and net-
tles straight to the water's edge. Information was then received
from a fellow workman of the deceased man that at about 1:55
P.M. that day he was sitting by the riverside about 100 yards
north of the spot and had seen someone swimming about in the
middle of the river. This person could not say for certain that it
was Bluck but thought it might have been him because only
that day Bluck had spoken about his ability as a swimmer and

under water swimmer in his earlier days and had even mentioned going in for a swim.

Since this case had likely ended in tragedy, P.C. Terry offered his unique help to Inspector Drakeley.

There appeared little doubt that Bluck had been drowned, and P.C. Terry then stated he would attempt to locate the body if possible, and for this purpose he cut a strong hazel fork from a bush nearby. He then took an under vest belonging to the deceased and wrapped this round his right hand and the hazel fork.

We then crossed the river in a punt and P.C. Terry stood at a point approximately 25 feet south of a line from the clothing to the opposite bank. With his back to the river, P.C. Terry slowly turned anti-clockwise towards the river. I was standing immediately behind him.

At that point something truly remarkable occurred, as Drakeley was careful to note.

When the hazel fork was pointing about 15 feet to the south of the clothing on the opposite bank, it commenced to quiver violently and twisted round P.C. Terry's hand with such force that he was compelled to release it and it shot out of his hands towards the river. Sergt. Wild, who was standing on the opposite bank, noted where the hazel fork was directed at this moment and stood at the spot. I knocked a stake in the ground where P.C. Terry was standing and a direct bearing to Sergt. Wild on the opposite side passed through the centre of a willow tree at the water's edge. I was able to accurately check this bearing as I was immediately behind P.C. Terry. P.C. Terry then walked 25 feet north, i.e. towards the clothing and repeated the procedure. The same thing happened again only the reaction on the hazel fork was even more violent. Another stake was knocked in the ground where he stood and cross bearings again pointed directly to the tree referred to. P.C. Terry again walked 25 feet north and once more repeated the procedure. This time the reaction on the hazel fork was about the same as in the first instance, not so violent as in the second (which pointed directly across the river to the willow tree) but the direction was exactly the same and cross bearings pointed directly to the tree.

I then took P.C. Terry along the bank for a distance of 150 yards to the north and south of a direct line across the river from the tree referred to. He was unable to get any reaction until he reached the two outside stakes and at that stage informed me the body was undoubtedly lying at or near the apex of the three bearings.

Inspector Drakeley explained that he and P.C. Terry then traveled one hundred and fifty yards upstream. As they approached the willow tree

The hazel fork he was holding suddenly twisted so violently that it snapped in half and so tightly wound itself round the under vest that it was several minutes before he could get it free. At this stage P.C. Terry maintained that the body lay immediately in front of the tree 6 ft. from the bank. The test was continued for 150 yards down stream but there was no reaction beyond the outer stake.

I was now convinced that P.C. Terry's information was correct and at 7:15 P.M. dragging operations were commenced.

The river, which in parts was 120 feet wide and 20 feet deep, was searched without success for almost three hours. The situation changed the following day.

Operations were continued at 8 A.M. the following morning but beforehand I had P.C. Terry make further test with the hazel fork. The reactions were exactly the same, and although I did everything possible to deter him from his conviction he still maintained that the body was where he indicated. Later on in the morning I had three drags fixed to an iron bar and these were pulled by ropes from one side of the river to the other, starting at the south stake and working up river to the north stake. Just before 1 P.M. I found a small particle of human flesh on the point of one drag. This was exactly over the spot indicated by P.C. Terry. Operations were continued and at 2:45 P.M. the body was recovered. It was in exactly the spot where P.C. Terry has indicated it should lie.

The body was subsequently identified as that of Lewis Bluck. Inspector Drakeley heaped praise on Police Constable Terry for his contribution, which Drakeley believed had led directly to the recovery of Bluck's body.

Apart from the finding of the clothes upon the bank, P.C. Terry had nothing else to help him and no one had any idea where the body lay. He was, however, so convinced with the result of his divining that he told me it was useless dragging anywhere else other than the spot he had indicated.

The intersection of the lines taken from the stakes across the river in the direction of the clothing revealed the exact position of the body.

P.C. Terry has previously located bodies by means of a hazel fork, when two men were buried on the Warwick Common as the result of enemy action. In this instance again he indicated the exact position of the bodies, although previously it was not known for certain whether there were any bodies underneath.

His assistance in this matter undoubtedly saved many hours, and probably days, of dragging operations and the accuracy of the information he is able to give unquestionably proves that his methods have so far withstood all tests he had undertaken.

On July 8 an article appeared in the local newspaper, *The Morning News*, that discussed the death of Lewis Bluck, the recovery of the body by the local police, and the inquest that followed. At no point in the article, however, was any mention made of the highly significant contribution made by Police Constable Terry. Apparently some people within the corridors of power did not wish to see the worlds of the paranormal and officialdom becoming intertwined.

On July 14, 1941, Dr. R. E. Stradling of the Ministry of Home Security interviewed Dr. E. J. Dingwell of Cambridge, England. Dingwell was described as a man of independent means who had devoted his life to the scientific study of a wide range of problems associated with psychical research. Stradling contacted Dingwell to discuss the dowsing activities of P.C. Terry.

Dingwell informed Stradling that the police statements were typical of a large number of similar incidents that he thought were due to "an unconscious appreciation of ordinary physical pointers." Water divining was undoubtedly a fact, said Dingwell, but little evidence, except from an unnamed German source, existed to show that it was a useful tool for locating dead bodies. Dingwell advised checking for an obvious explanation of the site where the body was found. The spot might be associated with natural currents that caused an "accumulation of things at the point and would thus be visible if the perception was keen enough," added Dingwell.

The final paragraph of Stradling's letter written two days after the interview had a major bearing on the apparent decision not to inform the local media of the role played by P.C. Terry in the case.

He agreed with me in strongly deprecating any official support to matters which could in any way be connected with spiritualism and although in the mind of the average person water divining is not usually connected in this way, yet if the mysterious comes into it, it does give a certain amount of support to the more extreme claims and in war time this is particularly dangerous.

Once again, we see officials fearful that the "mysterious" might be utilized as a tool of psychological warfare by the enemy during times of hostility.

Two weeks later, Professor W. E. Curtis interjected himself into the controversy once again. He submitted a two-page report to the Ministry of Home Security on July 29, 1941.

I visited the site on July 21 in company with Sergt. Wild and P.C. Terry. I verified the details given in Insp. Drakeley's report except for one slight discrepancy, namely, that the third observation was made on the opposite side of the first from the second, i.e. the first observation was midway between the other two, not on the same side of them as stated in the report. Both men were certain of this, and also that the first observation was made at a point almost exactly opposite the spot where the body was located. This point was selected by P.C. Terry himself, and it would thus appear probable that he had formed some expectation, subconsciously, it may be, of the probable position of the body before commencing operations with the hazel fork. It should be noted that he had examined the east bank (where the clothes and body were found) before crossing to the west bank to make his observation.

The river is quite straight for some hundreds of yards in each direction and I could not discover any indication, such as eddies for example, which would suggest one spot rather than another as a likely position of the body. It was of course probable that it would be downstream relative to the clothes, and it

was no doubt natural to select a position for the first observation immediately opposite the first bank (i.e. the tree) on that
side of the clothes.

But these indications appear to be too slight to account for
the extremely positive conclusion reached by P.C. Terry. There
is so far as I can see only one alternative to admitting this is a
genuine case of divining. I was informed that the depth of
water where the body was found was about six feet. It could not
well have been much more, as the man evidently dived in from
the bank, which is only a foot or so high, and could not have become imbedded in the mud had the water been appreciably
deeper than this. It is therefore likely that a slight eddy will
have existed immediately above the body, and it is possible that
this was the basis of P.C. Terry's (? subconscious) expectation
referred to above.

I submit however that there is justification for an investigation of the occurrence by an experienced worker in this field.
Meanwhile I propose, if you approve, to ask the police authorities to inform me in advance of any future operations of this
kind by P.C. Terry, so that I may be able to observe them in
progress.

This report generated further debate and controversy, including
the following letter to Dr. R. E. Stradling from Dr. E. J. Dingwell,
who had seen a copy of Professor Curtis's report.

In matters of this kind it is, of course, necessary to exclude all
normal sources of information before we can begin to assume
the presence of some factor which might compel us to suspect
that the information was derived "supernormally." Now in the
present instance it can hardly be maintained, I think, that we
have reached this stage, or indeed anywhere near it.

We have a starting point from where the clothes were discovered. We are told that the east bank is much overgrown, and, from the plan drawn up by Professor Curtis, it appears that some 20 yards down stream from where the clothes lay there is a small tree. Unfortunately there is no scale given but it seems possible that this tree along with other vegetation may have projected roots towards the water and offered some small obstructions along the edge of the bank. In the report you had with you there was some mention of other objects being recovered from this spot, and I should have liked to have heard more about these and how it would appear that they got there.

Had *we* been investigating the case (apart from any divining) I think it is probable that we should have gone down stream from where the clothes were found and stopped at the first tree as a spot most likely to offer some obstruction to an object being carried down stream. I do not of course say that we should have done so: I merely suggest the possibility.

Dr. Dingwell concurred with Professor Curtis that an eddy may have been present where the body of Lewis George Bluck was retrieved and addressed the vital importance of undertaking controlled experiments in areas of such controversy.

This seems to me quite likely, and plus the point I have outlined above we have one normal source of information which cannot be excluded. Of course this *may* not be the explanation at all: we can only say that it is not excluded, and that it is much to be preferred to any "psychic" or similar theory. Other normal theories might be advanced; and, indeed, in these cases it is almost impossible to exclude every normal source without rigidly controlled experiments and statistical checks by which it may be estimated how far the successes exceed those expected on the theory of chance coincidence.

In his conclusion, the doctor further emphasized that P.C. Terry's role in locating the body need not be attributed to the presence of a mysterious force or skill.

It would doubtless be possible to have a series of experiments with Terry, but I think that you may be inclined to agree that the present is not the best time for them. On the other hand, if you see no objection to it, it might be of interest and possibly of service to use Terry in cases where his alleged faculty might be allowed to be present at the operations if all publicity can be avoided.

I do not want in any way to discourage Terry, but, as I am sure you will agree, it must not be imagined that it is any way likely that we shall be convinced of anything supernormal in the procedure as long as the experiments are of the kind hitherto reported. Do not think that I deny the possibility. It is merely that they are not the kind of experiments that the scientific observer demands before he commits himself to theories which suggest something beyond the normal.

Aside from a brief memorandum of August 8, 1941, from the Ministry of Home Security recommending that Professor Curtis keep in touch with the police in the event that P.C. Terry's powers were to be used again, there the file ends, and so does the remarkable story of this all-too-brief liaison between two worlds that were otherwise poles apart.[1]

Was Police Constable Philip Terry's skill evidence of true dowsing, as his colleagues and superiors in the Warwickshire Police Force certainly seemed to believe? Or can the answers be found within the theories of the distinctly more skeptical pair, Dr. Dingwell and Professor Curtis? How relevant were the comments of Dr. Stradling with respect to ensuring that "support" for "the mysterious" should be avoided at all costs during such a "particularly dangerous" time? And did those same comments have an effect on the opinions of those tasked with examining the evidence for and against Police Constable Terry's alleged abilities?

More than sixty years have now passed since the strange events of the summer of 1941 in the heart of the picturesque English countryside. It is tempting to imagine that British police might still be employing dowsers in some of their more baffling cases. Farfetched? We don't think so.

Part Four

X-CREATURES

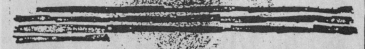

Part of Police report [illegible]

approximately 25 pounds [redacted] fence between four and five feet in height [redacted] and over several other fences of approximately [redacted] into a paddock approximately 50 yards away [redacted] involvement of any known animals most unlikely.

No pattern is discernible in the dates of the incidents, which appear to have all occurred in the later part of the night or just before first light. Moon phases have also been examined for any pattern but this is not consistent.

Shortly after the [redacted] staff found a knife in undergrowth at the Zoo [redacted] of the article and it was then subsequently used in the food preparation room. I have examined this knife which is approximately 12 inches overall length with a 7½ inch blade with a serrated edge. The blade is marked Saufax Inoxydable and the handle is of rough wood.

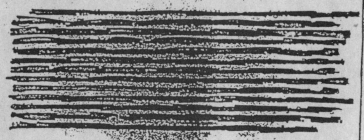

There are no persons known to be strongly opposed to the Zoo or any of a mental state known to the Curator or staff.

The only apparent link in these incidents is the removal of the head, and in the case of the swan and wallaby is the absence of any blood. In this respect, enquiries are being pursued into any possible link with black magic ceremonies.

There are a number of other incidents which have occurred in recent years involving the disappearance of animals and wild fowl from the Zoo but generally these were put down to foxes and other marauding animals and consequently no firm dates or information were recorded. However, if added to the recent series of incidents, these would make a very long catalogue of animals and wild fowl which have been destroyed at the premises in the last few years.

Heavily censored British police files of 1978 detail attacks on animals that may have been caused by large, predatory cats roaming the countryside.

Thirteen

THE MONSTER FILES

Situated only a few miles outside central London, England, is a large building called the Public Record Office. Not unlike the U.S. National Archives and Records Administration in Maryland, the PRO serves as a repository for both still classified and declassified files from a wealth of British government agencies, departments, and services, including the three intelligence branches MI5, MI6, and the Government Communications Headquarters; the Royal Air Force; the British Army; the Home Office; the police; and numerous other official bodies.

For the most part, the material available for public consumption at the PRO is precisely what you would expect to see at an archive housing both military and governmental files: records on the activities of the British military during World Wars I and II; Cold War spy scandals; the Cuban missile crisis; ministerial records that for the most part are mind-numbingly tedious; and much more of a bureaucratic, intelligence, and military nature that has been declassified via the terms of the government's Thirty Year ruling (named after the time that must pass before an official document can be released). But that is not all. Deep within the cavernous bowels of the

PRO, something else lurks—something ancient and terrifying: the never-before-seen files on what we have affectionately dubbed the X-creatures.

It was Sunday, May 9, 1830, and the Royal Navy barque *Rob Roy* was homeward-bound for Britain after a long and arduous journey—a journey that was, for the most part, incident-free. Until, that is, the *Rob Roy* approached the island of St. Helena.

From recently uncovered British Admiralty files held at the Public Record Office comes the following, startling account of one Captain James Stockdale, who takes up the story. Regrettably due to the passage of time, the details concerning to whom within the Admiralty the report was sent and precisely why have been lost. Nevertheless it makes for fascinating reading.

Light winds and fine clean weather. Strong [illegible] on the surface. Wind SSE with a light swell. Saw several very large whales—some of them very light coloured. About five P.M. all at once while I was walking on the poop my attention was drawn to the water on the port bow by a scuffling noise. Likewise all the watch on deck were drawn to it (being Sunday there was nothing doing).

Judge my amazement when what should stare us all in the face as if not knowing whether to come over the deck or to go around to the stern—but the great thundering big sea snake!

Now I had heard of the fellow before—and I have killed snakes twenty-four feet long in the straits of Malaca, but they would go in his mouth.

I think he must have been asleep for we were going along very softly two knots an hour, and he seemed as much alarmed as we were—and taken all aback for about fifteen seconds. But he soon was underway and, when fairly off, his head was square with our topsail and his tail was square with the foremast.

My ship is 171 feet long overall—and the foremast is 42 feet from the stern which would make the monster about 129 feet long. If I had not seen it I could not have believed it but there was no mistake or doubt of its length—for the brute was so close I could even smell his nasty fishy smell.

When underway he carried his head about six feet out of water—with a fin between the shoulders about two feet long. I think he was swimming about five miles an hour—for I watched him from the topsail yard till I lost sight of him in about fifty minutes. The thickened part of his body seemed to be as large round as a beef [illegible]. I hope never to see him more. It is enough to frighten the strong at heart.

James Stockdale, Captain.

Precisely what fearsome beast Captain Stockdale saw has never been satisfactorily explained, and the details of the incident were apparently quietly filed away and conveniently forgotten by a distinctly puzzled Admiralty. One presumes, however, that the image of a monstrous, snakelike creature no less than 129 feet long charging along the high seas remained with Captain Stockdale until his dying day. As for the Admiralty—and perhaps much to its regret—its sea-serpent file failed to stay closed.

In an Admiralty record dated 1857 and titled "Bombay to Liverpool: Sea Serpent," we learn about another strange beast from Commander George Henry Harrington, Ship's Officer William Davies, and Second Officer E. Wheeler of the 1,063-ton ship the *Castilan*. On December 13 of that year at 6:30 P.M. in the evening, according to the captain, a horrific-looking creature loomed into view—once again, interestingly enough, in the vicinity of St. Helena.

While myself and officers were standing on the lee side of the poop—looking toward the island—we were startled by the sight of a huge marine animal which reared its head out of the water within twenty yards of the ship—when it suddenly disappeared for about half a minute and then made a reappearance in the same manner again—showing us distinctly its neck and head about ten or twenty feet out of the water.

Its head was shaped like a long buoy—and I should suppose the diameter to have been seven or eight feet in the largest part with a kind of scroll or ruff encircling it about two feet from the top. The water was discoloured for several hundred feet from the head, so much so that on its first appearance my impression was that the ship was in broken waters, produced, as I supposed, by some volcanic agency, since I passed the island before.

But the second appearance completely dispelled those fears and assured us that it was a monster of extraordinary length and appeared to be moving slowly towards the land. The ship was going too fast to enable us to reach the masthead in time to form a correct estimate of this extreme length—but from what we saw from the deck we conclude that he must have been over two hundred feet long.

The Boatswain and several of the crew, who observed it from the forecastle, state that it was more than double the length of the ship, in which case it must have been five hundred feet.

Be that as it may—I am convinced that it belonged to the serpent tribe. It was of a dark colour about the head and covered with several white spots. Having [illegible] of the ship at the time I was unable to round-to without risk, and therefore was precluded from getting another sight of this Leviathan of the Deep.

Is it truly possible that a mere 150 years ago our oceans were home to *Jurassic Park*–like beasts five hundred feet in length? If not for the commander's own admission of numerous witnesses to this notable encounter with this wonderfully titled "Leviathan of the Deep," we might consider the report to be exaggerated in the extreme. But who knows? And the encounters do not end there, as the following report from an unidentified newspaper of 1863 titled "The Great Sea Serpent Again," which also found its way into Admiralty files at the Public Record Office, amply proves.

The existence of this extraordinary object of curiosity, if not also of terror, has received additional corroboration in the subjoined letter, which has been received in Liverpool from one of the officers of the African mail steamer Athenian, Cape Palmas, May 16th 1863—All doubts may be set at rest about the Great Sea Serpent. On the 6th of May the African Royal Mail steamer Athenian, on her passage from Tenerife to Bathhurst, fell in with one. About 7 A.M. John Chapple, quartermaster, at the wheel, saw something floating towards the ship. He called the attention of the Rev. Mr Smith and another passenger who were on deck at the time, to it. On nearing the steamer it was discovered to be a huge snake, about 100 feet long, of a dark brown colour, head and tail out of the water, the body slightly under. On its head was something like a mane, and the body was about the size of our mainmast.[1]

That a newspaper clipping pertaining to sea monsters should turn up in the archives of the Admiralty is intriguing, since it suggests that someone was actively scanning media outlets as well as official logbooks in attempt to collect and collate such material. Why?

The deep sea and the large creatures it may hold may still be of interest to the military today. In June 2002, *New Scientist* magazine revealed that, in 1997, U.S. Navy underwater sensors designed at the height of the Cold War as tools of surveillance had inadvertently picked up the sounds of what was possibly some form of huge undersea beast, nicknamed Bloop. The creature's sonic frequencies convinced marine experts that it was far bigger than any known species of whale.

In the 1960s the U.S. Navy established an array of underwater microphones, or hydrophones, around the globe to track Soviet submarines. The network was known as SOSUS, short for *Sound Surveillance System*. To this day, the listening stations lie hundreds of yards below the ocean surface, at a depth where sound waves become trapped in a layer of water known as the deep sound channel. Here temperature and pressure cause sound waves to keep moving without being scattered by the ocean surface or bottom. Needless to say, the vast majority of the sounds detected can be attributed to whales, ships, or earthquakes, but not all of them—including the mysterious Bloop.

Could the creature have been a giant squid perhaps? The largest squid (or cephalopod) ever officially recorded was approximately sixty feet in length. However, Phil Lobel, a marine biologist at Boston University, Massachusetts, doubted that giant squid were the source of Bloop.

"Cephalopods have no gas-filled sac, so they have no way to make that type of noise," he said. "Though you can never rule anything out completely, I doubt it." He did, however, admit that the likely source of the signal was something "biological in origin." And the U.S. Navy remains equally baffled too.

Christopher Fox of the U.S. National Oceanic and Atmospheric Administration's Acoustic Monitoring Project at Portland, Oregon, has given the signals names such as Train, Whistle, Slowdown, Upsweep, and even Gregorian Chant. He told *New Scientist* that most can be explained by ocean currents and volcanic activity: Upsweep, for example, was tracked to an undersea South Pacific mountain that has not been identified as "live."

The sound waves, explained Fox, are similar to voiceprints: "You're able to look at the characteristics of the sound and say, 'There's a blue whale, there's a fin whale, there's a boat, there's a humpback whale, and here comes an earthquake.'" But for now at least, Bloop continues to mystify.[2]

But sea serpents are not the only type of unidentified creature to attract the attention and interest of the British military.

No less than 250 million years ago, movements in the earth's crust led to the creation of a huge rift across Scotland that, today, is known as the Great Glen. As the centuries passed, the deeper parts of the Glen filled with water, and it now exists in the form of three main lakes, or *lochs*, to give them their correct title: Loch Oich, Loch Lochy, and Loch Ness. For more than a century and a half they have been connected by the sixty-mile-long Caledonian Canal, which provides passage for small marine vehicles from the North Sea to the Atlantic Ocean.

By far the largest of the three lochs is Loch Ness. Twenty-four miles in length and almost a mile wide, it contains more water than any other British lake, and at its deepest point the loch extends to a mind-boggling depth of almost one thousand feet. Surrounded by trees, mountains, and with water as black as ink, it is little wonder that Loch Ness is viewed by many as both a magical and a sinister location. And as practically anyone who has ever marveled at the mysteries of our world will be only too well aware, the loch is the alleged home of Nessie—arguably the world's most famous lake-monster.

As with other mysterious phenomena such as UFOs, ghosts, the occult, and extrasensory perception, the debate about precisely what does or does not live in Loch Ness has raged for decades—if not centuries even.

The earliest account of what may conceivably have been an encounter with one of the legendary beasts of Loch Ness reputedly occurred in A.D. 565 when St. Columbus was reported to have saved a swimmer from almost becoming the creature's dinner and commanded it to "go back with all speed." Of course, the fog of time, the lack of corroborating accounts, and that some researchers have disputed the nature of the encounter and even its supposed location means that we will never really know how relevant this case is to the overall mystery of what may lurk within the depths of the loch. There can be no doubt, however, that Loch Ness has a rich history of monster sightings.

In 1908, John Macleod observed a strange creature, estimated to be approximately thirty feet in length, which had an eel-like head, in the River Moriston, which later swam into the connecting loch. And on June 17, 1933, Edna MacInnes and David Mackay of Inverness saw a forty-foot-long creature with a giraffelike neck swimming in the loch.

Three years later a Mr. and Mrs. MacMillan viewed a similar long neck and two humps out in the loch for no less than fifteen minutes; and in 1938 Mr. John MacLean witnessed the neck and head of an unidentified animal rear up out of the water at a distance of only sixty feet and appear to swallow something. Moments later, said MacLean, the creature's body—complete with two humps again—appeared floating on the surface for several minutes.

Perhaps strangest and most spectacular of all, however, are those reports where the creatures have reportedly been seen on land in the vicinity of the loch. If the small number of such encounters in hand are not hoaxes, then they demonstrate the reality of a highly unusual breed of creature within Loch Ness.

In 1923, for example, a twenty-five-foot-long creature with a large, humped body and a "pug-nosed" head was seen on the road near the loch by a Mr. Alfred Cruickshank. It should be noted, however, that Cruickshank did not discuss his experience until after there was a media blitz on the Loch Ness monster story in 1933. At this time other land-based encounters were reported, including that of a Mr. and Mrs. George Spicer. It was July 22, 1933, and the Spicers were on holiday and driving along the Loch Ness Lakeshore Road when they claimed to have seen a strange-looking beast, which they could only describe as a "prehistoric animal," lumber across the road.

Of course, encounters similar to these could fill a plethora of books—and indeed have. For our purposes, however, we will focus on a celebrated incident from 1960 that, aside from the remarkable nature of the report itself, attracted the interest and attention of an elite division of Britain's military.

Early on the morning of Saturday, April 23, 1960, an English-man named Tim Dinsdale was driving along the shores of Loch Ness. Dinsdale was a self-described monster hunter and had been at the loch for five days, rising at the break of dawn and setting out to patrol various sectors of the vast expanse of water—and up until that point without success whatsoever. On the morning in question, however, which was to be his final day at the loch before returning to his regular career as an aeronautical engineer, his life would well and truly be turned upside down.

At approximately 8:30 A.M. he decided to cut short his watch and return to his hotel. Thirty minutes later he was driving through the nearby village of Upper Foyers and approaching his hotel. While passing Foyers Bay at a relatively slow speed, Dinsdale turned his head toward the loch and noticed something moving on the surface of the water at a distance of around four thousand feet.

Said Dinsdale, "Unhurriedly I stopped the car and raising my binoculars, focused them carefully upon it. The object was per-fectly clear and now quite large, and although when first I had seen it, it lay sideways on, during the few seconds I had taken with the binoculars it seemed to have turned away from me. It lay motionless on the water, a long oval shape, a distinct mahogany color, and on the left flank a huge dark blotch could be seen, like the dapple on a cow. For some reason it reminded me of the back of an African buf-falo—it had fullness and girth and stood well above the water, and although I could see it from end to end there was no visible sign of a dorsal fin upon it; and then, abruptly, it began to move. I saw ripples break away from the further end and I knew at once I was looking at the extraordinary humped back of some huge living creature!"

Dinsdale scrambled to turn on his 16mm Bolex cine camera (complete with 135mm telephoto lens), which was perched on its tripod in the car next to him. Needless to say he wasted no time in filming the unusual spectacle. Dinsdale would later state that the creature traveled on an erratic course and left behind it an extensive V-shaped wake and appeared to be gently and slowly submerging.

Two to three hundred yards from the far shore, however, it suddenly and without warning altered direction and began heading south and parallel to the shore. By this time, it was almost totally beneath the surface of the loch, and Dinsdale was forced to make a nerve-racking decision.

In what can only be described as a monster hunter's worst night-mare, Dinsdale realized that, after having had his camera running for four minutes, he was running perilously short of film and knew that he had to get closer to the shore in the event that the "ani-mal"—if indeed that was what it truly was—turned and headed back across the loch. Dinsdale made his decision in a split second. He stopped filming and drove at a wild pace through Lower Foyers, across a field, and down to the edge of the loch itself. Dinsdale's nightmare was about to get even worse. The surface of the loch was as calm as could be and the "thing" was gone. He did have his four minutes of film, however.

Dinsdale tried to keep knowledge of the film to an absolute min-imum and hoped for a quiet, serious viewing of its contents by the world's scientific community. That was not to be, as the media caught wind of the story.

On June 13, 1960, the London *Daily Mail* newspaper published details of the story and included still photographs from the four-minute film. Later that day, Dinsdale appeared on BBC Television's *Panorama*, and the film was shown to one and all. Inevitably, the public was fascinated by the controversy, and Dinsdale was deluged with mail and inquiries from across the country and throughout the world. Dinsdale was now well and truly caught up in the mystery, and so eventually was the Joint Air Reconnaissance Intelligence Center—an elite branch of the British military.

The Joint Air Reconnaissance Intelligence Center (JARIC) is based at Royal Air Force Brampton, near Huntingdon, England, and has a total staff of about five hundred, comprising service per-sonnel from the British Army, Royal Air Force, and Royal Navy and more than a hundred civil servants. Its role is to exploit and analyze images from all available sources and produce intelligence products and services to meet the requirements of the British Ministry of Defense and the operational commands. It provides this intelligence to military commanders and the government in support of current military operations and wider intelligence matters.

In 1965, David James, a former member of the British Parliament intrigued by the mystery of Loch Ness, persuaded JARIC's expert photographic interpretation team to take a look at the Dinsdale film. James had had previous dealings with JARIC over the Loch Ness Monster. On October 18, 1962, James's first expedition to the loch with the Loch Ness Investigative Bureau captured on 35mm, black-and-white film for just over half a minute some form of animate, humped object swimming close to—but never quite breaking—the surface of the loch. In the following year, the JARIC team examined the film footage and concluded that it showed not a wave effect, as had been postulated, but a solid body, dark in tone with a surface that "glistened."

On June 6 of the following year another piece of film footage was submitted to JARIC after members of David James's team caught sight of and filmed a "dark cylindrical object" that emerged from the water and lay in the shallows on a beach two and a quarter miles distant on the opposite side of Loch Ness. Not only that, the eyewitnesses reported that they had also seen "a serpentine head and neck."

On this occasion, JARIC asserted that the object appeared to move slightly, but that it was impossible to determine if its movement was independent or due to the action of the waves near the shore. The film was then viewed by an independent panel, who agreed that the shape observed in the film footage *did* correspond closely with the eyewitness descriptions.

JARIC had yet another opportunity to examine footage from the James team when on August 1, 1965, Elizabeth Hall, a member of the Loch Ness Expedition, filmed nine seconds of crucial film. According to JARIC, the film showed two wakes proceeding parallel to one another. The wakes were, said JARIC, 3,846 feet from the camera and approximately nine feet from each other, with one being around seven and a half feet ahead of the other. The speed of the objects was roughly one mile per hour. The JARIC analyses certainly did not prove that large, unknown animals inhabited Loch Ness. But David James was convinced that JARIC's experts offered the best hope of obtaining something conclusive from film footage. That's how JARIC would eventually come to examine the Dinsdale film. Their report is dated December 21, 1965.

The object image has been measured on frames 1 and 6 and size confirmed on frame 120. What one has to measure is a solid, black, approximately triangular shape, with NO impression of perspective. If this shape is assumed to be a plane triangle, in the vertical plane (parallel to the negative plane) it is a triangle with a base 5.5 ft approx. and height 3.7 ft approx. If in the horizontal plane it would be a triangle with base 5.5 ft approx. and height (i.e. length) 9.2 ft approx.

Between frames 816 (34 secs) and 1440 (60 secs) the object is traveling approx. parallel to the loch shore. At this time it is approx. 100 yards from the loch shore. Measures made of several of the frames in this sequence suggest that the mean speed is at least 7 mph and, it seems likely the speed may be as high as 10 mph. A reasonable assumption would be that during the complete film sequence the object was traveling at or approaching 10 mph.

The interpretation is a more difficult problem, but first consider whether this may be a surface vessel of any kind. The object appears to submerge but it can readily be argued that under certain conditions of light, reflectivity and aspect angle etc. objects may NOT be visible on the photography. The triangular object has a solid look about it, as if in fact it was an object with a continuous surface.

During the sequence in which the triangle is visible it is

moving AWAY from the OP and if it were a surface vessel it would be a view from the stern and the measure of 5+ ft would be a beam measurement.

In small craft length and beam are closely related and it is doubtful if a hull with this beam would have a length in excess of 16 ft. With small craft with "non-planning" hulls, the maximum speed, regardless of propulsive power, is limited by the waterline length, e.g. the 14 ft boat with Seagull outboard at 6+ to 7 mph is probably at or near its maximum possible speed. The object is traveling at 10 mph and it is doubtful if a "non-planning" hull of under 16 ft. could achieve this speed. A power boat shell with planning hull could easily achieve and exceed this speed and the design is such that it could appear to have a continuous surface. However these craft are normally painted in such a way as to be photo visible at any time and in any case the existence of such a craft on the loch would scarcely be missed by an observer. The assumption is therefore that it is NOT a surface vessel. One can presumably rule out the idea that it is any sort of submarine vessel for various reasons which leaves the conclusion that it is probably an animate object.

Considering the shape and size of the object, it can obviously NOT be a plane triangle. It is an object with some "body." The base of the triangle is blurred as one would expect with breaking water behind it and the base measurement is probably a true expression of the width or beam of the object at the waterline. The height of the solid object will be somewhat obscured because in this type of view, with NO impression of perspective, part of the measure on the photo is a Y measure due to the fore and aft length of the object (depth of view). It is impossible to define this part without knowing the fore and aft length. However if ALL of the measure were a Y measure the fore and aft length would be 9.2 ft. It seems reasonable that the fore and aft length of that portion above water is considerably less than this and therefore the part of the measure due to Y is a small part and it may seem reasonable to believe that the height of the object above the water line is about 3 ft.

If animate, the surface shape of the object will NOT be angular. As expected the apex of the triangle has a rounded shape. The slope of the sides of the triangle suggests that there will be some increase in width below the water line and even if slight means the width of the object is at least 6 ft. Even if the object is relatively flat bellied, the normal body "rounding" in nature would suggest that there is at least 2 ft under the water from which it may be deduced that a cross section through the object would not be less than 6 ft wide and 5 ft high. This would certainly mean that when submerged the object was disturbing more water than the underwater surface of a small boat and would therefore give a more pronounced wake.

The conclusions of the JARIC study were welcomed with eager and open arms by the monster-hunting community. According to celebrated Loch Ness Monster expert Roy P. Mackal, "The JARIC analysis is important as an independent and expert study, free of either pro or con monster bias."

Mackal continued, "The Dinsdale film is a most important item of authentic data, agreeing with many eyewitness observations. The great distance at which the film was made makes the film grainy and disappointing as far as detail is concerned; nevertheless, it provides objective information as to size, speed, and propulsive behavior."

But not everyone was convinced or even impressed by the JARIC analysis. In his book *The Great Orm of Loch Ness*, the author and investigator F. W. Holiday wrote, "Like an old lady who is scandalized at something improper, the British Museum kept their faces averted from all this activity. However, Dr. Maurice Burton, the arch-critic, took an early opportunity of writing to the International Oceanographic Foundation at Miami, Florida, to cast doubts on JARIC's interpretation of the Dinsdale film which the Foundation had recently discussed with impartiality in its journal *Sea Secrets*. Once again he was unable to produce any specific evidence in support of his negative views. Indeed, he appeared to have made up his mind about this film long before it reached the JARIC experts since he wrote to me on December 9th, 1963, regarding 'Dinsdale's sighting of a red brown motor-boat.' This unconvincing attempt to cast doubts on the findings of some of the foremost photographic analysts in the world seemed to me rather tragic."

But had the JARIC team misinterpreted a boat or dinghy for something more exotic? Peter Costello, author of *In Search of Lake Monsters*, had an important point to make: "It is not clear whether these experts had seen the film or not, for it is quite clear from the shots of the monster, and of the boat taken a short time after, that the pattern of the wake and wash are very different. JARIC were emphatic that the 'hump' was not a boat: Dr. Burton was emphatic that it was. Yet another impasse." The work of JARIC was not yet over, however.

On June 13, 1967, Dick Raynor of the Loch Ness Investigation Bureau filmed a large V-shaped wake moving out of the Dores bay area of the loch. As he was filming at a height of fifty feet above the loch, the pleasure boat *Scott II* came into view and traveled on a parallel course with the object. Raynor's film was duly submitted to JARIC. Its conclusion: that the object filmed was approximately seven feet in length. While this may not sound like a description of something straight out of *The Lost World*, the loch is not home to anything of such proportions—unless, of course, Nessie is real.[3]

The JARIC analyses failed to accurately resolve the issue of what may exist in Loch Ness and actually served to increase the controversy rather than lay it to rest. But that is not all. While much of the work of the JARIC is classified, the results of the examination and analysis of alleged Nessie film footage were released into the public domain shortly after their completion. In this case at least, the British government wasn't hiding anything and neither did we claim it was, although people who heard about our work immediately assumed that the British government was hiding information on the beast. It speaks volumes about society's attitude toward government when people automatically assume that official interest or involvement in a subject equates to official secrecy. We all need to be reminded that this is not always the case. But are we any nearer to knowing what really exists within the inky depths of the loch?

Numerous theories have been advanced as to what the creatures of Loch Ness may be, if, of course, such animals exist and the many and varied reports on record cannot be relegated to the worlds of hoaxing and misperception. Richard Freeman is one of Britain's most respected, full-time monster hunters (or cryptozoologists, as they are "officially" known) and has spent years traveling the globe in pursuit of unidentified animals and mysterious beasts. Formerly a head keeper at Twycross Zoo, England, he is now a prime mover in the British-based Center for Fortean Zoology (which is named after the renowned chronicler of all things unexplained, Charles Fort). Freeman's take on the famous denizens of Loch Ness is unequivocal.

"The idea that Loch Ness is home to some form of dinosaur or plesiosaur—as has been suggested on many occasions—is absurd," says Freeman. "The ecosystem of the loch simply makes that impossible. It lacks a sufficient quantity of fish to allow a large group of such creatures to survive there. My own theory is that we are probably looking at a large and still unidentified type of eel. Now, that might disappoint some people, but an eel of thirty, forty, or fifty feet would still be considered a monster and the Godzilla of the eel family.

"Also, the sightings of the creatures out of the water strongly suggests an eel as the culprit as eels have the capability to move on land too. And the lack of regular, daily sightings of the creature breaking the surface of the loch totally rule out any sort of mammal as being responsible. So that's where I think the evidence is going to lead us: to a large and unidentified species of eel."

As Richard Freeman points out, if Loch Ness truly is home to a species of presently unidentified animal, then the only way that the issue is likely to be resolved is if one day the undisputable physical remains of such an animal are secured for scientific study. As Freeman also astutely notes, however, it would be an undeniable tragedy to have to resort to killing one of the creatures just to prove to one and all its existence. Perhaps it would, therefore, be far better for Loch Ness to retain its air of mystery and wonderment for future generations of monster hunters and thrill seekers. Certainly, the Scottish Board of Tourism would have no argument with that.[4]

In the early part of 1998, the British House of Commons held a debate on the existence, or otherwise, of yet another breed of mystery animal rumored to inhabit the confines of the British Isles: the so-called Alien Big Cats or ABCs. It goes without saying that Britain is *not* home to an indigenous species of large cat such as a panther or puma. However, for decades stories have circulated from some of the wilder parts of the countryside of sightings of large, predatory cats that feed on livestock and terrorize the local populace. In many cases such sightings can of course be relegated to misperception and hoaxing. There now exists, however, a credible body of data in support of the notion that Britain *does* have a thriving population of presently unidentified large cats in its midst—as official documents generated by the British government's House of Commons reveal.

The House of Commons is traditionally regarded as the "lower house," but it is the main parliamentary arena for political battle. A government can only remain in office for as long as it has the support of a majority in the House of Commons; and as with the House of Lords, the House of Commons debates new legislation. The Commons, however, has primacy over the nonelected House of Lords; it scrutinizes the work of the government by various means, including questioning government ministers; and the leader of the political party that wins the majority of Commons seats in an election is called upon to form the next government.

But what of the House of Commons and the Alien Big Cats? Official documentation that followed the February 2, 1998, debate on the controversy in the House of Commons begins with a statement from Mr. Keith Simpson, the member of parliament for mid-Norfolk.

Over the past twenty years, there has been a steady increase in the number of sightings of big cats in many parts of the United Kingdom. These are often described as pumas, leopards or panthers. A survey carried out in 1996 claimed sightings of big cats in 34 English counties.

Many sightings, Simpson continued, had been reported in his constituency by people out walking their dogs or driving down country roads, often at dawn or at dusk. Frequently the description given fitted that of a puma or leopard. Simpson also added that in a number of incidents it had been claimed that ewes, lambs, and even horses had been attacked—and in some cases killed—by the creatures. Simpson continued:

A number of distinguished wildlife experts have suggested that some pumas or leopards could have been released into the countryside when the Dangerous Wild Animals Act 1976 made it illegal to own such animals without a license. They would have been able to roam over a wide area of countryside, live off wild or domestic animals and possibly breed. So what is to be done? I should like to suggest two positive measures for the Minister to consider. At national and local levels, it is logical that the Ministry of Agriculture, Fisheries and Food should be the lead Government Department for coordinating the monitoring and evaluation of evidence concerning big cats.

In response, Mr. Elliot Morley, the parliamentary secretary to the Ministry of Agriculture, Fisheries and Food, conceded that the issue was serious.

The Ministry's main responsibility on big cats is confined to whether the presence of a big cat poses a threat to the safety of livestock. The Ministry is aware that a total of 16 big cats have escaped into the wild since 1977. They include lions, tigers, leopards, jaguars and pumas, but all but two animals were at large for only one day. Because there is a risk that big cats can escape into the wild and because of the threat that such animals could pose to livestock, the Ministry investigates each report in which it is alleged that livestock has been attacked. Reports to the Ministry are usually made by the farmers whose animals have been attacked. In addition, the Ministry takes note of articles in the press describing big cat incidents and will consider them if there is evidence that livestock are at risk.

On receipt of a report of a big cat, explained Morley, the ministry would ask the Farming and Rural Conservation Agency, the ministry's wildlife advisers, to contact the person who reported the sighting.

The FRCA will discuss the situation with the farmer and seek to establish whether the sighting is genuine and whether any evidence can be evaluated. It will follow up all cases where there is evidence of a big cat that can be corroborated and all cases where it is alleged that livestock are being taken. The FRCA will consider all forms of evidence, including photographs given to it by members of the public and farmers, plaster casts of paw prints and video footage. In addition, it will carry out field investigations of carcasses of alleged kills for field signs of the animal responsible.

In conclusion, stated Morley:

It is impossible to say categorically that no big cats are living wild in Britain, so it is only right and proper that the Ministry should continue to investigate serious claims of their existence—but only when there is a threat to livestock and when there is clear evidence that can be validated. I am afraid that, until we obtain stronger evidence, the reports of big cats are still in the category of mythical creatures.[5]

But there *is* evidence that more may be known about the big cat situation within the United Kingdom than has been openly admitted. Jonathan Downes, director of the aforementioned Center for Fortean Zoology, author of a number of groundbreaking books on monster hunting and unknown animals, and the editor of the acclaimed magazine *Animals & Men*, has several tales to tell that link officialdom with an infamous big cat known as the Beast of Exmoor, which is rumored to hunt Britain's West Country.

"For many years," Downes begins, "there have been persistent rumors of a government and military cover-up regarding the big cats seen on Exmoor and Bodmin. I have tended to disregard these reports as merely paranoid conspiracy theorizing. I had never been able to see any real reason why any such cover-up would or should take place. But a telephone call I received several years ago gives a reason why such a cover-up might have taken place.

"I am taking a totally neutral position as regards this report," stresses Downes. "The caller seemed plausible enough, although extremely paranoid. He was also obsessed with Princess Diana and was claiming that when he had been a Royal Marine he had been part of a detachment of security services sent to protect Her Royal Highness while she was paying illicit visits to the home of her lover Major James Hewitt—who I happened to go to school with—in the Devon village of Bratton Clovelly. It must be said, in his defense, that he told me this some weeks before the liaison became public knowledge. It was certainly the first that I had heard of the scandal that was later to rock both the nation and the monarchy.

"I mention this only because it does, to a certain extent at least, establish his bona fides as a Royal Marine and presents some corroboration for the story that he was to tell me. My informant claims that when the Royal Marines made their well-publicized and apparently fruitless hunt for the Beast of Exmoor in the mid-1980s, that he was a sergeant in charge of one of the small reconnaissance parties. He also claims that the marines were also searching for the beast in another unspecified location in the southwest. He further claims that the search was *not* the primary aim of the exercise, but that security implications forbade him from telling me what the marines were *really* doing there."

Downes elaborates, "Over my last decade as a Fortean pundit I have met a number of ex-military personnel, or more accurately people claiming to be ex-military personnel, who have told me that something unpleasant to do with national security has happened on Exmoor over the last twenty-five years. But the main claim of my mysterious caller is that three animals were shot at unspecified locations, and that at least one was shot on private ground by a party who were not only trespassing but who had not been given permission to carry firearms. He claimed that a relatively junior officer had panicked and that the cover-up had been perpetrated further up the chain of command in order to 'save face.'"

Downes has also been given access to various British police reports dealing with the bizarre mutilation and killing of animals at Newquay Zoo in 1978. One such report states that on the night of one of the killings "something" had "attempted to gain access to the lion's cage." Checks outside the cage, the report states, revealed prints that were thought possibly to be those of a large cat of some type; however, the modus operandi behind the killings suggested a degree of sophisticated intelligence, which leaves this particular aspect of the affair somewhat murky.[6]

And there the matter remains to this day. Perhaps one day the controversy will be resolved once and for all. Until that time arrives, however, like the creatures rumored to inhabit Loch Ness, Britain's big cats will continue to coexist with us in stealth, blissfully unaware that their activities have attracted the attention of the highest echelons of the British government.

Fourteen

BUTCHERS FROM BEYOND

For more than thirty-five years, rural America has played host to an uninvited, and most definitely unwelcome, guest. With remarkable stealth, it prowls the length and breadth of the country by night and day, committing atrocious acts of mutilation on innocent cattle. Blood, bodily organs, fluids, and glands are removed with disturbing speed and precision, giving every impression that a superior technology is at work.

In many instances of mutilation, strange aerial lights are reported in the same area, suggesting that the two phenomena, whatever their ultimate nature, have a common origin. Military and unmarked helicopters are also seen in the vicinity of these mutilation incidents, and stories abound of witnesses being threatened into silence by dark and shadowy forces. Who or what is responsible for committing these grisly acts has provoked intense debate—predators, satanic cults, UFOs, and covert biological warfare operations have all been suggested—and the mystery continues to rage.

For a brief period in the late 1970s, however, the Federal Bureau of Investigation found itself caught up in this truly bizarre mystery and perhaps more than anyone else came close to uncovering the

FBI

TRANSMIT VIA:
☐ Teletype
☐ Facsimile
☐ AIRTEL

PRECEDENCE:
☐ Immediate
☐ Priority
☐ Routine

CLASSIFICATION:
☐ TOP SECRET
☐ SECRET
☐ CONFIDENTIAL
☐ UNCLAS E F T O
☐ UNCLAS

Date _____ 2/16/79

TO: DIRECTOR, FBI

FROM: SAC, ALBUQUERQUE

UNSUBS;
CATTLE MUTILATIONS OCCURRING
IN WESTERN STATES
CIR - MISCELLANEOUS

For the past seven or eight years mysterious cattle mutilations have been occurring throughout the United States and for the past four years have been occurring within the State of New Mexico. Officer GABE VALDEZ, New Mexico State Police, has been handling investigations of these mutilations within New Mexico. Information furnished to this office by Officer VALDEZ indicates that the animals are being shot with some type of paralyzing drug and the blood is being drawn from the animal after an injection of an anti-coagulant. It appears that in some instances the cattle's legs have been broken and helicopters without any identifying numbers have reportedly been seen in the vicinity of these mutilations. Officer VALDEZ theorizes that clamps are being placed on the cow's legs and they are being lifted by helicopter to some remote area where the mutilations are taking place and then the animal is returned to its original pasture. The mutilations primarily consist of removal of the tongue, the lymph gland, lower lip and the sexual organs of the animal. Much mystery has surrounded these mutilations, but according to witnesses they give the appearance of being very professionally done with a surgical instrument, and according to VALDEZ, as the years progress, each surgical procedure appears to be more professional. Officer VALDEZ has advised that in no instance, to his knowledge, have these carcasses ever attacked by predator or scavenger animals, although there are tracks which would indicate that coyotes have been circling the carcass from a distance. He also advised that he has requested Los Alamos Scientific Laboratory to conduct investigation for him but until just recently has always been advised that the mutilations were done by predatory animals. Officer VALDEZ stated that just recently he has been told by two assistants at Los Alamos Scientific Laboratory that they were able to determine

2 - Bureau
1 - Albuquerque

For decades, someone or something has been mutilating and killing cattle across the United States. This FBI document of 1979 titled "Cattle Mutilations Occurring in Western States" demonstrates the scale of the mystery.

truth, as an examination of the extraordinary FBI files pertaining to this subject will reveal. But first, some necessary background.

Essentially, the first animal mutilation took place in September 1967, when Lady, a three-year-old horse belonging to Nellie Lewis, was found killed and mutilated under shocking circumstances on the ranch of Nellie's brother, Harry King, in southern Colorado. While Lady's body was left intact, the flesh from her neck and head had been completely removed in a surgical fashion.

From his Alamosa home, Nellie Lewis's husband, Berle, commented on the sudden increase in UFO sightings that accompanied Lady's death: "We see something, I won't say what it is, every night." A further account came one month after the events at the King ranch from two witnesses who caught sight of a pair of high-flying, cigar-shaped objects, each about half the size of a football field, on a course that would have taken them over the southern Colorado area.[1]

In mid-1974, at least five cattle were found slain and mutilated in Madison County, Nebraska. In all cases the genitalia of the animals were removed, and one cow was reported to be minus one ear and eye, as well as its nose, mouth, and tongue. Again, unusual aerial activity was reported in the vicinity. One witness, Harold Kester, described seeing an object that "looked as if it had a bluish green light on each side with a glow surrounding it. It was behind a tree and moved from one side of the tree to the other. We couldn't tell how close it was or how fast it was moving."[2]

In July 1975, six head of cattle were found mutilated forty miles north of Council, Idaho. Again, tongues, genitalia, and the udders of the animals were removed. In a series of similar findings in Colorado, the cattle had been entirely drained of blood. "We didn't find any [blood] at all," commented Sheriff Jim Hileman of Adams County. "It could have been washed away by rain, but I'd have to say that not finding any blood in this sort of a case is highly unusual."[3]

Following a series of mutilations that hit the town in June 1978, a citizen of Elsberry, Missouri reported, "I'm not scared, just uneasy."

As in Madison County, Nebraska, in 1974, and Council, Idaho, in 1975, the animals were missing vital organs and body parts including teeth, eyes, tongues, and ears. And, more baffling, the animals were again reported to have been drained of blood in some vampirelike fashion.[4]

Greeley, Colorado, became the target for mutilators in September 1980. A Briggsdale rancher, Roland Ball, commenting on two cattle found slaughtered, said, "That's the first one I've ever seen this way. We found another west of the one that had been dead for two days, but it had been dead for quite a while. But it had one ear gone and I could tell it wasn't a predator." In addition to the removed organs, one of the cattle had a four-inch-diameter circle of hide removed from around its navel. "They had just taken the navel out and everything around it. It was just as neat a cut as could be," said Ball.[5]

At 9:45 P.M. on December 13, 1993, Christopher O'Brien, a journalist of southern Colorado, received a telephone call from a Crestone resident house-sitting in the Baca Grants, who reported that a "glowing white object" had fallen to the ground south of the Baca, north of Hooper.

The next day, a 1,700-pound bull was found dead on the Dale and Clarence Vigil ranch in the nearby Costilla County. In addition to the usual signs of mutilation, broken tree branches were found where the animal lay, and six feet up, red hair and blood were found on the tips of other branches, giving the impression that the bull had been physically lifted off the ground.[6]

All the currently available evidence suggests that FBI knowledge of the phenomenon began in the early months of 1973, when a cluster of reports surfaced in Iowa. Later that year more incidents occurred in at least a dozen counties in Kansas, with some extending into Nebraska. Many of the killings were associated with sightings of unidentified aerial lights and unmarked helicopters. But absolutely lacking was any evidence to suggest who (or what) was perpetrating these disturbing crimes.

With public anxiety rising, rumors began to circulate that the mutilations were the work of a powerful and extraordinarily well-equipped band of devil worshipers who were killing the unfortunate cattle and excising various body parts for use in their satanic ceremonies. On September 4, 1974, U.S. senator Carl T. Curtis wrote to the FBI director, Clarence M. Kelley, and informed him that an article had appeared in the Hastings, Nebraska, *Daily Tribune* in which it was reported that in addition to cattle mutilation incidents in Hastings, sightings of unidentified flying objects had been reported in the counties of Antelope and Knox. According to Sheriff Herbert Thompson, who was quoted in the newspaper, it was unclear what all of the aerial objects were; however, at least two had been identified as helicopters.

Despite the phenomenal number of mutilations and the repeated sightings of anomalous aerial lights, all of which suggested that some form of coordinated operation was under way, the FBI was curiously reluctant to become involved in the investigations at that time: "It appears that no Federal Law within the investigative jurisdiction of the FBI has been violated, inasmuch as there is no indication of interstate transportation of the maimed animals," FBI director Kelley advised Senator Curtis.

Four months later, an Airtel (an intra-FBI communication with highest priority of those sent through the mail) was sent from the FBI office at Minneapolis to the FBI Laboratory, playing down the theory that the mutilations were the work of some unidentified entity, and asserting that, in all probability, they were caused by "other varmints, believed to be foxes." A brief report citing the testimony of Richard Hilde, chief agent with the North Dakota Crime Bureau, stated that "the dead animals in North Dakota had been found in scattered locations, and the Bureau believed they died of natural causes and then small animals such as foxes had eaten the soft part of the animals."

This "solution" does not account for the mystery helicopters, nor the strange lights reported time and again in the areas of mutilations. Nor does it explain the total lack of similar reports prior to the late 1960s. And when an alarming outbreak of mutilations occurred in Colorado in 1974 and 1975, it became more than apparent that this was not the work of the local animal population.

On August 29, 1975, Floyd K. Haskell, senator from Colorado, wrote an impassioned letter to Theodore P. Rosack, special agent in charge of the FBI at Denver, Colorado, imploring the FBI to make a full investigation into the cattle mutilations, in an attempt to resolve the matter once and for all.

For several months my office has been receiving reports of cattle mutilations throughout Colorado and other western states. At least 130 cases in Colorado alone have been reported to local officials and the Colorado Bureau of Investigation (CBI); the CBI has verified that the incidents have occurred for the last two years in nine states.

The ranchers and rural residents of Colorado are concerned and frightened by these incidents. The bizarre mutilations are frightening in themselves: in virtually all the cases, the left ear, rectum and sex organ of each animal has been cut away and the blood drained from the carcass, but with no traces of blood left on the ground and no footprints.

That unmarked helicopter was also out in force in Colorado, as Senator Haskell was only too well aware.

In Colorado's Morgan County area there has [sic] also been reports that a helicopter was used by those who mutilated the carcasses of the cattle, and several persons have reported being chased by a similar helicopter.

Because I am gravely concerned by this situation, I am asking that the Federal Bureau of Investigation enter the case. Although the CBI has been investigating the incidents, and local officials also have been involved, the lack of a central unified

direction has frustrated the investigation. It seems to have pro-
gressed little, except for the recognition at long last that the incidents must be taken seriously.

Now it appears that ranchers are arming themselves to protect their livestock, as well as their families and themselves,
because they are frustrated by the unsuccessful investigation.
Clearly something must be done before someone gets hurt.

The loss of livestock in at least twenty-one states under similar
circumstances suggested that an interstate operation was being coordinated. Senator Haskell closed his letter by urging the FBI to
begin its investigation as soon as possible.

Senator Haskell forced the issue by issuing a press release, informing the media that he had asked the FBI to investigate the mutilations. This caused the *Denver Post* newspaper to take up the
senator's plea on September 3: "If the Bureau will not enter the investigation of the mysterious livestock deaths in Colorado and some
adjacent states then Senator Floyd Haskell should take the matter to
Congress for resolution."

Aware of previous FBI statements that the killings were not
within the Bureau's jurisdiction, the *Denver Post* stated firmly, "The
incidents are too widespread—and potentially too dangerous to
public order—to ignore. Narrow interpretations of what the FBI's
role is vis-à-vis state authority are not adequate to the need."

The issue of possible disregard for the law should the Bureau not
wish to become involved was also high on the *Post*'s agenda. "There
is already federal involvement. Consider this: Because of the gun-
happy frame of mind developing in eastern Colorado (where most
of the incidents have been occurring), the U.S. Bureau of Land
Management (BLM) has had to cancel a helicopter inventory of its
lands in six counties. BLM officials are simply afraid their helicopters might be shot down by ranchers and others frightened by cattle
deaths."

On the day after publication, Special Agents Rosack and Sebesta of the Colorado FBI made a visit to the offices of the *Denver Post*, where, in a meeting with three *Post* representatives, Charles R. Buxton, Lee Olson, and Robert Partridge, they spelled out the FBI's position with respect to mutilations: "Unless the FBI has investigative jurisdiction under federal statute, we cannot enter any investigation."

One week later, on September 11, Senator Haskell telephoned Clarence M. Kelley at the FBI to discuss the issue of cattle and animal mutilation and the possibility of the FBI becoming involved in determining who, exactly, was responsible. Again, the FBI asserted that this was a matter outside its jurisdiction.

"Senator Haskell [said that] he understood our statutory limitations but he wished there was something we could do," reported an FBI official, R. J. Gallagher. Haskell had additional reasons for wanting the mutilation issue resolved swiftly, as Gallagher recorded in an internal memorandum of September 12, 1975.

Senator Haskell recontacted me this afternoon and said that he had received a call from Dane Edwards, editor of the paper in Brush, Colorado, who furnished information that US Army helicopters had been seen in the vicinity of where some of the cattle were mutilated and that he, Edwards, had been threatened but Senator Haskell did not know what sort of threats Edwards had received or by whom. He was advised that this information would be furnished to our Denver Office and that Denver would closely follow the situation.

The FBI ultimately determined that the unidentified-helicopter issue was also outside its jurisdiction. Curiously, however, during this same time, numerous reports of both UFOs and unidentified helicopters surfaced in the immediate vicinity of strategic military installations around the USA, and evidence suggests that someone within the FBI was fully aware of this and was taking more than a cursory interest in these sightings. Proof comes via a number of Air

Force reports forwarded to the FBI only weeks after its contact with Senator Haskell. One report from December 1975 states:

On 7 Nov 75 an off duty missile launch officer reported that unidentified aircraft resembling a helicopter had approached and hovered near a USAF missile launch control facility, near Lewistown. Source explained that at about 0020, 7 Nov 75, source and his deputy officer had just retired from crew rest in the Soft Support Building (SSB) at the LCF, when both heard the sound of a helicopter rotor above the SSB. The Deputy observed two red-and-white lights on the front of the aircraft, a white light on the bottom, and a white light on the rear.

On 7 Nov 75, Roscoe E. III, Captain, 341 Strategic Missile Wing, advised that during the hours of 6–7 Nov 75, two adjacent LCFs, approximately 50 miles south of aforementioned LCF, reported moving lights as unidentified flying objects (UFO). During this period there were no reports of helicopter noises from personnel at these LCFs.

This office was recently notified of a message received by security police MAFB, MT., detailing a similar nocturnal approach by a helicopter at a USAF weapons storage area located at another USAF base in the Northern Tier states. Local authorities denied the use of their helicopters during the period 6–7 Nov 75.

It's curious that these reports should have been of interest to the FBI, given the statements made to Senator Haskell that the unidentified-helicopter sightings reported in Colorado were outside the FBI's jurisdiction. It is also notable that a currently unauthenticated document leaked to researcher William Moore refers to the Northern Tier helicopter and UFO sightings of 1975 and expresses concern that, since the media had picked up on the stories, some authority needed to develop an effective disinformation plan to counter the developing interest surrounding the sightings. Could this be why the FBI professed no interest in the Colorado helicopter encounters?[7]

The next indication of FBI involvement in mutilations came in the final months of 1976. In September of that year, *Oui* magazine published a large and comprehensive article outlining the history of the cattle mutilations, the theories surrounding who or what was responsible, and the opinions of numerous persons involved in the whole affair. A copy of the article was sent to FBI headquarters in Washington, D.C., by the special agent in charge at the Springfield, Illinois, FBI office, "in view of numerous references in this article to Federal investigative agencies and also theories that these mutilations of cattle are only a forerunner for later mutilations of human beings."

This reference to the animal mutilations as a forerunner for later mutilations of human beings is notable for one particular reason. Don Ecker spent ten years as a police investigator and is now a writer living in Los Angeles. While looking into claims that human beings had been mutilated, Ecker contacted an active police detective friend, Scot, who had been involved in the investigation of a number of cattle mutilations. "I relayed my various information on human mutes to [Scot] and asked if he would be willing to send an inquiry through his department's computer to the National Crime Information Center, operated and maintained by the FBI in Washington, D.C.," states Ecker.

Several days later, Scot, sounding troubled, got back in touch with Ecker. "Someone is sitting on something, big as hell." Contact was made with a further source, this time in the Department of Justice, who would only state that "if all were smart, they would simply leave this issue alone."[8] Something about this had captured the FBI's interest.

An examination of the animal mutilation files that the FBI has declassified reveals that between September 1976 and early 1978, the Bureau had no further involvement with the mutilation issue. By mid-1978, the FBI could no longer afford to ignore the issue.

With the assistance of local police authorities, medical sources, and concerned ranchers, the FBI slowly came to accept that this sickening mystery was all too real, even as the perpetrators remained disturbingly anonymous and free to conduct their butchery countrywide.

The turning point came when the mutilators focused their attention on Rio Arriba County, New Mexico. This incident convinced the FBI that, whoever was responsible for the strange killings, they were here to stay. Following a series of mutilations between 1976 and 1978, Manuel S. Gomez, a rancher who had himself lost a number of cattle, approached the senator for New Mexico (and a former astronaut) Harrison Schmitt and requested that inquiries be made to determine if, finally, some form of investigation could be instigated to settle the problem.

Schmitt duly complied and on July 10, 1978, wrote to Chief Martin E. Vigil of the New Mexico State Police and informed him of the concerns of Manuel Gomez and other ranchers in the area, many of whom were also losing livestock with worrying regularity to the elusive mutilators.

Aware that Police Officer Gabe Valdez of Espanola had investigated a number of such cases, Vigil asked Captain P. Anaya of the Espanola police to forward him copies of all relevant paperwork, which could in turn be made available to Senator Schmitt, should he wish to take matters further. As a result, by October 1978, Schmitt was in receipt of Valdez's files and, armed with the evidence that something truly mind-blowing was taking place, mailed a letter voicing his concern to the attorney general of the Department of Justice, Griffin B. Bell.

During the past several years, ranchers throughout the West, including my home state of New Mexico, have been victimized by a series of cattle mutilations. As a result, these ranchers have as a group and individually suffered serious economic losses. While an individual cattle mutilation may not be a fed-

eral offense, I am very concerned at what appears to be a continued pattern of an organized interstate criminal activity.
Therefore, I am requesting that the Justice Department re-
examine its jurisdiction in this area with respect to the possible reopening of this investigation.

Attorney General Bell responded with speed and assured Senator Schmitt, "I have asked Philip Heymann, head of the Criminal
Division to look into our jurisdiction over the cattle mutilation
problem with which you are concerned. I must say that the materials sent me indicate the existence of one of the strangest phenome-
nons [sic] in my memory."

That Bell took all of this seriously is evident from the following
note attached to a letter to Heymann: "Please have someone look
into this matter at an early date. Senator Schmitt is our friend and
there have been about 60 mutilations in New Mexico in recent
months."

On March 2, 1979, Assistant Attorney General Heymann wrote a
one-page memorandum for the attention of the FBI and attached
copies of Officer Gabe Valdez's files.

For several years the Criminal Division has been aware of the
phenomenon of animals being mutilated in a manner that
could indicate that such acts are performed by persons as part
of a ritual or ceremony. The report that some of the mutilations
have occurred in Indian country is our first indication that
Federal Law may have been violated. It is requested that the
Federal Bureau of Investigation conduct an appropriate investigation of the 15 mutilations and any others that occur in Indian country as a possible crime on an Indian reservation.

And so the FBI's deep involvement in the animal mystery began
in earnest. For the men and women of the FBI assigned to deal with

the animal mutilations, the first step was to review the files of Police Office Gabe Valdez. Between August 1975 and the summer of 1978, almost thirty cases of animal mutilation had been recorded in the Rio Arriba area, with many seemingly the work of some well-equipped intelligence. One report, filed by Valdez in June 1976, stands out and demonstrates that the genuine mutilations are not the work of predators.

At 8:00 P.M. on June 13, Valdez was contacted by the rancher Manuel Gomez and advised that he had found a three-year-old cow on his ranch that bore all the classic signs of mutilation. As Valdez listened, Gomez stated that the cow's left ear, tongue, udder, and rectum had been removed with what appeared to be a sharp instrument. Yet there was absolutely no blood in the immediate vicinity of the cow, nor were there any footprints in evidence; however, some marks gave every impression that an aerial object had landed and carried out a grisly attack on the unfortunate animal.

At 5:00 A.M. on the following day, Valdez set off for the Gomez ranch along with Paul Riley of the New Mexico Cattle Sanitary Board. On arriving, Officer Valdez and Riley confronted a scene of carnage. The cow was just as Gomez had described: three years old, lying on its right side, vital body parts having been removed with the utmost precision. But that was not all. There were also strange landing marks. Valdez recorded the details in a two-page report written shortly afterward and now declassified by the FBI.

Investigations continued around the area and revealed that a suspected aircraft of some type had landed twice, leaving three pod marks positioned in a triangular shape. The diameter of each pod was 14 inches. Emanating from the two landings were smaller triangular shaped tripods 28 inches and 4 inches in diameter. Investigation at the scene showed that these small tripods had followed the cow for approximately 600 feet. Tracks of the cow showed where she had struggled and fallen.

The small tripod tracks were all around the cow. Other evidence showed that grass around the tripods, as they followed the cow, had been scorched. Also a yellow oily substance was located in two places under the small tripods. This substance was submitted to the State Police Lab. The Lab was unable to detect the content of the substance.

A sample of the substance was submitted to a private lab and they were unable to analyze the substance due to the fact that it disappeared or disintegrated. Skin samples were analyzed by the State Police Lab and the Medical Examiner's Office. It was reported that the skin had been cut with a sharp instrument.

Three days later, Valdez contacted Dr. Howard Burgess, a retired scientist from Sandia Laboratories, and asked him to conduct a radiation test at the scene. The results were astounding. All around the tripod marks and in the immediate tracks, the radiation count was twice that of normal. Valdez came up with an intriguing hypothesis for this: "It is the opinion of this writer that radiation findings are deliberately being left at the scene to confuse investigators."

Valdez discovered something else, too. In the days between his first visit to the Gomez ranch and the second visit with Dr. Howard Burgess, the mysterious aerial object had returned. It led to a distressing discovery.

There was also evidence that the tripod marks had returned and removed the left ear. Tripod marks were found over Mr. Gomez's tire tracks of his original visit. The left ear was intact when Mr. Gomez first found the cow. The cow had a 3-month-old calf which has not been located since the incident. This appears strange since a small calf normally stays around the mother even though the cow is dead.

Valdez noted in his report that this incident was typical of those he had investigated over sixteen months. "They all carry the same pattern," he asserted. Perhaps most pertinent, Valdez had determined that in at least one case, the animal in question had a high dose of atropine in its blood. "This substance is a tranquilizing drug," reported Valdez.

Valdez was also concerned that government-associated laboratories were not reporting complete findings on the controversy. For that reason, Valdez ensured that samples from the slain cattle were later submitted to private chemists for analysis.

Valdez was fully aware of the theories that all of the mutilations were the work of either satanic cults or natural predators, but he dismissed them.

Both [theories] have been ruled out due to expertise and preciseness and the cost involved to conduct such a sophisticated and secretive operation. It should also be noted that during the spring of 1974 when a tremendous amount of cattle were lost due to heavy snowfalls, the carcasses had been eaten by predators. These carcasses did not resemble the carcasses of the mutilated cows. Investigation has narrowed down to these theories which involve (1) Experimental use of Vitamin B12 and (2) The testing of the lymph node system. During this investigation an intensive study has been made of (3) What is involved in germ warfare testing, and the possible correlation of these 3 factors (germ warfare testing, use of Vitamin B12, testing of the lymph node system).

As Valdez's files make abundantly clear, such reports proliferated, including a case from May 1978.

This four year old cross Hereford and Black Angus native cow was found lying on left side with rectum, sex organs, tongue, and ears removed. Pinkish blood from [illegible] was visible, and after two days the blood still had not coagulated. Left front and left rear leg were pulled out of their sockets apparently from the weight of the cow which indicates that it was lifted and dropped back to the ground. The ground around and under the cow was soft and showed indentations where the cow had been dropped. 600 yards away from the cow were the 4-inch circular indentations similar to the ones found at the Manuel Gomez ranch on 4-24-78. This cow had been dead approximately [illegible] hours and was too decomposed to extract samples. This is the first in a series of mutilations in which the cows' legs are broken. Previously the animals had been lifted from the brisket with a strap. These mutilated animals all dehydrate rapidly (in one or two days).

Another document from May 1978 refers to a second incident where abnormal radiation traces were found.

It is believed that this type of radiation is not harmful to humans, although approximately 7 people who visited the mutilation site complained of nausea and headaches. However, this writer has had no such symptoms after checking approximately 11 mutilations in the past 4 months. Identical mutilations have been taking place all over the Southwest. It is strange that no eye witnesses have come forward or that no accidents [have] occurred. One has to admit that whoever is responsible for the mutilations is very well organized with boundless financing and secrecy. Writer is presently getting equipment through the efforts of Mr. Howard Burgess, Albuquerque, N.M. to detect substances on the cattle which might mark them and be picked up by infra-red rays but not visible to the naked eye.

Strange landing marks, elevated radiation readings, tranquilizing drugs, animals covertly airlifted out of the area, what on earth (or off it) was going on? What had Officer Valdez stumbled upon? Was this a highly secret U.S. government or military operation centered on germ warfare testing, or something even more bizarre? The FBI documentation generated as a result of Valdez's police reports suggests that the Bureau took seriously the evidence and official testimony that the officer had collected. A four-page Airtel from Forrest S. Putman, FBI special agent in charge at Albuquerque, to the director of the FBI described the way in which Valdez theorized the mutilations took place.

Information furnished to this office by Officer Valdez indicates that the animals are being shot with some type of paralyzing drug and the blood is being drawn from the animal after an injection of an anti-coagulant. It appears that in some instances the cattle's legs have been broken and helicopters without any identifying numbers have reportedly been seen in the vicinity of these mutilations. Officer Valdez theorizes that clamps are being placed on the cow's legs and they are being lifted by helicopter to some remote area where the mutilations are taking place and then the animal is returned to its original pasture. The mutilations primarily consist of removal of the tongue, the lymph gland, lower lip and the sexual organs of the animal. Much mystery has surrounded these mutilations, but according to witnesses they give the appearance of being very professionally done with a surgical instrument, and according to Valdez, as the years progress, each surgical procedure appears to be more professional. Officer Valdez has advised that in no instance, to his knowledge, are these carcasses ever attacked by predator or scavenger animals, although there are tracks which would indicate that coyotes have been circling the carcass from a distance.

Special Agent Putman then informed the director of the outcome of Valdez's run-ins with officials.

He also advised that he has requested Los Alamos Scientific Laboratory to conduct investigation for him but until just recently has always been advised that the mutilations were done by predatory animals. Officer Valdez stated that just recently he has been told by two assistants at Los Alamos Scientific Laboratory that they were able to determine the type of tranquilizer and blood anti-coagulant that have been utilized.

Putman then spelled out for the director the sheer scale of events.

Officer Valdez stated that Colorado probably has the most mutilations occurring within their State and that over the past four years approximately 30 have occurred in New Mexico. He stated that of these 30, 15 have occurred on Indian Reservations but he did know that many mutilations have gone unreported which have occurred on the Indian reservations because the Indians, particularly in the Pueblos, are extremely superstitious and will not even allow officers in to investigate in some instances. Officer Valdez stated since the outset of these mutilations there have been an estimated 8,000 animals mutilated which would place the loss at approximately $1,000,000.

Putman further informed the director that on the previous day, February 15, 1979, he had met with Officer Gabe Valdez, Senator Harrison Schmitt, R. E. Thompson, United States Attorney (USA), and Bureau special agent Samuel Jones, and it had been decided that the best course of action was for a conference to be convened in Albuquerque, no later than April, where those who had suffered cattle mutilation could discuss this matter to determine what had been developed to date and to recommend further steps to solve the problem.

It is obvious if mutilations are to be solved there is a need for a coordinated effort so that all material available can be gathered and analyzed and further efforts synchronized. Whether the FBI should assume this role is a matter to be decided. If we are merely to investigate and direct our efforts toward the 15 mutilated cattle on the Indian reservation we, I believe, will be in the same position as the other law enforcement agencies at this time and would be seeking to achieve an almost impossible task. It is my belief that if we are to participate in any manner that we should do so fully, although this office and the USA's office are at a loss to determine what statute our investigative jurisdiction would be in this matter. If we are to act solely as a coordinator or in any other official capacity the sooner we can place this information in the computer bank, the better off we would be and in this regard it would be my recommendation that an expert in the computer field at the Bureau travel to Albuquerque in the very near future so that we can determine what type of information will be needed so that when the invitation for the April conference is submitted from Senator Schmitt's Office that the surrounding States will be aware of the information that is needed to place in the computer. It should be noted that Senator Schmitt's Office is coordinating the April conference and will submit the appropriate invitations and with the cooperation of the USA, Mr. Thompson will chair this conference. The FBI will act only as a participant.

Up until this point, Putman had not discussed with the director who might be responsible for the mutilations. That situation was about to change.

Since this has not been investigated by the FBI in any manner we have no theories whatsoever as to why or what is responsible for these cattle mutilations. Officer Gabe Valdez is very adamant in his opinion that these mutilations are the work of the U.S. Government and that it is some clandestine operation either by the CIA or the Department of Energy and in all probability is connected with some type of research into biological warfare. His main reason for these beliefs is that he feels that he was given the "run around" by Los Alamos Scientific Laboratory and they are attempting to cover up this situation. There are also theories that these are cults (religious) of some type of Indian rituals resulting in these mutilations and the wildest theory advanced is that they have some connection with unidentified flying objects.

In his conclusion, Putman laid out the enormous task ahead.

If we are to assume an investigative posture into this area, the matter of manpower, of course, becomes a consideration and I am unable to determine at this time the amount of manpower that would be needed to give this our full attention so that a rapid conclusion could be reached. The Bureau is requested to furnish its comments and guidance on this whole situation including, if desired, the Legal Counsel's assessment of jurisdictional question. An early response would be needed, however, so that we might properly, if requested to do so, obtain the data bank information. If it appears that we are going to become involved in this matter, it is obvious that there would be a large amount of correspondence necessary and Albuquerque would suggest a code name be established of BOVMUT.

On April 20, 1979, the proposed conference came to pass. Nearly two hundred people attended the meeting, which was held at the Albuquerque Public Library. A report to FBI headquarters from Albuquerque, dated April 25, outlines the flavor of the conference and addresses the various opinions of those in attendance.

Forrest S. Putman, Special Agent in Charge (SAC), Albuquerque Office of the FBI, explained to the conference that the Justice Department had given the FBI authority to investigate those cattle mutilations which have occurred or might occur on Indian lands. He further explained that the Albuquerque FBI would look at such mutilations in connection with mutilations occurring off Indian lands for the purpose of comparison and control, especially where the same methods of operation are noted. SAC Putman said that in order for this matter to be resolved, the facts surrounding such mutilations should be gathered and computerized.

District Attorney Eloy Martinez, Santa Fe, New Mexico, told the conference that his judicial district had made application for a $50,000 Law Enforcement Assistance Administration (LEAA) Grant for the purpose of investigating the cattle mutilations. He explained that there is hope that with the funds from this grant, an investigative unit can be established for the sole purpose of resolving the mutilation problem. He said it is his view that such an investigative unit could serve as a headquarters for all law enforcement officials investigating the mutilations and, in particular, would serve as a repository for information developed in order that this information could be coordinated properly. He said such a unit would not only coordinate this information, but also handle submissions to a qualified lab for both evidence and photographs. Mr. Martinez said a hearing will be held on April 24, 1979, for the purpose of determining whether this grant will be approved.

Gabe Valdez, New Mexico State Police, Dulce, New Mexico, reported he has investigated the death of 90 cattle during the past three years, as well as six horses. Officer Valdez said he is convinced that the mutilations of the animals have not been the work of predators because of the precise manner of the cuts. Officer Valdez said he had investigated mutilations of several animals which had occurred on the ranch of Manuel Gomez of Dulce, New Mexico.

Manuel Gomez addressed the conference and explained he had lost six animals to unexplained deaths which were found in a mutilated condition within the last two years. Further, Gomez said that he and his family are experiencing fear and mental anguish because of the mutilations.

The FBI then reported on the lectures delivered by a variety of speakers who had been invited to the conference. Their opinions make for notable reading.

David Perkins, Director of the Department of Research at Libre School in Farasita, Colorado, exhibited a map of the United States which contained hundreds of colored pins identifying mutilation sites. He commented that he had been making a systematic collection of data since 1975, and has never met a greater challenge. He said, "The only thing that makes sense about the mutilations is that they make no sense at all."

Tom Adams of Paris, Texas, who has been independently examining mutilations for six years, said his investigation has shown that helicopters are almost always observed in the area of the mutilations. He said that the helicopters do not have identifying markings and they fly at abnormal, unsafe, or illegal altitudes.

Dr. Peter Van Arsdale, Ph.D., Assistant Professor, Department of Anthropology, University of Denver, suggested that those investigating the cattle mutilations take a systematic approach and look at all types of evidence and is discounting any of the theories such as responsibility by extraterrestrial visitors or satanic cults.

Richard Sigismund, Social Scientist, Boulder, Colorado, presented an argument which advanced the theory that the cattle mutilations are possibly related to activity of UFOs. Numerous other persons made similar type presentations expounding on their theories regarding the possibility that the mutilations are the responsibility of extraterrestrial visitors, members of Satanic cults, or some unknown government agency.

Dr. Richard Prine, Forensic Veterinarian, Los Alamos Scientific Laboratory (LASL), Los Alamos, New Mexico, discounted the possibility that the mutilations had been done by anything but predators. He said he had examined six carcasses and in his opinion predators were responsible for the mutilation of all six.

Dr. Claire Hibbs, a representative of the State Veterinary Diagnostic Laboratory, New Mexico State University, Las Cruces, New Mexico, said he recently came to New Mexico, but that prior to that he examined some mutilation findings in Kansas and Nebraska. Dr. Hibbs said the mutilations fell into three categories: animals killed and mutilated by predators and scavengers, animals mutilated after death by "sharp instruments" and animals mutilated by pranksters.

Tommy Blann, Lewisville, Texas, told the conference he has been studying UFO activities for twenty-two years and mutilations for twelve years. He explained that animal mutilations date back to the early 1800's in England and Scotland. He also pointed out that animal mutilations are not confined to cattle, but cited incidents of mutilation of horses, dogs, sheep, and rabbits. He also said the mutilations are not only nationwide, but international in scope.

Chief Raleigh Tafoya, Jicarilla Apache Tribe, and Walter Dasheno, Governor, Santa Clara Pueblo, each spoke briefly to the conference. Both spoke of the cattle which had been found mutilated on their respective Indian lands. Chief Tafoya said some of his people who have lost livestock have been threatened.

Carl W. Whiteside, Investigator, Colorado Bureau of Investigation, told the conference that between April and December

1975, his Bureau investigated 203 reports of cattle mutilations.

At the conclusion of the conference, a meeting was convened in Albuquerque, which was heavily attended by the FBI, law enforcement officers from New Mexico, and numerous official investigators from Nebraska, Colorado, Montana, and Arkansas. One of the highlights of the meeting, which had not been divulged during the public conference, was the revelation that, in Arkansas, the authorities had investigated twenty-eight cases of cattle mutilation, all of which "were the work of intentional mutilators and not of predators." The investigator from Montana concurred.

As a result, during May 1979, the District Attorney's Office for Santa Fe, New Mexico, received a $50,000 Law Enforcement Assistance Administration (LEAA) grant, to enable a comprehensive review of the evidence. The investigation would be limited to a study of those livestock found solely on Indian land in New Mexico, however. Oddly, an FBI memorandum of June 1, 1979, stated that, following the announcement that an official investigation was to begin, "there have been no new cattle mutilations in Indian country."

Four days later, however, the FBI's low-profile approach was shattered when the *National Enquirer* devoted a page of its June 5 edition to a discussion of the FBI's involvement in the mutilation issue. Among those cited by the *Enquirer* was Henry Monteith, an engineering physicist at Sandia Laboratories. Having spoken with a number of Indians, Monteith had no doubt that the mutilations were the work of extraterrestrials and disclosed that among those Indians with whom he had spoken, some claimed to have seen "spaceships land and unload star people who chase down animals and take them back to the spaceship." Going along for the ride, District Attorney Eloy Martinez of Espanola, New Mexico, admitted that "UFOs are a possibility" and stated, "I might be the first district attorney in the country to prosecute an alien from outer space."

Armed with the $50,000 LEAA grant, investigations began in earnest, under the three-person team of Director Kenneth M. Rommel Jr., who had served with the FBI for twenty-eight years. But in July 1979, the *Rio Grande Sun* reported that "the county's freshest mutilation so far" had curiously gone uninvestigated. "I was really disgusted," said Dennis Martinez, a rancher, who had discovered the mutilated carcass within three hundred yards of his Truchas farm. "The news media said investigators would come as soon as they were called." For seven hours Martinez waited, but no investigator arrived.

"I don't blame them for being upset," commented Senator Harrison Schmitt, expressing his concern that the finding on the Martinez ranch remained practically unacknowledged. And when advised that Kenneth Rommel had yet to contact Officer Gabe Valdez, who had prompted Schmitt to initiate high-level inquiries with the FBI, he responded, "That doesn't sound like complete investigating."[9]

Other stories were in circulation too concerning the LEAA-funded investigation, as the *Rio Grande Sun* was only too well aware. Citing a number of confidential sources who had expressed dissatisfaction with the Rommel study, the *Sun* stated, "Persons who have spoken to the investigator complain he is brusque or too flippant, or he doesn't take their ideas or their reports seriously, and they'd rather not discuss with him further mutilation phenomena."

While this may represent nothing more than a marked difference of opinion over the source of the mutilations, darker rumors were also in circulation. "Other persons express fears that not only Rommel, but the District Attorney and the State Police, are working together to cover up whatever is behind the mutilations and rumors are spreading fast," added the newspaper.[10]

On July 17, 1979, Senator Schmitt announced that the Senate

Appropriations Committee had directed the FBI to continue its investigations. Such action, said Schmitt, is "necessary due to the continuing widespread problem of cattle mutilations and the need for federal coordination of the investigation. I hope that the committee's endorsement of this proposal will increase the FBI's investigative activity so that the answer to this bizarre and grisly mystery will be found." This was not to be. A lack of new mutilations on Indian lands in New Mexico led the Albuquerque FBI office to place the matter in "a closed status." Rommel would find little out of the ordinary, according to a January 1980 FBI document.

On January 15, 1980, Kenneth M. Rommel advised [that] his office has pursued numerous investigative leads regarding the possible mutilation of animals in New Mexico. He said that to date, his investigative unit has determined that none of the reported cases has involved what appear to be mutilations by other than common predators. Rommel said he has traveled to other states and conferred with investigators in those areas regarding mutilations, and to date has received no information which would justify the belief that any animals have been intentionally mutilated by human beings. Rommel added that regarding all the dead animals he had examined, the damage to the carcasses has always been consistent with predator action.

On January 15, 1980, this matter was discussed with Assistant US Attorney Richard J. Smith, US Attorney's Office, Albuquerque. Assistant US Attorney Smith said that in his opinion there is no Federal interest in continuing an investigation in this matter in the absence of further reports of acts of suspected mutilation of animals on Indian land in New Mexico.

Two months later Rommel summed up his conclusions in a letter to the FBI Laboratory in Washington.

For your information, since approximately 1975, New Mexico and other states, primarily those located in close proximity to

New Mexico, have had incidents referred to by many as "the cattle mutilation phenomena."

Stock animals, primarily cattle, have been found dead with various parts of the carcass missing such as one eye, one ear, the udder, and normally a cored anus. Most credible sources have attributed this damage to normal predator and scavenger activity. However, certain segments of the population have attributed the damage to many other causes ranging from UFOs to a giant governmental conspiracy, the exact nature of which is never fully explained. No factual data has been supplied supporting these theories.

In the same letter, Rommel requested that an analysis be carried out on some material that was believed to be identical to flakes found on the hides of cattle in the Dulce, New Mexico, area. He stated, "I would appreciate it if through the use of a GS Mas spectroscopy test or any other logical test, that these flakes can be identified. This in itself would go a long way to assisting me to discredit the UFO–Cow Mutilation association theory." Rommel was informed that the flakes were nothing more than enamel paint.

By the summer of 1980, Rommel had prepared a final bound report, entitled *Operation Animal Mutilation*, copies of which were circulated throughout the FBI. The final entry in the FBI's cattle mutilation file reads: "A perusal of this report reflects it adds nothing new in regard to potential investigation by the Albuquerque FBI of alleged mutilations on Indian lands in New Mexico."

And there matters stand to this day. For all the efforts of Senators Harrison Schmitt and Floyd Haskell, Police Officer Gabe Valdez, numerous ranchers, media sources, private and official investigators, the final report generated by the LEAA's $50,000 grant concluded that the mutilations were the work of nothing more than scavengers. A detailed study of the data set forth in FBI files, however, clashes acutely with the conclusions of *Operation Animal Mutilation*.

Firstly, the decision to limit investigations to those cattle found mutilated on Indian land in New Mexico makes no sense, particularly since, when it was announced that Rommel's study was beginning in earnest, such killings ceased. While individual mutilations outside Indian land might not technically have been within the FBI's jurisdiction, surely a detailed comparison of cases nationwide would have been warranted. Forrest S. Putman, special agent in charge of the FBI at Albuquerque, had made this point back in early February 1979: "If we are merely to investigate and direct our efforts toward the 15 mutilated cattle on the Indian reservation we, I believe, will be in the same position as the other law enforcement agencies at this time and would be seeking to achieve an almost impossible task. It is my belief that if we are to participate in any manner that we should do so fully."

Other questions remain. In his letter of March 5, 1980, to the FBI, Kenneth Rommel wrote that there was no factual data to support the claims that the mutilations were the work of UFOs or a "giant government conspiracy." Granted the UFO angle of the mystery may be a stretch, but what of the files of Police Officer Gabe Valdez? They may not confirm that aliens from some far-off world are systematically butchering our cattle, but they do confirm the presence of unidentified aerial vehicles in the immediate vicinity of mutilation sites.

The disturbing report written up by Valdez after his visit to the ranch of Manuel Gomez on June 14, 1976, is a perfect example: "Investigations continued around the area and revealed that a suspected aircraft of some type had landed twice." And what of the pod marks, scorched ground, elevated radiation readings, and the unidentified yellow, oily substance found at the site? Is this not the factual data that Rommel asserted was so noticeably absent?

Moreover, the reports collected by Valdez in 1978, implying that animals had actually been lifted into the air by some unknown object, are also convincing evidence of a phenomenon beyond mere predators. "Both cows were laying on their left side with left front leg and left rear leg broken which indicates that animals were lifted by their extremities," reported Valdez.

We also note that investigations in Arkansas had concluded that no fewer than twenty-eight cases of cattle mutilation had been recorded, and that in Colorado, a phenomenal 203 accounts had surfaced. Yet, the project sponsored by the Law Enforcement Assistance Administration insisted on focusing solely on the aforementioned fifteen New Mexico–based incidents. And it should not be forgotten that Dane Edwards, editor of a Brush, Colorado–based newspaper, had informed Senator Floyd Haskell that not only had U.S. Army helicopters been seen in the vicinity of local cattle mutilations, but that he too had been "threatened" by unknown parties.

Not surprisingly, some people believed that not only Rommel but the district attorney and the state police were working to cover up whatever was behind the mutilations.

Did the FBI uncover something about the mutilations that was deemed so shocking that the public and the media had to be kept in the dark at all costs? Emil P. Moschella of the FBI has informed us that the Bureau has not conducted any investigation of cattle mutilation since 1980 and that all material on the FBI's involvement in the New Mexican mutilations has been released into the public domain without any deletions. A similar assurance comes from the Justice Department. So how can we explain what the FBI appears to have shoved under the rug?

What was certainly one of the most controversial statements ever made with respect to animal and cattle mutilations came in 1997 from Lieutenant Colonel Philip J. Corso, who served on President Eisenhower's National Security Council staff, the Operations Coordination Board, and the U.S. Army Staff's Foreign Technology Division. "In the Pentagon from 1961 to 1963," wrote Corso, "I reviewed field reports from local and state police agencies about the discoveries of dead cattle whose carcasses looked as though they had been systematically mutilated.

"Local police reported that when veterinarians were called to the scene to examine the dead cattle left in fields, they often found evidence not just that the animal's blood had been drained but that the entire organs were removed with such surgical skill that it couldn't have been the work of predators or vandals removing the organs for some depraved ritual."

According to Corso, the first thought on the part of the U.S. military was that these mutilations were the work of the Soviets. However, it was not the Soviets going after U.S. cattle but the EBEs or extraterrestrial biological entities—a term allegedly used within U.S. intelligence circles to describe alien beings. The EBEs, said Corso, "were experimenting with organ harvesting, possibly for transplant into other species or for processing into some sort of nutrient package or even to create some sort of hybrid biological entity."[11]

Is it really the case, as suggested by the late Colonel Philip J. Corso, that alien creatures are carrying out these macabre acts? Or is there a more down-to-earth possibility? There is. And it is even more terrifying in its implications.

As a police officer in Fyffe, Alabama, Ted Oliphant investigated over thirty cases of cattle mutilation from October 1992 to May 1993. Oliphant has reported that in a number of such cases, pharmaceuticals had been found in bovine blood, including barbiturates, anticoagulants, and synthetic amphetamines. The drugs were *not* veterinary drugs, stresses Oliphant: they are pharmaceuticals used in human beings. Among those law enforcement agents who have thoroughly investigated these bovine excision sites, the consensus is, says Oliphant, that some kind of medical testing is taking place.

Oliphant makes the noteworthy observation that the jaws, which are often excised from the animals, are where enzymes are produced. He also notes that the digestive tract acts as a filter that absorbs, collects, and stores traces of any chemical or toxin introduced. The rectum and the ears store traces of toxins and chemicals like a library. Because many diseases like Creutzfeldt-Jakob disease (CJD) and bovine spongiform encephalopathy (BSE) can be inherited, the reproductive system may be a good place to look for clues on how they are passed to the next generation, Oliphant notes. "With BSE and CJD being such devastating new diseases, is it possible that many alleged cases of cattle mutilation are actually evidence of our tax dollars at work?" he asks.[12]

Could it really be the case that U.S. authorities are concerned by—and are covertly monitoring—the possible spread of nightmarish diseases such as BSE and CJD in the American food chain and even among the population at large? Such a scenario would explain the overwhelming secrecy surrounding the cattle mutilation mystery.

We have seen how the U.S. military may have utilized the UFO mystery as a convenient cover to test-fly its own flying saucers. It may not be beyond the bounds of credibility, therefore, to suggest that some of the UFO-related animal mutilation stories in circulation have deliberately been spread as a tool of disinformation to mask the truth about those mutilations.

The U.S. government has long feared that the country's cattle herds may become infected with rampant diseases. Top secret papers have surfaced under the terms of the U.S. Freedom of Information Act showing that more than fifty years ago, American authorities were concerned that a potentially hostile nation would attempt to cripple the U.S. food chain by deliberately infecting the country's cattle herds with foot-and-mouth and other diseases.

Prepared by the Committee on Biological Warfare at the request of the American government's elite Research and Development Board, this fifty-page file dates from March 1947 to the latter part of 1948 and makes for disturbing reading in view of what we know about cattle mutilations. In September 1947, the Research and Development Board prepared an in-depth report, also classified top secret, that outlined its concerns with respect to biological warfare.

Preparations for biological warfare can be hidden under a variety of guises. The agents of biological warfare are being studied in every country of the world because they are also the agents of diseases of man, domestic animals and crop plants. The techniques used in developing biological warfare agents are essentially similar to the techniques used in routine bacteriological studies and in the production of vaccines, toxoids and other beneficial materials.

By the latter part of 1948, biological warfare was seen as a major threat to the United States by the Research and Development Board. Moreover, the fear that a hostile nation would attempt to ravage the U.S. food supply by deliberately infecting its cattle herds with diseases such as foot-and-mouth ran high in official circles. A 1948 document states:

Biological warfare lends itself especially well to undercover operations, particularly because of the difficulty in detecting such operations and because of the versatility possible by the proper selection of biological warfare agents. Within the last few years there have been several outbreaks of exotic diseases and insect pests which are believed to have been introduced accidentally but which could have been introduced intentionally had someone wished to do so. The use of epizootic agents against our animal population by sabotage methods is a very real and immediate danger. Foot-and-mouth disease and rinderpest are among those which would spread rapidly, and unless effective counter-measures were immediately applied, would seriously affect the food supply of animal origin.

Since foot-and-mouth is now present in Mexico, it would be relatively easy for saboteurs to introduce the disease into the United States and have this introduction appear as natural spread from Mexico. Since rinderpest and foot-and-mouth disease are not present in the United States, our animal population is extremely vulnerable to these diseases.

Alarmingly, the papers reveal, the United States was in no position to prevent a large-scale biological attack on its cattle herds had it indeed occurred.

The United States is particularly vulnerable to this type of attack. It is believed generally that espionage agents of foreign countries which are potential enemies of the United States are present already in this country. There appears to be no great barrier to prevent additional espionage agents from becoming established here and there is no control over the movements of people within the United States. North America is an isolated land mass and hence specific areas therein present feasible biological warfare targets for an extra-continental enemy since fear of backfiring is minimized.

Most disturbing, however, was the potential outlook for the USA in the event of a countrywide biological warfare attack on its cattle herds.

The food supply of the nation could be depleted to an extent which materially would reduce the nation's capacity to defend itself and to wage war. Serious outbreaks of disease of man, animals or plants also would result in profound psychological disturbances.

But how would a covert introduction of disease into the U.S. food chain be undertaken? The committee had a number of ideas: via "water contamination"; "fodder and food"; "infected bait"; "contamination of soil"; "Biological Warfare aerosols", and deliberate "contamination of veterinary pharmaceuticals and equipment."

Realizing the grave implications such a scenario presented, the U.S. government carefully and quietly began to initiate a number of plans to detect such an attack on the continental United States. The committee asserted that ventilation shafts, subway systems, and water supplies throughout the country should be carefully monitored. Similarly, the committee recommended that steps be taken to determine the extent to which contamination of stamps, envelopes, money, cosmetics, food, and beverages as a means of subversively disseminating biological agents was possible.

The conclusions of the committee's report on the use of diseases as a biological weapon spelled out the utter lack of defense against such an attack.

It is concluded that: (1) biological agents would appear to be well adapted to subversive use. (2) The United States is particularly susceptible to attack by special BW operations. (3) The subversive use of biological agents by a potential enemy prior to a declaration of war presents a grave danger to the United States. (4) The biological warfare research and development program is not now authorized to meet the requirements necessary to prepare defensive measures against special BW operations.

Indeed, such was the concern shown that even the FBI got in on the act. A confidential memorandum to FBI director J. Edgar Hoover on May 9, 1950, from Raymond P. Whearty, Chairman, Interdepartmental Committee on Internal Security, titled "Alerting of Public Health Agencies re Biological Warfare," makes this very apparent.

The Public Health Service should be the chief agency on which NSRB [National Security Resources Board] will rely as a source of advice to these agencies on biological warfare matters in so far as they are a part of civil defense of people. NSRB will rely on the Bureau of Animal Industry in the same manner for defense of animals against BW. The National Security Resources Board has kept the Public Health Service fully informed as to biological warfare plans. In developing these plans the NSRB created an Interdepartmental Committee on Defense Against Biological Warfare. The Public Health Service and BAI are, of course, represented on this committee. Definite plans are being made in this field, as shown by the two attached "Restricted" documents. The Public Health Service and Bureau of Animal Industry are planning the training course for civil defense against biological warfare and will conduct such courses if and when appropriations are available. Approximately fifty Public Health Service top administrative officers recently spent one week at Camp Detrick for orientation in BW as part of the training, for Public Health Service officers in this particular field.

As this document makes abundantly clear, numerous U.S. government agencies in the late 1940s and early 1950s were referenced on the biological warfare issue as it related to animals and specifically to cattle. But that is not all. Also contained within the released files are various "withdrawal notices" where documents have been withheld from public consumption and scrutiny on the grounds of national security. More than half a century later, it seems, some of the U.S. government's findings on biological warfare as they relate to animals—and particularly cattle—remain classified.

Given the U.S. government's very real fear in the late 1940s that some form of bioterrorism campaign could be directed at the nation's cattle herds, the idea that regular and covert checks of those same cattle herds may have been conducted in the decades to follow seems not so strange at all and downright sensible.

It goes without saying that the spread, whether by accident or design, of emerging diseases—and particularly CJD, the human form of mad cow disease—could have major implications for our future as a species. If the targeting of ranch animals to ascertain if new strains of killer diseases are beginning to surface is justified, then what better way to do so than behind a "predator" or "UFO" smoke screen?

Fifteen

CONCLUSIONS

Having now examined and digested an absolute wealth of files from a wide and varied range of agencies and departments—and on an even wider range of unusual phenomena—what conclusions can we reach about how these phenomena have been of interest to elements of the government, military, and intelligence communities of the United States, the United Kingdom, and the Soviet Union?

The public has an innate distrust of the workings of government, which is at times entirely justified. The consensus is that if "they" are interested in an issue and have collated files on it, then "they" *must* have all the answers and *must* be hiding something of profound importance from us. While that is certainly the case sometimes—as in the X-creatures examples we cited—it is not necessarily always so.

The CIA files on remote viewing, the U.S. Army papers on witchcraft and sorcery, and the Defense Intelligence Agency records on ESP and other psychic phenomena in both humans and animals show that the prime reason for official interest was to determine if these phenomena could be skillfully utilized as tools of warfare and espionage at the height of the Cold War.

Similarly, the British Air Ministry's involvement in the Foo Fighter puzzle of the Second World War had less to do with an *X-Files*–style secret hunt for aliens and more to do with determining if the Nazis had succeeded in perfecting a frightening and poorly understood new weapon of war. This also seems to have been the motive of many of those tasked with evaluating the evidence for and against the existence of flying saucers—could they be Nazi- or Soviet-built? And it was largely the fear of Communism and the Soviet menace that led the FBI to investigate the "contactees" of the 1950s and 1960s such as George Adamski and George Van Tassel. The UFO nature of their alleged experiences was secondary. In these cases, official interest in the unexplained was stimulated by regional and global conflicts, the fear of Reds-under-the-beds, and by forward thinkers in the Pentagon and the Kremlin looking for new and novel weapons of war.

But what of the other mysteries that we have addressed? There was *never* any official secrecy surrounding the Loch Ness Monster, although, as we have demonstrated, the same possibly cannot be said for the big cat sightings in the United Kingdom. However, that the British military sought to offer genuine help and assistance in resolving the Loch Ness conundrum, only to find itself—nearly forty years later—accused of hiding the truth simply because it maintains files on the subject, is, sadly, indicative of the times that we live in. Sometimes a file is just a file.

Clearly, in some cases profound secrets may be being kept from us. The Central Intelligence Agency's files on Noah's Ark, for example, are a perfect case in point. Based on the available testimony and circumstantial evidence alluded to in the declassified documentation on the Ark, the information that has surfaced into the public domain only tells a fraction of the story. And, of course, *why* would the CIA be interested in a biblical mystery dating back thousands of years? On this issue we are left with more questions than answers.

A similar situation exists with the "cattle mutilation" mystery. Although many have seen fit to dismiss this subject, the little-known and highly detailed FBI records on this particularly grisly mystery suggest that a demonstrably real phenomenon is at work. Moreover, the work of Ted Oliphant and the newly publicized files of the U.S. government's Committee on Biological Warfare, prepared in 1947–48, point toward the possible existence of a well-hidden and incredibly well funded operation designed to monitor the nation's cattle herds that even the FBI was unable to penetrate the inner sanctum of.

With the Men in Black, we see a similar scenario. There are examples of MIB-style reports in the hands of agencies such as the FBI, but the records of the CIA and the British Royal Air Force's Provost and Security Services suggest the existence of covert MIB-style operatives stealthily investigating UFO encounters for their own—presently unknown—purposes that, again, the FBI was unaware of. The MIB mystery and the cattle mutilations are perfect examples that agencies not only keep secrets from the public at large, they also keep them from each other.

On the issue of water-divining or dowsing, the British government's files of the Second World War seemingly offer convincing evidence that dowsing really did work. However, the reluctance to be seen embracing what was described as "the mysterious" at a time of war offers yet another line of thinking on the nature of how and why secrets are kept.

The same could apply to the crop-circle mystery. The long-standing claim is that the much rumored British government study into the puzzle in the late 1980s was initiated and kept secret because of the totally unexplained nature of the circles. But, we have seen that—based on similar historical precedents from the files of MI5—the latter study might, in fact, have been conducted in an effort to determine if the circles were made by enemies of the country.

On the other hand, the official files on spontaneous human combustion suggest that perhaps we have little to fear. We can all sleep a little sounder at night knowing that it is unlikely that we will burst into flames.

Officials have investigated the mysteries of our planet for a variety of reasons and have, in many cases, classified their findings for a variety of reasons also. Their curiosity and concern is likely to continue and the files are likely to accumulate.

Meanwhile cryptozoologists will continue to explore the wilds of South America, the jungles of Africa, the great forests of Washington State, and the Australian outback in search of fantastic creatures and beasts; UFO researchers will still scan the heavens in search of our alleged cosmic cousins; archaeologists will continue to excavate some of the most ancient biblical sites that pepper our globe; and those fascinated by the inner workings of the mind will still wonder exactly what we as a species may really be capable of.

In light of what we have seen, however, it is entirely possible that, within the bowels of a cavernous, secret government archive somewhere, there is evidence that some need wonder about no longer and for whom there are no more mysteries to be explained.

REFERENCES

1. AROUND IN CIRCLES
1. *Wall Street Journal*, August 28, 1989.
2. Timothy Good, ed., *The UFO Report 1992* (Sidgwick & Jackson, 1991).
3. Letter to Nick Redfern from Jonathan Turner, September 21, 1994.
4. Dr. David Clarke and Andy Roberts, *Out of the Shadows* (Piatkus, 2002).
5. Public Record Office files: WO 199/1982, KV 4/28 and KV 4/11. Crown copyright exists.
6. Public Record Office file: AIR 2/17526. Crown copyright exists.
7. *New Ufologist* 5 (1996).

2. THE ARARAT ANOMALY
1. Professor Porcher Taylor III, "The Origin of and Planned Search for the Mount Ararat 'Anomaly' in Turkey," Anthony Montasano, "The Ararat Anomaly," January 9, 1996, www.eomonline.com; *Daily Mail*, November 20, 1997, www.cia.gov.
2. www.noahsarksearch.com.
3. Fernand Navarra, edited with David Balsager, *Noah's Ark: I Touched It* (Logo International, 1974).
4. Charles Berlitz, *The Lost Ship of Noah: In Search of the Ark at Ararat* (G. P. Putnam & Sons, 1987).
5. *Fortean Times* 120 (March 1999). Robin Simmons, *Riddle of Ararat* (video), 2000.
6. *Washington Times*, November 18, 1997.
7. Ibid.

8. Taylor, "Origin of and Planned Search for the Mount Ararat 'Anomaly.' "

9. Ibid.; and Montasano, "Ararat Anomaly."

10. Leonard David, "Satellites Search for Noah's Ark," www.space.com.

3. ASHES TO ASHES

1. Michael Harrison, *Fire From Heaven* (Sidgwick & Jackson, 1976). Charles Dickens, *Bleak House* (Everyman Library, 1972). Joe Nickell with John F. Fischer, *Secrets of the Supernatural* (Prometheus, 1988). Todd Venezia, "FBI Debunks Spontaneous Human Combustion," August 1, 2000, www.apbonline.com. *The Saturday Magazine*, August 1832. Dr. Wilton Marion Krogman, "The Strange Case of the Cinder Lady," *Pageant*, October 1952.

4. GREAT BALLS OF FIRE!

1. Public Record Office file: Admiralty 131/119. Crown copyright exists.

2. *UFOs 1947–1987*, compiled and edited by Hilary Evans with John Spencer (Fortean Tomes, 1987).

3. *Western Morning News*, February 16 and 19, 1932. Jonathan Downes, *The Owlman and Others* (Domra Publications, 1997).

4. Ibid.

5. Harold T. Wilkins, *Flying Saucers on the Attack* (Ace Books, Inc., 1954).

6. Timothy Good, *Beyond Top Secret* (Sidgwick & Jackson, 1996).

7. Jenny Randles, *Something in the Air* (Robert Hale Ltd., 1998).

8. Warren Smith, *UFO Trek* (Sphere Books Ltd, 1977).

9. Documentation made available to the authors via the Central Intelligence Agency, 1997.

10. *UFO* 12, no. 1 (1997).

11. *Ovni*, 1998.

12. *Flying Saucer Review* 24, no. 1 (1978).

13. Public Record Office files: AIR 14/2076 and Air 2/5010. Crown copyright exists.

14. Ibid.

15. Ibid.

16. Public Record Office file: AIR 14/2076. Crown copyright exists.

17. Public Record Office file: AIR 14/2800. Crown copyright exists.

18. Martin Caidin, *Ghosts of the Air* (Bantam Books, 1991).

19. Public Record Office file: 40/464. Crown copyright exists.

20. Public Record Office file: AIR 14/2076.

21. Ibid.

22. Aime Michel, *The Truth About Flying Saucers* (Robert Hale Ltd., 1957).

23. Wilkins, *Flying Saucers on the Attack*.

24. *Sightings* 1, no. 8 (1996).

25. Project Grudge, Technical Report, August 1948.

5. WHO FLIES THE SAUCERS?

1. Public Record Office file: AIR 20/9321. Crown copyright exists.

2. Public Record Office files: DEFE 41/117 and DEFE 41/118. Crown copyright exists.

6. COSMIC COMMIES

1. Edward Ashpole, *The UFO Phenomenon* (Headline, 1995).

2. Jack Stoneley and A. T. Lawton, *Is Anyone Out There?* (Star Books, 1975).

3. FBI files on George Van Tassel.

4. Truman Bethurum and Mary Kay Tennison, *Aboard a Flying Saucer* (DeVores & Co., 1954).

5. George Hunt Williamson and Alfred C. Bailey, *The Saucers Speak!* (New Age, 1954). *UFO Magazine*, September/October 1995.

6. Daniel Fry, *The White Sands Incident* (Horus House Press, Inc., 1992).

7. Desmond Leslie and George Adamski, *Flying Saucers Have Landed* (Werner Laurie, 1953). Lou Zinsstag and Timothy Good, *George Adamski: The Untold Story* (Ceti Publications, 1983). George Adamski, *Behind the Flying Saucers* (Paperback Library, Inc., 1967). Colin Bennett, *Looking for Orthon* (Paraview Press, 2001).

7. THE REAL MEN IN BLACK

1. Interview with source, 1995.

2. Lecture give by John Keel, 1998.

3. Gray Barker, *They Knew Too Much About Flying Saucers* (University Books, Inc., 1956). Albert K. Bender, *Flying Saucers and the Three Men* (Saucerian Books, 1962).

4. *Oklahoma MUFONEWS*, April 1993.

5. *Far Out* 2, no. 6 (1993).

6. Nick Redfern, *Cosmic Crashes* (Simon & Schuster, 1999). Public Record Office file: AIR 2/16918; Crown copyright exists. Interview with Anne Leamon (née Henson), February 2, 1998.

8. WARFARE AND WITCHCRAFT

1. U.S. Air Force biography.

2. Jon Elliston, "Psywar Terror Tactics," www.parascope.com

3. Joint Public Affairs Office, "The Use of Superstitions in Psychological Operations in Vietnam," 1967.

9. ANIMALS AND ESPIONAGE

1. *Daily Telegraph*, June 30, 2001.
2. *Daily Telegraph*, November 4, 2001.

10. MIND WARS

1. Tim Rifat, *Remote Viewing* (Vision Paperback, 2001).
2. W. Adam Mandelbaum, *The Psychic Battlefield* (Thomas Dunne Books, 2000).

12. THE DOWSING DETECTIVES

1. Public Record Office file: HO 199/480. Crown copyright exists.

13. THE MONSTER FILES

1. Public Record Office files: BJ 7/49 and MT/9/207. Crown copyright exists.
2. *New Scientist*, June 2002.
3. Nicholas Witchell, *The Loch Ness Story* (Corgi Books, 1989). Tim Dinsdale, *Loch Ness Monster* (Routledge, Kegan & Paul, 1989). Daniel Cohen, *A Modern Look at Monsters* (Tower Books, 1977). Roy P. Mackal, *The Monsters of Loch Ness* (McDonald & Janes, 1976). F. W. Holiday, *The Great Orm of Loch Ness* (Faber & Faber, 1968). Paul Harrison, *The Encyclopedia of the Loch Ness Monster* (Hale, 1999). Peter Costello, *In Search of Lake Monsters* (Garnstone Press, 1974). William Atkins, *The Loch Ness Monster* (Signet, 1977). Ulrich Magin, *Waves Without Wind and a Swimming Island*, Fortean Studies, vol. 7 (John Brown Publishing Ltd., 2001). Joint Air Reconnaissance Intelligence Center file: Photographic Interpretation Report Number 66/1. The Web site www.lochness.com provides useful data on the entire controversy surrounding the Loch Ness Monster.
4. Interview with Richard Freeman, June 6, 2002. For information on the Center for Fortean Zoology, write 15 Holne Court, Exwick, Exeter, EX4 2NA, England. Alternatively, contact the CFZ via its Web site: www.cfz.org.uk.
5. Parliamentary copyright material from Commons Hansard, February 2, 1998, is reproduced with the permission of the controller of Her Majesty's Stationery Office on behalf of Parliament.
6. Jonathan Downes, *The Owlman and Others* (CFZ Publications, 2002). Interview with Jonathan Downes, June 16, 2002. Jonathan Downes, *Monster Hunter* (publication pending).

14. BUTCHERS FROM BEYOND

1. *Pueblo Chieftain*, October 7, 1967. Linda Moulton Howe, *An Alien Harvest* (Linda Moulton Howe Productions, 1989).
2. *Argus Leader*, August 30, 1974.
3. *Idaho Statesman*, July 6, 1975.

4. *Elsberry Democrat*, June 22, 1978.

5. *Greeley Tribune*, September 18, 1980.

6. *The Leading Edge* 66 (1994).

7. William L. Moore and Jaime H. Shandera, *The MJ-12 Documents: An Analytical Report*, 1990.

8. *UFO* 4, no. 3, and *UFO* 5, no. 2.

9. *Rio Grande Sun*, various editions (some undated in FBI records), July 1979.

10. Ibid.

11. Lieutenant Colonel Philip J. Corso and William J. Birnes, *The Day After Roswell* (Simon & Schuster, 1997).

12. *The Anomalist* 6 (1998).

INDEX